Struts
Essential Skills

Struts
Essential Skills

Steven Holzner

McGraw-Hill/Osborne

New York Chicago San Francisco
Lisbon London Madrid Mexico City
Milan New Delhi San Juan
Seoul Singapore Sydney Toronto

The McGraw-Hill Companies

McGraw-Hill/Osborne
2100 Powell Street, 10th Floor
Emeryville, California 94608
U.S.A.

To arrange bulk purchase discounts for sales promotions, premiums, or fund-raisers, please contact **McGraw-Hill**/Osborne at the above address. For information on translations or book distributors outside the U.S.A., please see the International Contact Information page immediately following the index of this book.

Struts: Essential Skills

1234567890 CUS CUS 01987654

ISBN 0-07-225659-1

Publisher Brandon A. Nordin
Vice President & Associate Publisher Scott Rogers
Acquisitions Editor Lisa McClain
Project Editors LeeAnn Pickrell, Mark Karmendy
Acquisitions Coordinator Athena Honore
Technical Editor James Mitchell
Copy Editor Sally Engelfried
Proofreader Susie Elkind
Indexer Jean Skipp
Composition John Patrus, Jean Butterfield
Illustrators Kathleen Edwards, Melinda Lytle
Series Design Jean Butterfield
Cover Design Jeff Weeks

This book was composed with Corel VENTURA™ Publisher.

To Nancy—always and forever my sweetheart.

Contents at a Glance

About the Author

Steven Holzner is the award-winning author of 85 computer books. His books have sold over 1.5 million copies, and they've been translated into 18 languages around the world. He has served as contributing editor for *PC Magazine* and has written a number of computing bestsellers and Computer Book of the Month club selections. He has also written extensively on Java and on Struts.

Steve got his B.S. at MIT and his Ph.D. from Cornell University. He's been on the faculty of both MIT and Cornell. He also teaches classes on Java Web programming for professional programmers in corporations around the country.

Contents

Acknowledgments

Thanks to James Mitchell, who was the technical reviewer for this material. Thanks also go to Nancy Maragioglio, Lisa McClain, Athena Honore, LeeAnn Pickrell, and Jean Butterfield at McGraw-Hill/Osborne for their help in publishing this book.

Introduction

Welcome to *Struts: Essential Skills*. This book is designed to be as accessible and complete as it is possible for a first book on Struts to be. It puts Struts to work in depth, pushing the envelope and working with allied standards as well. The best way to learn any topic like Struts is by example, and this is an example-oriented book.

There aren't many topics that are gaining popularity as fast as Struts these days. More and more Web applications are being built using Struts. With Struts, you have a great deal of control over how those applications work because you have a framework that you can plug components into.

You're getting into Struts at the right time—the excitement level is high and new developments appear frequently. This book tries to be true to that spirit and capture as much of the excitement and power of Struts as possible.

Who Is this Book For?

This book is for you if you want to develop the power that Struts applications are capable of. What you'll see here lets you take control of the server side of things. If you already know how to handle JSP and servlet programming and want to go on to the next step in creating Web applications, then this is the book for you.

To use this book profitably, you'll need to be acquainted with Java, JavaServer Pages (JSP), servlets, and HTML. We'll review the skills you need in this book in Module 1. If you don't feel comfortable with the level of discussion there, it's a good idea to take a look at an introductory JSP/servlet book before pressing on. Check out *JSP: A Beginner's Guide* (McGraw-Hill/Osborne, 2001) for more information.

What's Inside?

This book is filled with examples, because seeing a working example is the best way to learn Struts; there's nothing like seeing it work for yourself. Here are a few of the topics we'll cover:

- The parts of a Struts application
- Model/View/Controller architecture
- Accepting user input, processing it, and displaying results
- Storing data in beans
- Passing bean data to views
- Handling exceptions
- Understanding struts-config.xml
- Creating Struts forms in the view
- The ActionForm class
- Handling errors
- Connecting to beans and action servlets
- Message resources
- Property files

- Form beans
- Business rules
- Using the Action class
- User validation
- Action mappings
- Forwards
- Creating custom JSP tags
- <html:text>
- <html:submit>
- <html:select>
- All other <html> tags
- <bean:cookie>
- <bean:message>
- <bean:write>
- <logic:equal>
- <logic:lessThan>
- <logic:match>
- <logic:messagePresent>
- Validators: automatic field checking
- Checking data with validators
- Introducing Tiles
- Building applications with Tiles
- Writing JSP for Tiles
- Creating DynaForms
- Using Eclipse to write Struts applications
- Using Ant to build Struts applications

What Do You Need?

Besides a familiarity with JSP, servlets, Java, and HTML, you'll need some software to work with this book. The good news is that the software is available for free on the Internet.

As it's needed, you'll see where to download the software for this book. We're going to use Java, the Tomcat Web server, and Struts itself (including both Struts 1.1 and early release versions of 1.2, as well as the Validator and Tiles frameworks that now come with Struts). In Module 11, we'll use the Eclipse Java Integrated Development Environment to make Struts development easier.

All of this software is available for free; all you need to have to get it is a Web browser and connection to the Internet.

Where to Download the Code for this Book

The code in this book is available for download on the McGraw-Hill/Osborne web site at www.osborne.com.

All the code examples have been tested both by the author and the tech editor, using different machines. Installing the examples so you can use them with Tomcat is easy—take a look at the readme.txt file that comes with the downloadable code.

Conventions Used in this Book

There are some conventions used in this book that you should know about:

- Terms that I wish to emphasize in text appear in boldface.
- You find Notes and Tips filled with useful information.
- When an example is being developed step by step, you'll see the newly added section of code displayed in bold to distinguish it from what's already there, like this:

```
package ch03;
public class DataAction extends Action {

  public ActionForward execute(ActionMapping mapping,
    ActionForm form,
    HttpServletRequest request,
    HttpServletResponse response)
    throws IOException, ServletException {
```

```
        if ( form != null ) {
          DataForm dataForm = (DataForm)form;
            .
            .
            .
        }
    }
```

The three dots arranged vertically above indicate that more code is coming.

And that's it, we're ready to go with Module 1, where we review the Java, JSP, and servlet skills you'll need in this book.

Module 1

Creating Web Applications

CRITICAL SKILLS

1.1 Get and Install Tomcat

1.2 Use JSP

1.3 Work with JavaBeans

1.4 Work with Servlets

Welcome to Struts, the dynamic application framework that's taken the online Java community by storm. Java programming has been online for years with JavaServer Pages (JSP) and servlets—in fact, as long ago as Java applets—but not until now, not until Struts, has it been possible to create such powerful web applications. We've come far from the days of simple web pages that displayed a guestbook or maybe an online mailer; today, web applications are being created that demand thousands of lines of code. To create extended applications like that, you need something more substantial than the ad hoc programming that used to pass muster. You need an application framework designed to host larger applications, and that framework is Struts.

When you start developing web applications beyond the most basic, it helps to have a well-defined framework for your application. We're going to see how that works in this book. We'll start in this module with an overview of Struts and then review the foundation that will be essential for the coming chapters where we put Struts to work. That foundation is built on three pillars of online Java programming: JSP, JavaBeans, and Java servlets. We'll get up to speed on all three topics in this module; this module is intended primarily as review to make sure we have the skills we'll need under our belt.

If you already feel confident of your JSP/servlets skills, feel free to skip this module. On the other hand, if this module leaves you behind, it might be a good idea to take a look at a JSP/servlets book before going on, because we'll need the foundation built in this module before pressing on. We'll start with an overview of Struts itself.

All About Struts

Take a look at Figure 1-1; that's a Struts web application. In the next module, we'll go through the structure of a Struts application in detail to ensure you have a solid understanding of it. For now, note what this sample web application is doing; it's using HTML controls (check boxes, text fields, and so on) in a web page to ask the user what they'd like to order, a pizza or a sandwich. The user can customize their order with the check boxes at left, and select a pizza or sandwich in the drop-down list box at right.

When the user clicks the Place Your Order! button, the web application we've set up using the Struts framework reads the data they've entered, processes it, and returns a summary, as you can see in Figure 1-2.

Even though it looks simple, there's a lot going on behind the scenes. This application uses about a dozen files to make it work, including JSPs, servlets, and beans, which is to say that Struts is not a lightweight application framework. Sometimes, web applications are fine when built using a few JSPs and perhaps a JavaBean or two. In such cases, you probably don't need Struts. However, when you go beyond the most simple web applications, things can get complex very fast, and the Struts framework makes it easier to create web applications in a well-defined, easily maintained way.

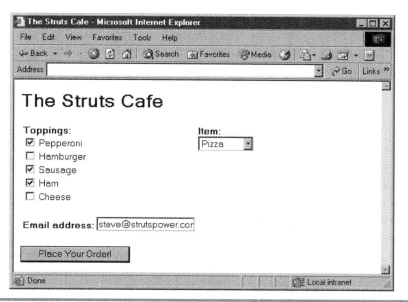

Figure 1-1 A sample Struts application

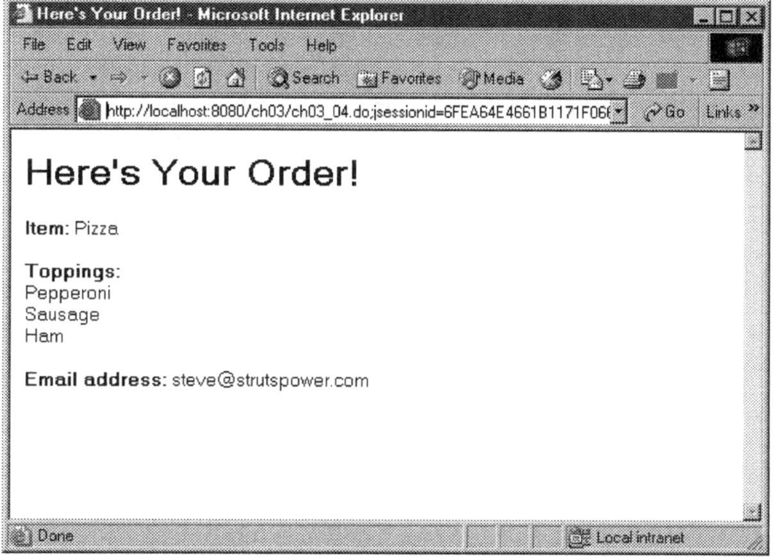

Figure 1-2 Displaying the processed data

Why "Struts"?

What about the origin of the name Struts? Contrary to what a lot of people think, the term "Struts" isn't an acronym. It's intended to stand for the struts that you can use as underpinnings for construction projects—in this case, for constructing web applications. Struts was originally created by a team of developers and released in June 2000 as Struts 1. The primary developer was Craig R. McClanahan, who has also been the main developer behind some editions of Tomcat, the web server we're going to use with this book; McClanahan is also the lead developer on Sun's Java Web Services Developer Pack.

Originally, web applications were built in an ad hoc manner, with data mixed in with the HTML to present an interface to the user. That kind of programming, as we'll see in the next module, is now called Model 1 programming. Struts' job is to implement Model 2 programming, in which you use the building blocks discussed in this module: JSPs, JavaBeans, and servlets. In a Struts application, a servlet acts as the *controller* of the application, delegating user requests as needed. JSPs handle the user interface, called the *view*, and JavaBeans implement the so-called *model*, which is where the hardcore data handling goes on. You use Model 2 programming when you want to create more than a simple web application, and Struts' genius is to provide a framework that implements a well-defined way to create Model 2 applications.

The current Struts version is 1.1; we'll also get a look at the upcoming Struts 1.2.

Who Creates and Maintains Struts?

Struts is an open source framework, which means its source code is available freely, and you can even modify it as you want. It's hosted by the Apache Software Foundation (ASF), as are some of the other products we'll need, like the Tomcat web server and the Ant build tool. You can get Struts for free from http://jakarta.apache.org/struts/; just click the links under the Download section on the left. In particular, we'll use the Binaries link in the next module to download the prebuilt version of Struts. Click the Source link if you want to build Struts yourself.

All software produced by the Apache Software Foundation is licensed according to the terms of Apache License, currently in version 2, which you can find at http://www.apache.org/licenses/LICENSE-2.0. The license makes it clear that you don't have to pay to get Struts or to use it. The license is friendly to businesses as well; you can use Struts in commercial projects.

You're going to need Java to run Tomcat. If you don't have Java installed, you can get it for free from http://java.sun.com/j2se/1.4/install.html.

Progress Check

1. What does "Struts" stand for?[1]
2. Who maintains Struts?[2]

CRITICAL SKILL 1.1

Get and Install Tomcat

To create Struts-based applications, we need a web server that can handle online Java applications. We're going to use the Tomcat web server in this book. If you don't have it, you can download it for free from http://jakarta.apache.org/tomcat/index.html.

NOTE

Although we're using it in this book, you don't have to use Tomcat. As long as your web server can act as a JSP/servlet container, you'll be fine. We're using Tomcat because it's free, it's the official reference server for JSP/servlets, and it works well with Struts.

We'll be using the latest version of Tomcat, which is version 5.0.19 as of this writing. When you download Tomcat, just pick the appropriate version for your system—for example, if you're using Windows, it's jakarta-tomcat-5.0.19.zip—and unzip/untar it in a directory of your choosing. In this book, we'll decompress Tomcat in a directory named tomcat. When you decompress Tomcat, it'll create a subdirectory named jakarta-tomcat-5.0.19; here is the directory structure created when you expand the download in a directory named tomcat:

```
tomcat
 |__jakarta-tomcat-5.0.19
     |__bin               Binary executable files
     |__common            Common classes available to Web applications
     |    |__classes      Common Java classes
     |    |__lib          Common Java classes in Java Archive (JAR) format
     |__conf              Configuration files (such as passwords)
     |__logs              The server's log files
     |__server            Internal Tomcat classes
     |__shared            Shared files
     |__temp              Temporary files
     |__webapps           Directory for Web applications
     |__work              Scratch directory for holding temporary files
```

1. It's not an acronym; it's meant to evoke the struts you use to build applications with.
2. The Apache Software Foundation.

We'll get very familiar with this directory structure while working through this book. The webapps directory is perhaps the most important one, because that's where the web applications you create go, making them accessible to the browser. For instance, the examples from this module, Module 1, will go into the ch01 directory, which we'll add to webapps as follows:

```
webapps
|__ch01                     Directory for Day 1 examples
```

The directory containing web applications also has to contain a directory named WEB-INF, with two subdirectories, classes and lib. WEB-INF, classes, and lib can all be empty, but Tomcat will expect them to be there before running your application:

```
webapps
|__ch01                        Our folder for Day 1 examples
    |__WEB-INF                 Information about Day 1's Web applications
        |__classes             Java classes used by Day 1's Web applications
        |__lib                 JAR files used by Day 1's Web applications
```

We'll see many path specifications in this book, such as jakarta-tomcat-5.0.19\webapps\ch01 in Windows, or jakarta-tomcat-5.0.19/webapps/ch01 in Unix. If you're using Unix and you see backslashes (\) in a path, it's a Windows path—just substitute forward slashes (/) instead. And vice versa if you're a Windows user who sees forward slashes.

We'll create the ch01, WEB-INF, classes, and lib directories we need in a moment, but first we'll get Tomcat running.

Running Tomcat

In order to run Tomcat, you have to set a couple of environment variables; these environment variables let Tomcat find Java and the Tomcat installation. You can find the details on these environment variables in the file RUNNING.txt, which is included in the Tomcat download. The environment variables to set are as follows:

- **JAVA_HOME** Points to the installation directory of Java; for example, that might be C:\jdk1.4 in Windows.
- **CATALINA_HOME** Points to the installation directory of Tomcat; for example, that might be C:\tomcat\jakarta-tomcat-5.0.19 (you get this path when you unzip Tomcat 5.0.19 in C:\tomcat) in Windows.

How you set these environment variables depends on your operating system. You can find instructions on setting environment variables for all operating systems that run Java in the installation notes on the Java download page, http://java.sun.com/j2se/1.4/install.html.

One way to set these environment variables is when you start Tomcat itself (you'll find the directions for starting Tomcat in the RUNNING.txt document that comes with Tomcat). To start Tomcat, you'll need a command prompt (in Windows, that's the DOS prompt, which you get in a DOS window). To set the environment variables when you start Tomcat in Windows, you can type the following at a DOS prompt, making the version numbers and paths here match what you have installed:

```
SET JAVA_HOME=C:\jdk1.4
SET CATALINA_HOME=C:\tomcat\jakarta-tomcat-5.0.19
```

In the Unix bash shell, this might look something like this in your .bashrc file (start a new shell to make the changes take effect):

```
JAVA_HOME=/jdk1.4
export JAVA_HOME
SET CATALINA_HOME=/tomcat/jakarta-tomcat-5.0.19
export CATALINA_HOME
SET PATH=/usr/local/bin:/jdk1.4/bin
export PATH
```

In the Unix tcsh shell, it might look like this in your .tcshrc file (start a new shell to make the changes take effect):

```
setenv JAVA_HOME /jdk1.4
setenv CATALINA_HOME /tomcat/jakarta-tomcat-5.0.19
setenv PATH /usr/local/bin:/jdk1.4/bin
```

You're ready to start Tomcat. This process is also operating-system dependent; see the Tomcat document RUNNING.txt for more details. In Windows, move to the Tomcat bin directory (under the directory that Tomcat was unzipped to, such as C:\tomcat\jakarta-tomcat-5.0.19\bin) and type **startup**, as follows:

```
C:\tomcat\jakarta-tomcat-5.0.19\bin\>startup
```

In the various different forms of Unix, that command might look like this:

```
/tomcat/jakarta-tomcat-5.0.19/bin/startup.sh
```

That starts Tomcat (in Windows, you'll see a new DOS window open; don't close this new window; that's where Tomcat is running). To verify that Tomcat is running, start a browser and navigate to the URL http://localhost:8080. You should see the Tomcat Welcome page that appears in Figure 1-3.

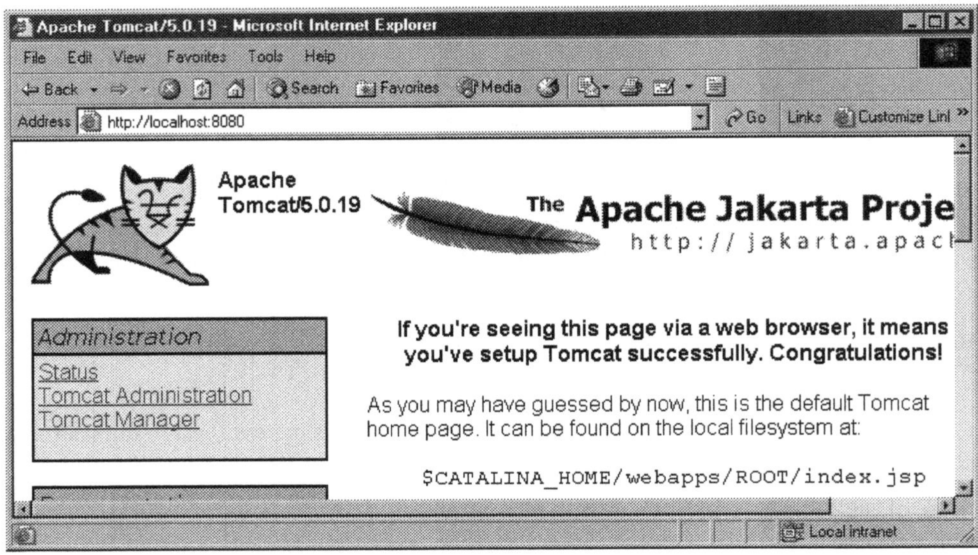

Figure 1-3 The Tomcat Welcome page

Note the URL we've used here, http://localhost:8080. The *localhost* part corresponds to a web server running on your own machine (IP address 127.0.0.1). 8080 is the port number. Each web server uses a port number to keep it separate from other web servers; most web servers use port 80, but Tomcat uses port 8080 so it won't interfere with other web servers. To stop Tomcat, use the shutdown command. That looks something like this in Windows,

```
C:\tomcat\jakarta-tomcat-5.0.19\bin\>shutdown
```

and this in Unix:

```
/tomcat/jakarta-tomcat-5.0.19/bin/shutdown.sh
```

We've got our JSP/servlet container going—we're ready for some JSP programming.

Use JSP

JSP lets you embed Java code in HTML. For example, take a look at this JSP, which prints the text "No worries." to a web page:

```
<HTML>
  <HEAD>
    <TITLE>A JSP Example</TITLE>
```

```
    </HEAD>
    <BODY>
      <H1>Using JSP</H1>
      <% out.println("No worries."); %>
    </BODY>
</HTML>
```

The Java code here, **out.println("No worries.");**, appears inside a JSP *scriplet*. In this case, we're using the **println()** method of the **out** object available to you in JSP scriptlets to display the text "No worries." in the web page that the server will send back to the browser. You can see the results in Figure 1-4.

Because this module is meant as a review, we'll discuss JSP in overview. There are four different types of elements you can use in JSP:

- **Scripting elements** Your Java code, as in the scriptlets we've already seen.
- **Comments** Text you add to annotate a JSP document—ignored by the web server.
- **Directives** Instructions to the web server. For example, a directive can indicate that you want the output of a page to be XML, not HTML.
- **Actions** Perform some operation, such as including other pages in the current page.

We'll take a brief look at these different elements here, starting with scripting elements.

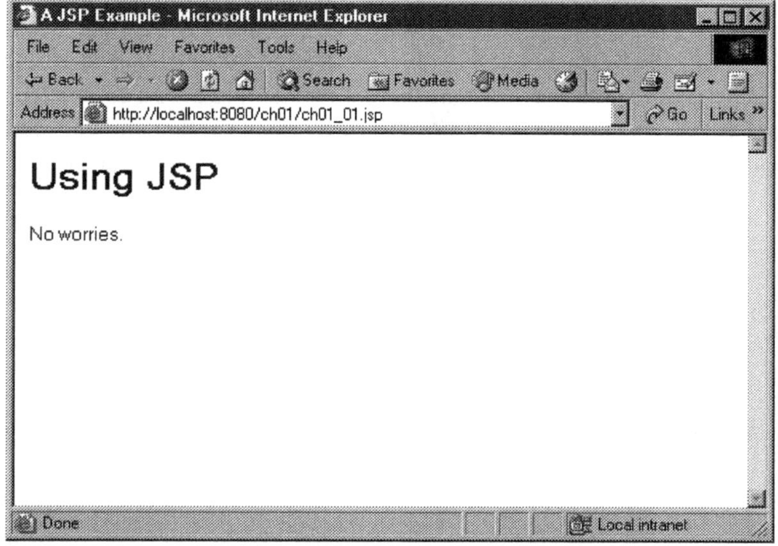

Figure 1-4 A first JSP

Progress Check

1. What object do you use to print to a web page from JSP code?

2. What are the four types of elements you can use in JSP?

Scripting Elements

JSP has three scripting elements:

- **Scriptlets** The most general of all scripting elements; scriptlets can contain Java code.
- **Declarations** Declare a variable or a method for use in Java code.
- **Expressions** Contain a Java expression that the server evaluates. The result of the expression is inserted into the web page.

Of these, *scriptlets* are the most general, and they can hold general Java code. You enclose scriptlets with the markup <% and %>. We used a scriptlet to display text in our first JSP example: **<% out.println("No worries."); %>**. This scriptlet contained only a single Java statement, but there's no limit to the number of statements you can have—which is what makes scriptlets the most general of all the JSP scripting elements. In fact, scriptlets are what many JSP programmers think of when they think of JSP.

You can also use JSP *declarations*. A declaration can declare anything you can declare in Java: variables, methods, classes, and so on. You can declare data items in scriptlets, such as variables, but you can't declare types or methods—for that, you need a declaration. You enclose declarations with the markup <%! and %>. Here's an example; the following code declares the variable **message** in a declaration (note that simple variables like this can also be declared in scriptlets):

```
<HTML>
  <HEAD>
    <TITLE>A JSP Example</TITLE>
  </HEAD>

  <BODY>
    <%! String msg = "No worries."; %>
</BODY>
</HTML>
```

1. The **out** object.

2. Scripting elements, comments, directives, and actions.

After declaring this variable, you can use it in a scriptlet. For example, here's how you can display the text in **message** in a web page:

```
<HTML>
  <HEAD>
    <TITLE>A JSP Example</TITLE>
  </HEAD>

  <BODY>
    <%! String msg = "No worries."; %>
    <% out.println(message); %>
</BODY>
</HTML>
```

A JSP *expression* is any Java code fragment that can be evaluated to yield a value. For example, the expression 2 + 2 yields a value of 4, the expression 40 – 10 yields 30, and so on. In JSP, you can surround a Java expression in the tags <%= and %>. The expression's value is inserted into the web page as text by the server.

Here's an example; if we had stored our string "No worries." in a variable named **message**, we could insert that string into the web page simply by using the variable as an expression this way:

```
<HTML>
  <HEAD>
    <TITLE>A JSP Example</TITLE>
  </HEAD>

  <BODY>
    <%! String message = "No worries."; %>
    <%= message %>
</BODY>
</HTML>
```

Note that expressions like this must result in a single value when they're evaluated.

Comments

Comments in JSP are just like comments in any programming language; they act as annotations, and they're ignored by the web server. In JSP, you enclose the text in a comment between the tags <%-- and --%>. Here's an example; in this case, the code includes the comment "Now print the message." to this JSP example:

```
<HTML>
  <HEAD>
    <TITLE>A JSP Example</TITLE>
  </HEAD>
```

```
  <BODY>
    <%-- Now print the message. --%>
<% out.println("No worries."); %>
  </BODY>
</HTML>
```

Directives

JSP *directives* let you give directions to the server on how a page should be processed. There are three directives in JSP; we'll see them throughout the book, but here's an overview:

- **page** Lets you configure an entire JSP page, such as whether its output is HTML or XML.
- **include** Lets you include another page or resource in a JSP page.
- **taglib** Lets you use a set of custom JSP tags as defined in a tag library.

You use the special markup <%@ and %> with directives. For example, to create a **page** directive, you include the keyword "page" like this: <%@ page ... %>.

To get an idea of what directives can do, we'll take a look at the **page** directive. In this example, we're specifying that we want to make the output of this page XML not the default HTML, we want to import java.sql.* so our Java code can use it, and if there are any errors, the server should pass them to an error page, error.html. You can do all that using attributes of the **page** directive. Here's how that looks:

```
<%@ page errorPage="error.jsp" language="java"
    contentType="application/xml" import="java.sql.*" %>
<HTML>
    <HEAD>
        .
        .
        .
```

It's important to note that if you use the **page** directive, it must come at the very beginning of the page.

Actions

In JSP, you can also use *actions* (not to be confused with Struts actions, which are classes used by the Struts controller). As their name implies, these perform some action, such as forwarding a request from a browser to a new location. In JSP, there are two types of actions: standard actions, which are built into JSP, and custom actions, which you create yourself. The standard actions are as follows:

- **<jsp:forward>** Forwards the browser request to a new location. Using forwards, you can delegate browser requests to various parts of your web applications.
- **<jsp:include>** Includes the output of a web component such as an HTML page, JSP, or servlet at the current location.
- **<jsp:plugin>** Lets you execute applets or JavaBeans with a plug-in.
- **<jsp:getProperty>**, **<jsp:setProperty>**, and **<jsp:useBean>** Designed to be used with JavaBean components.

We'll learn more on these actions as we need them.

Reading Data from Web Pages

JSP specializes in reading data from web pages. For example, say that you have a web page, ch01_02.html, which uses an HTML **<FORM>** element to display HTML controls and asks the user to enter their name into an HTML text field we've named **text1**:

```
<HTML>
    <HEAD>
        <TITLE>Submitting Text Fields</TITLE>x
    </HEAD>

    <BODY>
        <H1>Submitting Text Fields</H1>
        <FORM ACTION="ch04_05.jsp" METHOD="POST">
            Please enter your name:
            <INPUT TYPE="TEXT" NAME="text1">
            <BR>
            <INPUT TYPE="SUBMIT" value="Submit">
        </FORM>
    </BODY>
</HTML>
```

You can see this web page at work in Figure 1.5.

When the user clicks the Submit button, a request object is sent to the JSP named in the HTML form's **ACTION** attribute, ch01_03.jsp. In that JSP, you can use the **request** object's **getParameter()** method to recover the text from the text field named **text1**. Here's how that works:

```
<HTML>
  <HEAD>
    <TITLE>Reading Data From Text Fields</TITLE>
  </HEAD>
```

```
    <BODY>
        <H1>Reading Data From Text Fields</H1>
        Your name is
        <% out.println(request.getParameter("text1")); %>
    </BODY>
</HTML>
```

The results appear in Figure 1-6, where we've recovered the text from the text field using JSP. We'll look at how to connect JSP to JavaBeans next, using Java code inside JSP scriptlets.

CRITICAL SKILL 1.3

Work with JavaBeans

JSPs are fine for presenting your data and interacting with the user, but as your code gets longer, it's hard to keep fitting it into scriptlets and JSPs where that code mingles with HTML. When your code gets longer than a few lines, it's time to put it into a JavaBean, where you can use straight Java code, with no intermingled HTML needed (picture trying to debug 30 pages of code and mixed HTML).

And that's where we're going to go next.

At its most basic, a bean is just a unit of reusable Java code based on a public Java class that includes a constructor with no arguments. Beans can also expose properties, and we'll review how that works as well. Using Java code in beans means you can reuse that code, organize it into manageable components, and let multiple JSPs use the same code. Further JavaBeans are an integral part of Model 2 and, therefore, Struts programming.

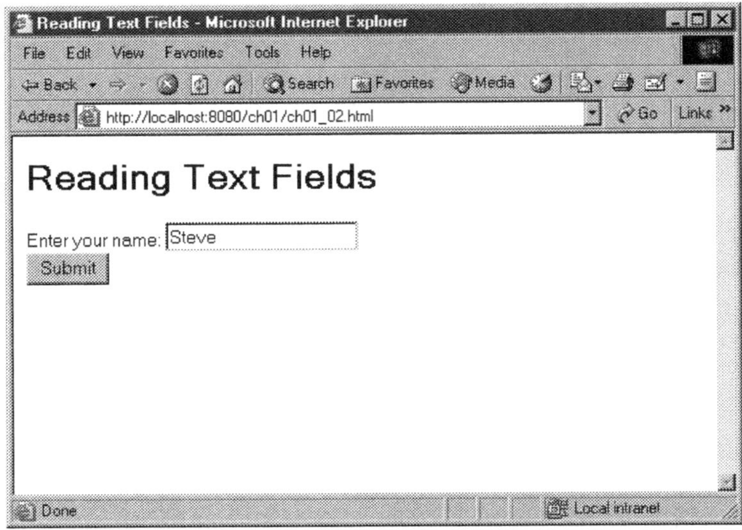

Figure 1-5 A text field

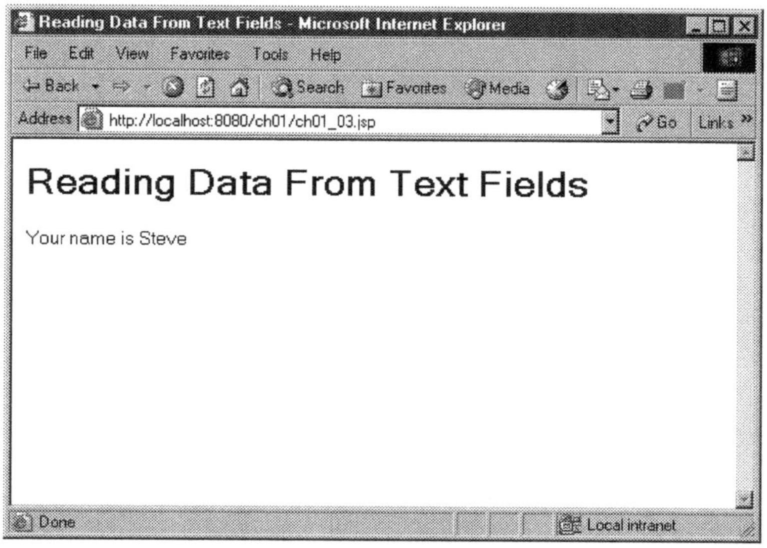

Figure 1-6 Reading data from a text field

Creating a Bean

As an example, we'll create a bean now named ch01_04.java that will expose a method named **message()**, which will simply return the text "No worries." We'll interface to that bean in a JSP and call that method from our Java code, displaying the returned message in a web page we'll send back to the browser.

In this example, we'll start by putting our code into a Java package named **beans**:

```
package beans;
        .
        .
        .
```

Our class will be named ch01_04, and we'll have a default constructor that takes no arguments:

```
package beans;
public class ch01_04
        .
        .
        .
  public ch01_04()
  {
  }
}
```

All that's left is to create the **message()** method that will return the text "No worries.", which looks like this:

```
package beans;
public class ch01_04
{
  public String message() {
    return "No worries.";
  }

public ch01_04()
  {
  }
}
```

This method is declared **public()** because a public method can be called from outside a class and any other classes based on this class. So how do you install this bean where JSP can access it and put it to work?

The first step is to compile ch01_04.java into ch01_04.class using the Java compiler javac. If you've set your machine's path to include the Java bin directory, you can move to the directory containing ch01_04.java and use the javac command directly like this. As discussed in the Introduction, I use % as a generic command-line prompt in this book to stand for the command-line prompt in either Unix or Windows:

```
%javac ch01_04.java
```

If you haven't set your machine's path to include the Java bin directory, qualify the name javac with the correct path to invoke it. That might look something like this in Windows: C:\jdk1.4\bin\javac ch01_04.java.

This compiles ch01_04.java to ch01_04.class. Where do you place ch01_04.class so that you'll have access to it in your JSPs? As you recall, this module's examples go into the Tomcat webapps/ch01 directory. This directory has a subdirectory named WEB-INF, which in turn has two subdirectories, classes and lib:

```
webapps
|_____ch01
     |_____WEB-INF
          |_____classes
          |_____lib
```

The .class files you want to use in web applications go into the classes directory (or subdirectories of that directory). When you work with Java packages, such as the **beans** package we placed our code in, the directory structure must mirror the package structure, so instead of placing ch01_04.class directly in the classes directory, we place it in classes/beans:

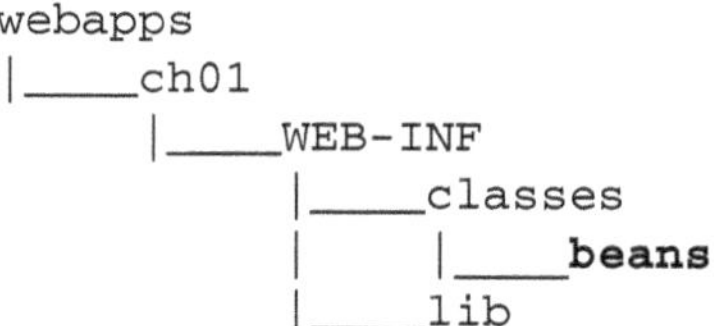

```
webapps
|____ch01
     |____WEB-INF
          |____classes
          |    |____beans
          |____lib
```

If you had placed your code in a package named **here.are.the.beans**, then you'd store the .class file in the directory classes\here\are\the\beans:

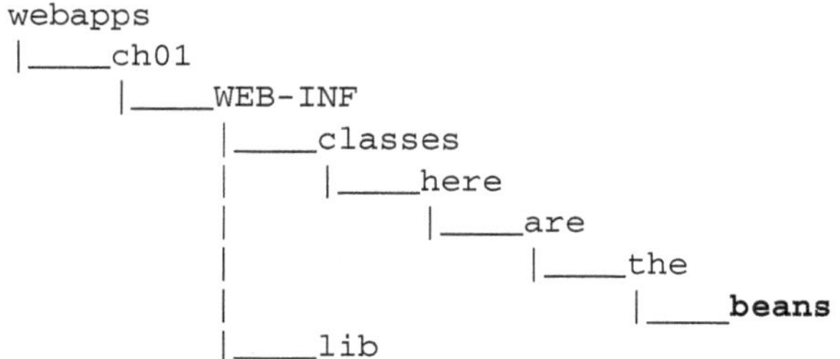

```
webapps
|____ch01
     |____WEB-INF
          |____classes
          |    |____here
          |         |____are
          |              |____the
          |                   |____beans
          |____lib
```

When you recompile the new .class file in a Tomcat directory like this, you should restart Tomcat (stop it with the **shutdown** command, followed by the **startup** command; if you're running Windows, wait until the second DOS window has disappeared before entering **startup**). This ensures the new .class file is copied over to the Tomcat work directory, which is Tomcat's workspace. (You should also restart Tomcat after you've changed configuration files such as web.xml, which we'll see later in this module.)

There is a way to configure Tomcat so you don't have to restart it every time after changing .class or configuration files, but that's beyond the scope of this book; see the Tomcat documentation if you're interested.

Connecting to a Bean

So how do you access the newly installed ch01_04 class in JSP code? We'll do that in a new JSP file, ch01_05.jsp. In that JSP, we'll start by creating a new object, **messenger**, in a scriptlet of our **ch01_04** class, which we must qualify as **beans.ch01_04**:

```
<HTML>
        .
        .
        .
```

```
    <BODY>

    <% beans.ch01_04 messenger = new beans.ch01_04(); %>
        .
        .
        .
    </BODY>
</HTML>
```

Now you can use this new object, **messenger**, in your JSP code. We'll use a JSP expression to display the text returned by the **message()** method, like this:

```
<HTML>
    <HEAD>
        <TITLE>Using a Bean</TITLE>
    </HEAD>

    <BODY>
        <H1>Using a Bean</H1>

    <% beans.ch01_04 messenger = new beans.ch01_04(); %>
    The bean says: <%= messenger.message() %>
    </BODY>
</HTML>
```

Place this new JSP, ch01_05.jsp, in webapps\ch01. This JSP connects to our JavaBean. To see it at work, navigate to http://localhost:8080/ch01/ch01_05.jsp. The result appears in Figure 1-7, where the JavaBean is accessed from JSP code. Not bad!

Creating Bean Properties

JavaBeans also can support *properties*, and you can use those properties either directly in JSP code or by using the JSP actions **<jsp:useBean>**, **<jsp:getProperty>**, and **<jsp:setProperty>**. The example bean ch01_06.java will support a property. To create a property named **message** of type **String**, create a private **String** data member named **message** in a bean:

```
package beans;
public class ch01_06
{
    private String message = "No Worries.";
        .
        .
        .
}
```

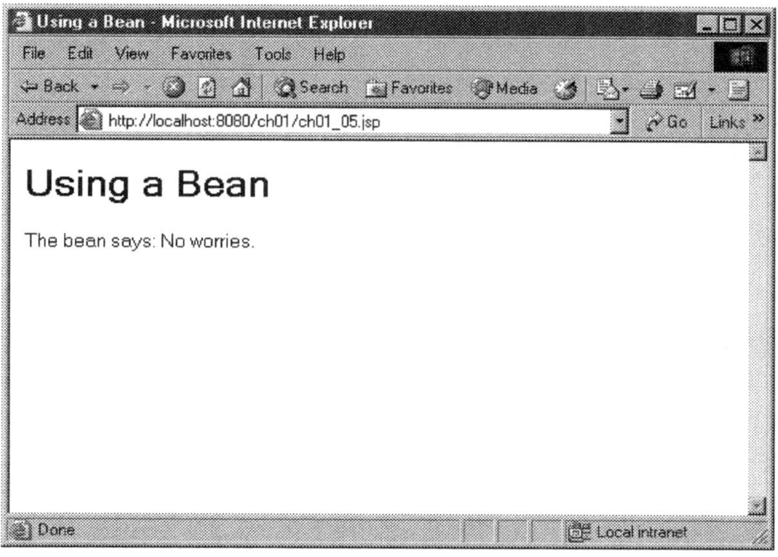

Figure 1-7 Reading text from a JavaBean

To let Java code read the value of the **message** property, add a getter method named **getMessage()**, which returns the value in the **message** variable:

```
package beans;
public class ch01_06
{
    private String message = "No Worries.";

    public String getMessage()
    {
        return message;
    }
        .
        .
        .
}
```

To let Java code set the value of the property, create a setter method named **setMessage()**, which sets the value stored in the internal variable **message**:

```
package beans;
public class ch01_06
{
```

```
    private String message = "No Worries.";

    public String getMessage()
    {
        return message;
    }

    public void setMessage(String text)
    {
        message = text;
    }
    public ch01_06()
    {
    }
}
```

That creates a new property, **message**, in this bean. How do you connect to this new property from Java code in JSPs? We'll explore that next.

Connecting to Bean Properties

You can connect to this new property by calling the **getMessage()** and **setMessage()** methods in your code directly, like this:

```
<% beans.ch01_06 messenger = new beans.ch01_06(); %>
The bean says: <%= messenger.getMessage() %>
```

You can also use the JSP actions **<jsp:useBean>**, **<jsp:getProperty>**, and **<jsp:setProperty>** to connect to bean properties, if you prefer. Here's an example, ch01_07.jsp, that shows how these actions work. We start by creating a bean object named **bean1** using **<jsp:useBean>**:

```
<HTML>
    <BODY>
        <H1>Using Bean Properties</H1>
        <jsp:useBean id="bean1" class="beans.ch01_06" />
        .
        .
        .
```

This new object, **bean1**, is now available to any JSP code in the page (just as the **messenger** object was available in the earlier code). We can use it in a

<jsp:getProperty> action to get the value of the message property and insert it into the web page this way:

```
<HTML>
    <BODY>
        <H1>Using Bean Properties</H1>
        <jsp:useBean id="bean1" class="beans.ch01_06" />
        The bean says: <jsp:getProperty name="bean1" property="message" />
        .
        .
        .
```

You can also use the **<jsp:setProperty>** action to set the value of a property. Here, we'll set the property to a new string, "No Problem.", and then display the new value:

```
<HTML>
    <HEAD>
        <TITLE>Using Bean Properties</TITLE>
    </HEAD>

    <BODY>
        <H1>Using Bean Properties</H1>
        <jsp:useBean id="bean1" class="beans.ch01_06" />
        The bean says: <jsp:getProperty name="bean1" property="message" />
        <BR>
        <jsp:setProperty name="bean1" property="message
            value="No Problem." />

        Now the beans says: <jsp:getProperty name="bean1"
            property="message" />
</BODY>
</HTML>
```

You can see the results in Figure 1-8, which show the JavaBean properties—first we display the current value of the bean's **message** property, then we reset that property to a new string and display the new value.

Using JavaBeans in your web application like this is easy, makes your code reusable, and lets you store that code in straight Java files, which are easier to handle than trying to cram long sections of code into JSPs. Struts-based web applications often rely heavily on beans.

As the final topic in this module, let's review Java servlets. Servlets are another of the essential building blocks of Struts applications, and we must know how they work in order to build and use them.

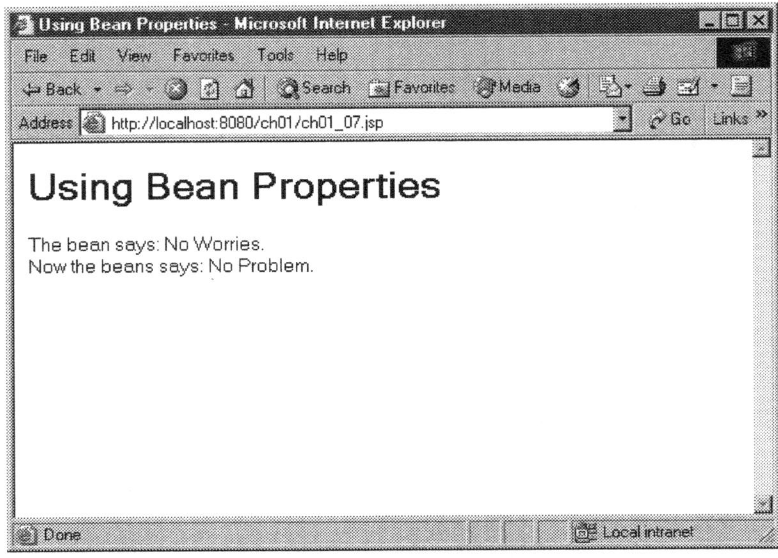

Figure 1-8 Using JavaBean properties

Progress Check

1. Where do you store compiled bean code so it can be accessed by JSPs?
2. If you had a property named **data**, what would its setter and getter methods be called?

CRITICAL SKILL 1.4

Work with Servlets

Servlets are the real core of online Java programming. In fact, JSPs themselves are translated into servlets before Tomcat runs them. JSPs were created to make servlet programming easier; instead of having to create all the objects you need in Java code yourself, as you have to do in a servlet, those objects are already created for you in JSPs (such as the **out** object you use to send text back to the browser). You can also mingle HTML with your Java code in JSPs if you use scriptlets, something you can't do in servlets. Sun wanted to bring online Java programming to the masses with JSPs, but it's all really centered on servlets, and there's no getting away from that fact. There's much you can do with servlets that you can't do with standard JSPs.

---

1. In the classes directory, or a subdirectory of the classes directory.
2. **setData** and **getData**.

If you want to see what the servlet code looks like for a JSP, take a look in the Tomcat work directory. The name of your JSP will have been changed, and the extension will be .java, but it's usually still recognizable.

Writing a Servlet

We're going to be working with servlets quite a bit in this book, so we'll review how they work here, beginning with an example servlet, ch01_08.java. This example will display our familiar web page with the text "No worries." You start by importing needed packages and creating the ch01_08 class, which extends the Java **HttpServlet** class:

```
import java.io.*;
import javax.servlet.*;
import javax.servlet.http.*;

public class ch01_08 extends HttpServlet
{
        .
        .
        .
}
```

In this new class, we'll override the **doGet()** method, which will be called when the user navigates to our servlet. That method is passed a request object of the **HttpServletRequest** class, which holds the data being passed to it from the browser, such as data in HTML controls. It's also passed a response object of the **HttpServletResponse** class, which it can use to create a web page to create its response that will be sent back to the browser:

```
import java.io.*;
import javax.servlet.*;
import javax.servlet.http.*;

public class ch01_08 extends HttpServlet
{
    public void doGet(HttpServletRequest request,
        HttpServletResponse response)
        throws IOException, ServletException
    {
        .
        .
        .
    }
}
```

The **doGet()** method handles data sent to the servlet when an HTML form has its **METHOD** attribute set to **GET**, which is the default. You can also use the **doPost()** method, which handles the case when an HTML form has its **METHOD** attribute set to **POST**. Or you can use the **service()** method, which handles both **GET** and **POST** methods.

In the **doGet()** method, we indicate that our response, which is to be sent back to the browser, is going to be in HTML. To send back that HTML to the browser, we'll create a **PrintWriter** object named **out** in the code. In JSP, the **out** object already exists as soon as the JSP starts executing, but in servlets you have to explicitly create it:

```
import java.io.*;
import javax.servlet.*;
import javax.servlet.http.*;

public class ch01_08 extends HttpServlet
{
    public void doGet(HttpServletRequest request,
        HttpServletResponse response)
        throws IOException, ServletException
    {
        response.setContentType("text/html");
        PrintWriter out = response.getWriter();
        .
        .
        .
    }
}
```

To send HTML back to the browser, you can use the **out** object's **println()** method. Here's how that works in the example:

```
import java.io.*;
import javax.servlet.*;
import javax.servlet.http.*;

public class ch01_08 extends HttpServlet
{
    public void doGet(HttpServletRequest request,
        HttpServletResponse response)
        throws IOException, ServletException
    {
        response.setContentType("text/html");
        PrintWriter out = response.getWriter();

        out.println("<HTML>");
```

```
            out.println("<HEAD>");
            out.println("<TITLE>");
            out.println("A Servlet Example");
            out.println("</TITLE>");
            out.println("</HEAD>");
            out.println("<BODY>");
            out.println("<H1>");
            out.println("A Servlet Example");
            out.println("</H1>");
            out.println("No worries.");
            out.println("</BODY>");
            out.println("</HTML>");
    }
}
```

That's the servlet's code; now we must get it running to see what will happen.

Compiling a Servlet

The next step is compile the servlet's code. That code imports various servlet packages like javax.servlet.*, so we'll need to include servlet-api.jar in the classpath (this .jar file was named servlet.jar in Tomcat 4.*x*, if you're working with an earlier release). The servlet-api.jar file comes with Tomcat, and you can find it in the Tomcat common\lib directory (e.g., c:\tomcat\jakarta-tomcat-5.0.19\common\lib\servlet-api.jar). To compile ch01_08.java, set the classpath to include servlet-api.jar like this:

```
%set classpath=servlet-api.jar
```

If you don't want to copy servlet-api.jar to the local directory, qualify the reference to servlet-api.jar with the full path; for example, **set classpath=c:\tomcat\jakarta-tomcat-5.0.19\common\lib\servlet-api.jar**. Then use the Java compiler to compile ch01_08.java to create ch01_08.class:

```
%javac ch01_08.java
```

Now we have the servlet's code file compiled. What's next?

Installing a Servlet

To give Tomcat access to ch01_08.class, place that file in webapps/ch01/WEB-INF/classes, which is where Tomcat will search for it when the user navigates to http://localhost:8080/ch01/ch01_08. That's all we need to do to install the servlet's code file itself.

There's one more step, however; we should still register the new servlet with Tomcat in a file named web.xml file, the *deployment descriptor*. This XML document goes into the ch01/WEB-INF directory, and it tells Tomcat where to look for the servlet's code when needed. This document begins with a standard heading and a **<web-app>** element, which we'll use to create a web application.

In our web application, we'll start by registering the ch01_08 servlet with a **<servlet>** element:

```
<?xml version="1.0" encoding="ISO-8859-1"?>
<!DOCTYPE web-app PUBLIC "-//Sun Microsystems, Inc.//DTD Web Application 2.3//EN"
    "http://java.sun.com/dtd/web-app_2_3.dtd">
<web-app>
  <servlet>
    <servlet-name>ch01_08</servlet-name>
    <servlet-class>ch01_08</servlet-class>
  </servlet>
        .
        .
        .
```

This ties the servlet to the ch01_08.class file. We also must map the URL pattern ch01_08 to this servlet so the server knows which servlet we want when we use ch01_08 in an URL. You can do that with a **<servlet-mapping>** element this way:

```
<?xml version="1.0" encoding="ISO-8859-1"?>
<!DOCTYPE web-app PUBLIC "-//Sun Microsystems, Inc.//DTD Web Application 2.3//EN"
    "http://java.sun.com/dtd/web-app_2_3.dtd">
<web-app>
  <servlet>
    <servlet-name>ch01_08</servlet-name>
    <servlet-class>ch01_08</servlet-class>
  </servlet>

  <servlet-mapping>
    <servlet-name>ch01_08</servlet-name>
    <url-pattern>/ch01_08</url-pattern>
  </servlet-mapping>

</web-app>
```

That's it; web.xml is complete. Now, place web.xml into webapps/ch01/WEB-INF, which gives us this directory structure for this example:

```
webapps
|__ch01
   |__WEB-INF                web.xml
        |__classes
           |__beans          ch01_08.class
        |__lib
```

Restart Tomcat and navigate to http://localhost:8080/ch01/ch01_08 to start the servlet. You should see the results in Figure 1-9, where the servlet is running. That concludes our overview of getting servlets started.

The Life Cycle of a Servlet

As our final servlet review topic, we'll discuss two special servlet methods: **init()** and **destroy()**. In the servlet lifecycle, **init()** is called first so you can perform any initialization you want, then the **doGet(), doPost(),** and **service()** methods are called as appropriate, followed by **destroy()**, where you can perform cleanup and deallocate resources.

Here's an example servlet, ch01_09.java, that uses the **init()** method to initialize the data in a **String** field named message to "No worries." After the call to **init()** method, the message variable is ready for use by the rest of the code, so we can display its text in the **doGet()** method, as you see in ch01_09.java:

```
import java.io.*;
import javax.servlet.*;
import javax.servlet.http.*;

public class ch01_09 extends HttpServlet
{
    String message = "";

    public void init(ServletConfig config)
```

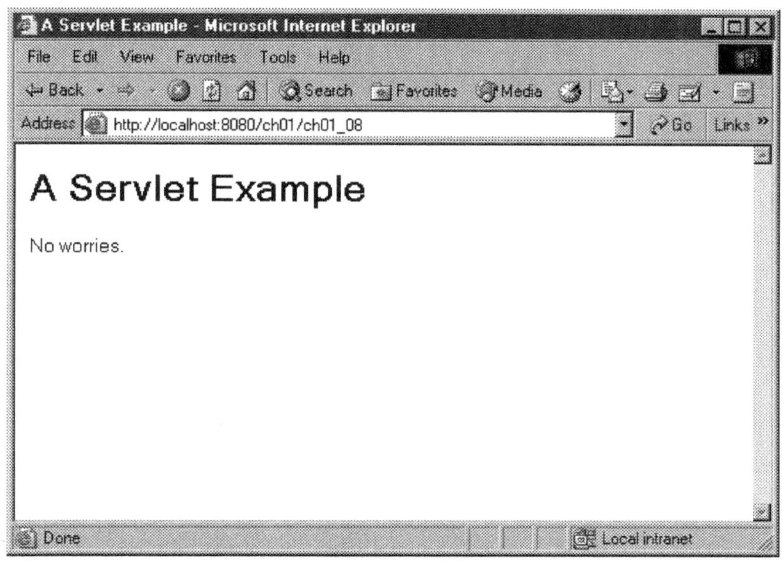

Figure 1-9 A sample servlet

```
    {
        message = "No worries.";
    }

    public void doGet(HttpServletRequest request,
        HttpServletResponse response)
        throws IOException, ServletException
    {
        response.setContentType("text/html");
        PrintWriter out = response.getWriter();

        out.println("<HTML>");
        out.println("<HEAD>");
        out.println("<TITLE>");
        out.println("Servlet Lifetime Example");
        out.println("</TITLE>");
        out.println("</HEAD>");
        out.println("<BODY>");
        out.println("<H1>Servlet Lifetime Example</H1>");
        out.println(message);
        out.println("</BODY>");
        out.println("</HTML>");
    }
}
```

We also have to update web.xml in the ch01 folder to register this new servlet, ch01_09, with the server. (Note that the **<servlet>** elements are grouped together and the **<servlet-mapping>** elements are grouped together; you can't intermingle these elements in web.xml.)

```
<?xml version="1.0" encoding="ISO-8859-1"?>
<!DOCTYPE web-app PUBLIC "-//Sun Microsystems, Inc.
    //DTD Web Application 2.3//EN"
    "http://java.sun.com/dtd/web-app_2_3.dtd">
<web-app>
  <servlet>
    <servlet-name>ch01_08</servlet-name>
    <servlet-class>ch01_08</servlet-class>
  </servlet>

  <servlet>
    <servlet-name>ch01_09</servlet-name>
    <servlet-class>ch01_09</servlet-class>
  </servlet>

  <servlet-mapping>
    <servlet-name>ch01_08</servlet-name>
    <url-pattern>/ch01_08</url-pattern>
```

```
  </servlet-mapping>

  <servlet-mapping>
    <servlet-name>ch01_09</servlet-name>
    <url-pattern>/ch01_09</url-pattern>
  </servlet-mapping>

</web-app>
```

That's all we need; the results appear in Figure 1-10; as you can see, the text in the message field was indeed initialized properly. We've used the **init()** method to initialize data as required before the rest of the servlet code ran.

Progress Check

1. What's the first method called in a servlet's code?
2. What .jar file do you use in Tomcat 5.*x* to import support for servlet code?

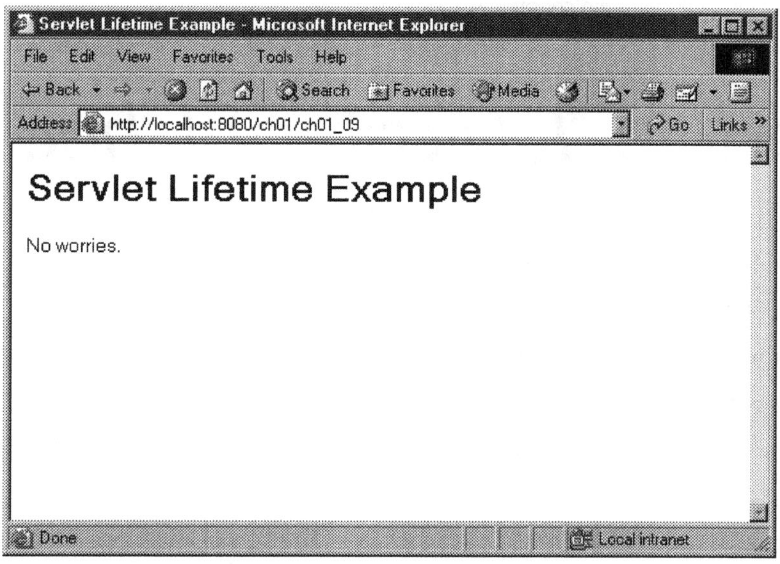

Figure 1-10 Initializing a servlet

---

1. The **import()** method.
2. servlet-api.jar.

In this module, we've reviewed the skills we'll need to work with Struts. We saw web applications using the Tomcat server built on JSP, JavaBeans, and servlets, the three pillars of Struts applications. Our foundation is complete, and we're ready to go.

If you want to brush up a little more, here's a starter list of online JSP and servlet tutorials:

- **http://java.sun.com/products/jsp/docs.html** Sun's "QuickStart" guides to JSP
- **http://java.sun.com/webservices/docs/ea2/tutorial/doc/JSPIntro.html** A Sun JSP tutorial
- **http://www.apl.jhu.edu/~hall/java/Servlet-Tutorial/** A Sun-recommended JSP tutorial
- **http://www.apl.jhu.edu/~hall/java/Servlet-Tutorial/** A tutorial on servlets and JSP
- **http://www.jspinsider.com/content/rcarnes/jspb_intro.view** The JSP Insider's tutorial
- **http://www.jsptut.com/** A JSP tutorial site
- **http://java.sun.com/products/jsp/tutorial/TagLibrariesTOC.html** A tag library tutorial

If you really didn't feel comfortable with the topics in this module, it's probably a good idea to take a look at a book on JSP and servlets before proceeding. The skills in this module will be built on in the chapters to follow.

✓ Module 1 Mastery Check

1. What are the different types of JSP elements?

   A. Scripting elements, methods, directives, and actions

   B. Scripting elements, comments, directives, and schema

   C. Scripting elements, comments, directives, and actions

   D. Scripting elements, comments, commands, and actions

2. What are the different types of JSP scripting elements?

   A. Scriptlets, comments, and expressions

   B. Scriptlets, directives, and expressions

   C. Scriptlets, declarations, and actions

   D. Scriptlets, declarations, and expressions

3. In order, what markup do you use to create JSP scriptlets, declarations, and expressions?

   A. <% and %>, <%! and %>, and <%= and %>

   B. <% and %>, <%? and %>, and <%= and %>

   C. <% and %>, <%$ and %>, and <%= and %>

   D. <% and %>, <%= and %>, and <%! and %>

4. What are the three JSP directives?

   A. page, include, and taglibrary

   B. page, subst, and taglibrary

   C. page, include, and taglib

   D. page, subst, and taglib

5. What JSP action can you use to create a Java object from a JavaBean?

   A. **<jsp:makeBean>**

   B. **<jsp:useBean>**

   C. **<jsp:instantiateBean>**

   D. **<jsp:createBean>**

6. What servlet methods can you use to handle data sent from a HTML form with the GET method?

   A. **doGet**

   B. **doRead**, **doGet**

   C. **doRead**, **service**

   D. **doGet**, **service**

7. Which of these methods can you use to send text back to a browser from a servlet?

   A. A PrintWriter object's **out** method

   B. A ServletWriter object's **out** method

   C. A ServletWriter object's **println** method

   D. A PrintWriter object's **println** method

8. What servlet method can you use to initialize your servlet?

   A. **initialize**

   B. **init**

   C. **start**

   D. **servlet**

9. What is the name of the directory in which you place .class files so they're accessible from JSP?

   A. lib

   B. library

   C. classes and subdirectories as needed to reflect package structure

   D. lib and subdirectories as needed to reflect package structure

10. In JSP, what request object method can you use to read text from a text field?

    A. **getValue**

    B. **getData**

    C. **getParameter**

    D. **getText**

Module 2

Struts Essentials

CRITICAL SKILLS

This module puts Struts to work for us. We'll get an overview of Struts in this module and write an example. The Struts learning curve is a steep one, and the skills discussed here are all essential. We'll start with an overview of the inspiration behind Struts: the Model-View-Controller architecture. Then we'll get a skeleton Struts application working, and finally, we'll implement a working, fleshed out Struts application.

CRITICAL SKILL 2.1

Use MVC Architecture

In the previous module, we used servlets, JSPs, and JavaBeans, and you can build web applications using these components. However, most such applications end up somewhat ad hoc, and as web applications grow larger and more involved, a better overall plan is needed. We'll start this module with an overview of how the ad hoc application, called Model 1 Architecture, works and then move on to Model 2.

Model 1 Architecture

Small web applications are typically built using Model 1 programming architecture. In a Java-based Model 1 application, you might use a JSP that calls a few JavaBeans that implement the application's logic. For example, you may want to present an online order form to the user and use JSPs to display items to the user and allow the user to search for additional items, move to new items, and so on. You can also use beans to calculate prices with shipping and tax.

In this case, the JSPs do everything but handle the actual logic used in the beans to calculate shipping costs and tax. That's fine as far as it goes, but where Java code and HTML are intermixed, JSPs don't work well for extensive programming. Servlets are a better choice when it comes to straight Java programming, but they are not that useful for displaying a user interface. So what's the best way of creating larger applications—with JSPs, servlets, or JavaBeans? The answer is with all three.

Model 2 Architecture

Model 2 architecture is very similar to what's called *Model View Controller* (MVC) architecture. Here, the *controller* (often a servlet) oversees the whole application, interacting with the user and calling code in the *model* (often JavaBeans) to handle the internal logic and business rules, and then sending the results to presentation code, the *view* (often JSPs), which displays data to the user. Here's an overview of these three components:

- The model implements the functionality, such as the "business rules" of the application. This is the core code that does the internal work, such as checking if an item is in stock, what its price and discount are, and so on. The model doesn't know anything about the view of the controller. The model is often implemented using JavaBeans.

- The view implements the presentation of data to the user. The view takes the data supplied to it (usually from the controller) and displays it. The designers of the view need to know HTML, but they don't need to know anything about the logic implemented in the model. The view is often implemented in JSP.
- The controller oversees the model and the view by reacting to the data the user sends. It accepts input from the user, calls the appropriate bean methods in the model, and sends data to the view for presentation. The controller is often implemented as a servlet.

In other words, a Model 2 web application can use all three programming techniques you reviewed in Module 1—a servlet controller, a JavaBean model, and a JSP view. This will be the basis of your Struts applications.

Struts applications are built using an architecture that is very close to Model 2 architecture, but there's some terminology you have to learn. That's coming up next.

CRITICAL SKILL 2.2

Understand How Struts Works

The hardest part of learning how Struts works is understanding the flow of control through a Struts application. There are a number of new terms here—ActionServlet, ActionForm, ActionMapping, and so on—and it's crucial that you master them. Because there's a lot to absorb here, we'll go through the whole control flow a number of times, first in overview here, then with working examples in code. You might have to come back and read this description a number of times as we progress, but don't give up; once you know how these concepts work, you've won half the battle.

We'll take a look at how a typical Struts application works now in overview, starting with a Welcome page and ending with a results page. There are many ways to build Struts applications, but this will give us a good start.

Ask the Expert

Q: Is the MVC architecture right for every web application?

A: No. If you're writing something simple, you probably don't need the explicit code separation involved in writing the different components—model, view, and controller—involved in an MVC application. The MVC advantages come into play principally in larger applications.

The Welcome Page

Struts applications often start with a Welcome page, which is often index.jsp (the default JSP that will be opened when you browse to a directory on the server if no other file is specified and no index.html is present). A Welcome page may contain HTML controls, such as text fields, check boxes, and so on, that the user can enter data into. When the user clicks the Submit button, that data is supposed to go back to your Struts application's controller.

In Struts, the controller is made up of an action servlet (an **ActionServlet** object) and an action object or objects. User requests are sent to the action servlet, which delegates those requests to the action object or objects for further processing. It's done this way instead of using a single servlet for the controller because the action servlet comes built into Struts and you don't usually modify it yourself. Instead, you modify the **Action** objects that handle requests sent to them from the action servlet.

So how do you make sure the data in the HTML controls in the Welcome page (or any other page) goes back to the action servlet (and then is sent on to the correct action object)? There are six custom JSP tag libraries that come with Struts 1.1, and you use them in JSPs to handle tasks like this for you. In this case, you use the **html** tag library to create a custom HTML form that will send its data back to the action servlet. You start the Welcome page, index.jsp, with a JSP **<%@taglib%>** directive to add support for the **html** tag library:

```
<%@ taglib uri="/tags/struts-html" prefix="html" %>
        .
        .
        .
```

Then you're able to create an HTML form to hold HTML controls using the **<html:form>** custom tag. You can set the **action** attribute of this form to the name of the action the action servlet should forward the form's data to:

```
<%@ taglib uri="/tags/struts-html" prefix="html" %>
        .
        .
        .
    <html:form action="Data">
          Please click the button:
          <html:submit />
    </html:form>
```

Note also the **<html:submit />** element here, which creates a Submit button. There are **<html:*xxxx*>** tags for the various HTML controls, such as **<html:text>**, to create an HTML text field and so on.

But how does this data get to the action servlet? As we'll see, that servlet is typically set up to handle URLs that end in **.do**, so the custom JSP tag **<html:form>** replaces the **action** attribute's value with the URL corresponding to the actual action the action servlet will forward this data to, **Data.do**:

```
<form name="dataForm" method="post" action="/ch02/Data.do">
      Please click the button:
      <input type="submit" value="Submit">
</form>
```

Because the action servlet is set up to handle all URLs that end in **.do**, it'll be called **Data.do** (that means the action servlet will know that it should forward the data from the form to the action you've named **Data**, and you'll see how that happens in a few pages). But how is the action servlet configured to handle all URLs with the extension **.do**?

The ActionServlet

The action servlet is indeed a servlet; it's an object of the **org.apache.struts.action .ActionServlet** class, which extends the standard **javax.servlet.HttpServlet** class. Servlets are configured in web.xml in the WEB-INF directory with **<servlet>** and **<servlet-mapping>** elements as reviewed in Module 1.

In web.xml, the action servlet is given the name action, and it's set up like this in the **<servlet>** element—note that various initialization parameters here set values the action servlet will need, such as the name of the configuration file, **struts-config.xml**, which we'll use soon:

```
<servlet>
    <servlet-name>action</servlet-name>
    <servlet-class>org.apache.struts.action.ActionServlet</servlet-class>
    <init-param>
      <param-name>config</param-name>
      <param-value>/WEB-INF/struts-config.xml</param-value>
    </init-param>
    <init-param>
      <param-name>debug</param-name>
      <param-value>2</param-value>
    </init-param>
    <init-param>
      <param-name>detail</param-name>
      <param-value>2</param-value>
    </init-param>
    <load-on-startup>2</load-on-startup>
  </servlet>
```

The action servlet, named action here, is connected to the URL *.do in a **<servlet-mapping>** element:

```
<servlet-mapping>
  <servlet-name>action</servlet-name>
  <url-pattern>*.do</url-pattern>
</servlet-mapping>
```

This connects the action servlet to the URL ***.do**, so when we submit our form's data to **Data.do**, the action servlet will get that data and know it's supposed to forward that data to the **Data** action. How does it find the Java code that corresponds to that action?

ActionMappings

Together with the action servlet, actions make up the controller in Struts applications. As discussed, the controller here is broken into two parts: the action servlet which comes built into Struts, and the actions that you customize yourself.

At this point in our application, the action servlet knows that it's supposed to send the data from your HTML form to the action named **Data**. An action is a Java object based on the **org.apache.struts.action.Action** class, and the action servlet needs only to call the action's **execute** method to pass all the data needed to it. How does it know where to find the action object? It checks the **<action-mappings>** element in the struts-config.xml file.

The struts-config.xml file doesn't have to have that name; you can set any name you want as long as you use that name in the **config** initialization parameter for the action servlet in web.xml.

As we've seen, the action servlet is set up in web.xml. When it loads, the action servlet reads in another configuration file, struts-config.xml. This file tells Struts how you've set up your application; in particular, the **<action-mappings>** element in struts-config.xml tells the action servlet where to find the actions it needs to pass data on to.

The **<action-mappings>** element contains **<action>** elements, one for each action you've created. For example, to set up an action named **Data**, you might set an **<action>** element's **path** attribute to that name. To give the name of the Java class that implements this action, you can use the **type** attribute. For example, to indicate that the **Data** action is supported by the **ch02.DataAction** class (which the action servlet will look for in your applications WEB-INF/classes directory), your **<action>** element might look like this:

```
<action-mappings>
    <action
      path="/Data"
      type="ch02.DataAction"
        .
        .
        .
    </action>
</action-mappings>
```

Now the action servlet knows what Java method to send the data from our HTML form to, **ch02.DataAction.execute**. But how does it actually send that data? That data will vary for each web application, so it's not easy to set things up so that a few set values are always passed to the action.

Instead, Struts is designed so that the action servlet sends data to an action using a JavaBean object. You write that bean object, an **ActionForm** object, to have a read/write property for every piece of data in the HTML form. For example, if you had an HTML text field named **text** in your HTML form, the corresponding bean would have a property named **setText**, which the action servlet calls to store the text from the text field. The action servlet then passes that bean on to the action, which can call the bean's **getText** method to recover that text.

Here's how using a bean works. You specify the name of the bean the action servlet should use when passing data on to an action in the **<action>** element's **name** attribute inside the **<action-mappings>** element. For example, we might make that name **dataForm**:

```
<action-mappings>
    <action
      path="/Data"
      type="ch02.DataAction"
      name="dataForm"
      input="/index.jsp">
    </action>
</action-mappings>
```

In the **<form-beans>** element in struts-config.xml, you create a <form-bean> element tying the name of this bean, **dataForm**, to a Java class, which we can name **ch02.DataForm** (which the action servlet will look for in your applications WEB-INF/classes directory):

```
<form-beans>
    <form-bean name="dataForm"
        type="ch02.DataForm"/>
</form-beans>
```

Now the action servlet knows what class to use to create the bean it needs to transfer data to the action. How do we actually write the code for that bean class?

Action Forms

The beans that action servlets stock with data to send on to actions are based on the **ActionForm** class. Here's how you can write such a bean:

```
package ch02;

import javax.servlet.http.HttpServletRequest;
import org.apache.struts.action.*;

public class DataForm extends ActionForm {
.
.
.
}
```

If your HTML form had HTML controls like a text field named **text**, you'd add code like this to support a **text** property:

```
package ch02;

import javax.servlet.http.HttpServletRequest;
import org.apache.struts.action.*;

public class DataForm extends ActionForm {

  private String text = null;

  public String getText()
  {
    return (text);
  }

  public void setText(String text)
  {
    this.text = text;
  }

  public void reset(ActionMapping mapping,
    HttpServletRequest request)
  {
    this.text = null;
  }
}
```

Now the action servlet can call this bean's **setText** method to store the text from the text field and pass the bean to the action we've specified. That action can read the text that was in the text field by calling the **getText** method. How do you write the code for actions like this? That's coming up next.

Actions

The action class is where you write your own customized part of the application's controller. The action servlet passes data on to you that you're supposed to work on, and as we'll see, you can pass back instructions to the action servlet.

In Struts 1.0, the **execute** method was the **perform** method. It was replaced in Struts 1.1 by **execute**, which has better exception handling (**perform** is not deprecated, however).

To create an action, you extend the **org.apache.struts.action.Action** class and override the **execute** method:

```
package ch02;

import java.io.IOException;
import javax.servlet.*;
import javax.servlet.http.*;
import org.apache.struts.action.*;

public class DataAction extends Action {

  public ActionForward execute(ActionMapping mapping,
    ActionForm form,
    HttpServletRequest request,
    HttpServletResponse response)
    throws IOException, ServletException {
        .
        .
        .
  }
}
```

The **execute** method is passed several objects: an **ActionMapping** object that it can use to tell the action servlet which view to use to display results in; an **ActionForm** object, which is the bean the action servlet uses to send data to the action; and the standard **request** and

response objects from the browser (which also contain the data passed to the action servlet from the browser).

The action can read data passed to it using the **form** variable. For example, if you wanted to read the data passed to you from the Welcome page's text field, you could use code like this:

```
package ch02;

import ch02.DataForm;
import java.io.IOException;
import javax.servlet.*;
import javax.servlet.http.*;
import org.apache.struts.action.*;

public class DataAction extends Action {

  public ActionForward execute(ActionMapping mapping,
    ActionForm form,
    HttpServletRequest request,
    HttpServletResponse response)
    throws IOException, ServletException {

    String text = ((DataForm) form).getText();
          .
          .
          .
  }
}
```

The action can read the data passed to it and, to work with that data, it can call the JavaBeans that implement the model. For example, if the code for the model was implemented in a JavaBean named **DataModel**, which had a method named **doWork()**, you could pass the data from the Welcome page on to that method this way in the action:

```
package ch02;

import ch02.DataForm;
import java.io.IOException;
import javax.servlet.*;
import javax.servlet.http.*;
import org.apache.struts.action.*;

public class DataAction extends Action {

  public ActionForward execute(ActionMapping mapping,
```

```
      ActionForm form,
      HttpServletRequest request,
      HttpServletResponse response)
      throws IOException, ServletException {

      String text = ((DataForm) form).getText();

      DataModel dataModel = new DataModel();
      dataModel.doWork(text);
    }
}
```

After the data has been processed and you want to send it to the view to display the results, you have to make sure the view has access to that data. There are a number of ways to do that. We've connected the bean **dataBean** to this action in the **<action>** element, so you can use the methods of that bean to store data like this:

```
package ch02;

import java.io.IOException;
import javax.servlet.*;
import javax.servlet.http.*;
import org.apache.struts.action.*;

public class DataAction extends Action {

  public ActionForward execute(ActionMapping mapping,
    ActionForm form,
    HttpServletRequest request,
    HttpServletResponse response)
    throws IOException, ServletException {

    ((DataForm) form).setText("No problem.");
  }
}
```

The view, a JSP, will be able to access the **dataBean** bean using the **<bean>** tag library elements and retrieve the data you've set in the bean.

You don't have to pass data to the view using a bean, however; you can also store data in the request object using the **setAttribute** method, making that data accessible to the view:

```
package ch02;

import java.io.IOException;
import javax.servlet.*;
```

```
import javax.servlet.http.*;
import org.apache.struts.action.*;

public class DataAction extends Action {

  public ActionForward execute(ActionMapping mapping,
    ActionForm form,
    HttpServletRequest request,
    HttpServletResponse response)
    throws IOException, ServletException {

    request.setAttribute("text", "No worries.");
  }
}
```

Now that you've stored some data for the view to display, using either the action's bean or the request object, how do you actually forward control on to the view? You do that in an action by creating an **ActionForward** object, which the **execute** method is intended to return. Here's how it works.

The various views that you can forward to are set up in the **<action>** element in struts-config.xml using **<forward>** elements. For example, if we wanted to define two forwards to handle success or failure, we might just name them success and failure using **<forward>** elements. You set the **path** attribute to the URL for these forwards like this—if we're successful, we'll forward the results to results.jsp; otherwise, we'll start over by forwarding to the original Welcome page, index.jsp:

```
<action-mappings>
<action
      path="/Data"
      type="ch02.DataAction"
      name="dataForm"
      input="/index.jsp">
      <forward name="success" path="/results.jsp"/>
      <forward name="failure" path="/index.jsp"/>
    </action>
</action-mappings>
```

Since an **ActionMapping** object, **mapping**, is passed to the **execute** method, you have access to these **<forward>** elements. All you have to do is to use the **mapping** object's **findForward** method and use that method to return a new **ActionForward** object to the action servlet, telling it where to go next. For example, here's how you might forward to our **success** page:

```
package ch02;

import java.io.IOException;
import javax.servlet.*;
import javax.servlet.http.*;
import org.apache.struts.action.*;

public class DataAction extends Action {

  public ActionForward execute(ActionMapping mapping,
    ActionForm form,
    HttpServletRequest request,
    HttpServletResponse response)
    throws IOException, ServletException {

    request.setAttribute("DATA", "No worries.");

    String target = new String("success");
    return (mapping.findForward(target));
  }
}
```

Returning an **ActionForward** object from the **execute** method makes the **execute** method pass control to the view we've requested, results.jsp.

The Results Page

The results page, results.jsp in this case, is usually a JSP page. In this page, you have access to the data in the form bean, **dataForm**, used by the action. For example, to get the value of the **text** property from this bean and display it, you could use the **<bean:write>** custom tag like this:

```
<html>
  <head>
    <title>A Results page</title>
  </head>
  <body>
  <h1>A Sample Results Page</h1>

  <bean:write name="dataForm" property="text"/>

  </body>
</html>
```

If you wanted to recover data that was stored as a servlet context attribute, you could use the request object's **getAttribute** method in a scriptlet:

```
<html>
  <head>
    <title>A Results page</title>
  </head>
  <body>
  <h1>A Sample Results Page</h1>

    <%= request.getAttribute("text") %>

  </body>
</html>
```

That completes the overview, from Welcome page all the way to the results page. Now you'll see this in operation in working examples.

Progress Check

1. A form bean object holding data from the action servlet is passed to each action. What's the name of the form bean class?
2. The **execute** method passes back an object of which class to the action servlet?

CRITICAL SKILL

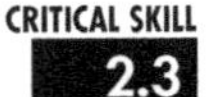

2.3 Develop a Struts Skeleton: struts-blank.war

It's easy enough to get a Struts example going, because there are some good ones already written for you that come with Struts. One example is struts-blank.war, which is a skeleton Struts example that acts as a sort of fill-in-the-blanks application. You'll find struts-blank.war in the Struts webapps directory when you expand the Struts download. You can use this example as the backbone of your application, developing it as you like.

Install .war files such as struts-blank.war by simply placing them in the Tomcat webapps directory.

---

1. The **ActionForm** class.
2. The **ActionForward** class.

Restart Tomcat. Tomcat will expand struts-blank.war and create a new directory in the webapps directory named struts-blank. Here's what's in that directory; note in particular all the Struts .jar files in the lib directory—those are the files that allow a Struts application to run:

```
tomcat
 |__jakarta-tomcat-5.0.19
    |__webapps
        |__struts-blank
            |__index.jsp
            |__META-INF
            |   |__MANIFEST.MF
            |
            |__pages
            |   |__Welcome.jsp
            |
            |__WEB-INF
                |__struts-bean.tld
                |__struts-config.xml
                |__struts-html.tld
                |__struts-logic.tld
                |__struts-nested.tld
                |__struts-template.tld
                |__struts-tiles.tld
                |__tiles-defs.xml
                |__validation.xml
                |__validator-rules.xml
                |__web.xml
                |
                |__classes
                |       |__resources
                |           |__application.properties
                |
                |__lib
                |   |__commons-beanutils.jar
                |   |__commons-collections.jar
                |   |__commons-digester.jar
                |   |__commons-fileupload.jar
                |   |__commons-lang.jar
                |   |__commons-logging.jar
                |   |__commons-validator.jar
                |   |__jakarta-oro.jar
                |   |__struts.jar
                |
                |__src
                    |__build.xml
                    |__README.txt
```

```
        |__java
           |__resources
               |__application.properties
```

Because it takes time to expand large .war files, after you've installed struts-blank.war, you might want to delete it from the Tomcat webapps directory. Otherwise, Tomcat will expand it every time it starts.

With Tomcat running, navigate to http://localhost:8080/struts-blank and you'll see the struts-blank application's Welcome page, as shown in Figure 2-1. That's what this application does; it sets up a skeleton application for you to fill in the blanks and sets up a forward to this Welcome page. It doesn't use any Java code for actions or forms—all that is up to you.

That's all it took to get our first Struts application going. How does this application work? We'll dissect its flow of control next. When you enter the URL http://localhost:8080/struts-blank, Tomcat looks for index.html or index.jsp in the webapps/struts-blank directory, and in this case finds index.jsp.

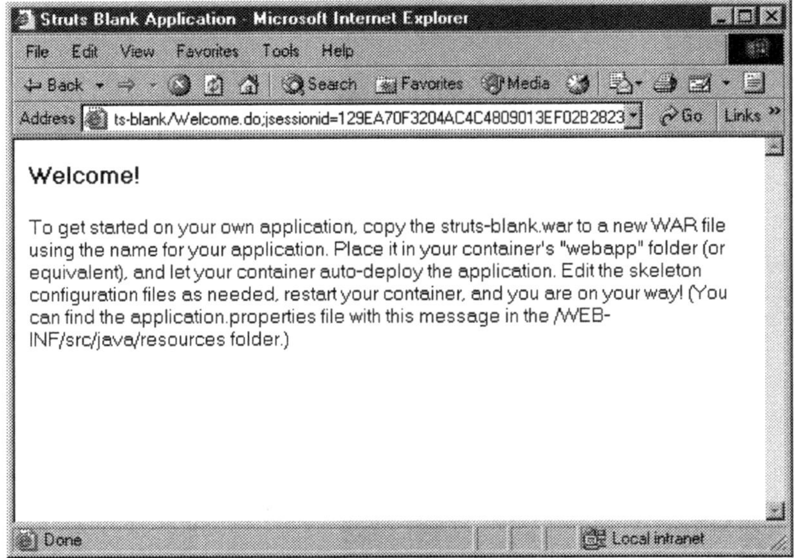

Figure 2-1 A blank Struts application

index.jsp

When you open some Struts applications, you navigate directly to a particular page to get things started. That's how we'll write most of the applications in this book. However, there's another way of opening a Struts application as well, where you don't have to specify a specific document. All you have to do is navigate to a subdirectory of the webapps directory.

That's how the struts-blank application works. It relies on a default index.jsp page that the browser will open first automatically and which will redirect the browser to a page inside the application itself. The index.jsp file does that with a forward named **welcome** using a Struts **<logic:redirect>** custom tag like this (we'll see custom **<logic>** tags like this one in this book):

```
<%@ taglib uri="/tags/struts-logic" prefix="logic" %>
<logic:redirect forward="welcome"/>

<%--

Redirect default requests to Welcome global ActionForward.
By using a redirect, the user-agent will change address to match the
path of our Welcome ActionForward.

--%>
```

struts-config.xml

You can set up a forward like this one with a **<forward>** element inside the **<global-forwards>** element in struts-config.xml. In the struts-blank application, this entry in struts-config.xml means that when the **<logic:redirect>** tag in index.jsp is processed by Tomcat, it will be expanded into a redirection header to Welcome.do:

```
<global-forwards>
    <!-- Default forward to "Welcome" action -->
    <!-- Demonstrates using index.jsp to forward -->
    <forward
        name="welcome"
        path="/Welcome.do"/>
</global-forwards>
```

In other words, the browser will now navigate to Welcome.do, which the action servlet will interpret as a request for the welcome action. That action is defined in struts-config.xml this way:

```
<action-mappings>
    <action
        path="/Welcome"
```

```
            type="org.apache.struts.actions.ForwardAction"
            parameter="/pages/Welcome.jsp"/>
    </action-mappings>
```

This action uses the predefined action class **org.apache.struts.actions.ForwardAction** instead of using a custom action you write yourself. It forwards you on to the URL given by the **parameter** attribute, which in this case is the document /pages/Welcome.jsp. That's the document you see in Figure 2-1.

Welcome.jsp

The Welcome.jsp file begins with a JSP **<%@taglib%>** element for each Struts tag library it uses, as well as an **<html:html>** tag, which starts the document in a locale-sensitive way like this:

```
<%@ taglib uri="/tags/struts-bean" prefix="bean" %>
<%@ taglib uri="/tags/struts-html" prefix="html" %>
<%@ taglib uri="/tags/struts-logic" prefix="logic" %>

<html:html locale="true">
<head>
        .
        .
        .
```

The text displayed in Welcome.jsp is actually stored in a file named application.properties, stored in /WEB-INF/src/java/resources. Using an application.properties file to store the text used by a Struts application is a common thing to do, and it makes internationalizing your applications easier. The text in this file is stored using *keys* like **welcome.title** and so forth, like this:

```
# -- standard errors --
errors.header=<UL>
errors.prefix=<LI>
errors.suffix=</LI>
errors.footer=</UL>
# -- validator --
errors.invalid={0} is invalid.
errors.maxlength={0} can not be greater than {1} characters.
errors.minlength={0} can not be less than {1} characters.
errors.range={0} is not in the range {1} through {2}.
errors.required={0} is required.
errors.byte={0} must be an byte.
errors.date={0} is not a date.
errors.double={0} must be an double.
errors.float={0} must be an float.
```

```
errors.integer={0} must be an integer.
errors.long={0} must be an long.
errors.short={0} must be an short.
errors.creditcard={0} is not a valid credit card number.
errors.email={0} is an invalid e-mail address.
# -- other --
errors.cancel=Operation cancelled.
errors.detail={0}
errors.general=The process did not complete. Details should follow.
errors.token=Request could not be completed. Operation is not in
sequence.
# -- welcome --
welcome.title=Struts Blank Application
welcome.heading=Welcome!
welcome.message=To get started on your own application, copy the
struts-blank.war to a new WAR file using the name for your
application. Place it in your container's "webapp" folder (or
equivalent), and let your container auto-deploy the application. Edit
the skeleton configuration files as needed, restart your container,
and you are on your way! (You can find the application.properties file
with this message in the /WEB-INF/src/java/resources folder.)
```

You can access this text by key using the **<bean:message>** custom Struts tag with the **key** attribute to specify which string you want. Here's how Welcome.jsp retrieves the title text, "Struts Blank Application", from application.properties and uses it:

```
<%@ taglib uri="/tags/struts-bean" prefix="bean" %>
<%@ taglib uri="/tags/struts-html" prefix="html" %>
<%@ taglib uri="/tags/struts-logic" prefix="logic" %>

<html:html locale="true">
<head>
<title><bean:message key="welcome.title"/></title>
        .
        .
        .
```

Welcome.jsp also uses the **<html:base>** custom tag, which sets the HTML "base" to the current URL, http://localhost:8080/struts-blank/pages/Welcome.jsp:

```
<%@ taglib uri="/tags/struts-bean" prefix="bean" %>
<%@ taglib uri="/tags/struts-html" prefix="html" %>
<%@ taglib uri="/tags/struts-logic" prefix="logic" %>

<html:html locale="true">
<head>
<title><bean:message key="welcome.title"/></title>
```

```
<html:base/>
        .
        .
        .
```

This is useful because it means you can use relative URLs from now on. JSPs like this can be copied to other directories before being executed, which can break relative URLs. Using the **<html:base>** tag resets the base URL to the current URL for use in all relative URLs, as we'll discuss later in this book.

Next, Welcome.jsp uses the **<logic:notPresent>** tag to make sure the **org.apache.struts .action.MESSAGE** bean is present for use in the servlet context; if not, the application's resources haven't been loaded, and Welcome.jsp displays an error:

```
<%@ taglib uri="/tags/struts-bean" prefix="bean" %>
<%@ taglib uri="/tags/struts-html" prefix="html" %>
<%@ taglib uri="/tags/struts-logic" prefix="logic" %>

<html:html locale="true">
<head>
<title><bean:message key="welcome.title"/></title>
<html:base/>
</head>
<body bgcolor="white">

<logic:notPresent name="org.apache.struts.action.MESSAGE" scope="application">
  <font color="red">
    ERROR:  Application resources not loaded -- check servlet container
    logs for error messages.
  </font>
</logic:notPresent>
        .
        .
        .
```

Error messages like this one are usually stored in application.properties, but this is an exception—clearly, if the resources haven't been loaded, you can't access an error message from them.

Finally, Welcome.jsp displays the welcome message's header and the message itself:

```
<%@ taglib uri="/tags/struts-bean" prefix="bean" %>
<%@ taglib uri="/tags/struts-html" prefix="html" %>
<%@ taglib uri="/tags/struts-logic" prefix="logic" %>
        .
        .
        .
```

```
<logic:notPresent name="org.apache.struts.action.MESSAGE"
scope="application">
  <font color="red">
    ERROR:  Application resources not loaded -- check servlet container
    logs for error messages.
  </font>
</logic:notPresent>

<h3><bean:message key="welcome.heading"/></h3>
<p><bean:message key="welcome.message"/></p>
</body>
</html:html>
```

That completes the structure of the struts-blank application. All it's designed to do is to set up an automatic forward to Welcome.jsp, including the needed web.xml and struts-config.xml files.

Creating your own actions and forms is up to you, and that's our next step: to make this application actually do something interesting, we'll modify it to support a button that the user can click and an action that will forward the user to a new page when the button is clicked.

Progress Check

1. What custom tag allows you to use relative URLs in a Struts JSP?
2. What custom JSP tag can you use to read strings from the application.properties file?

CRITICAL SKILL 2.4

Write Forms and Actions: a Struts Example

There's no customized Java code in the struts-blank application we just saw, and that hardly makes it a real Struts application. We'll now add a custom action and a form to implement the kind of application we discussed in overview in the beginning of this module, with **DataForm** and **DataAction** classes. You can reach this application as http://localhost:8080/ch02/, as shown in Figure 2-2.

---

1. **<html:base>**.
2. **<bean:message key="your key here">**.

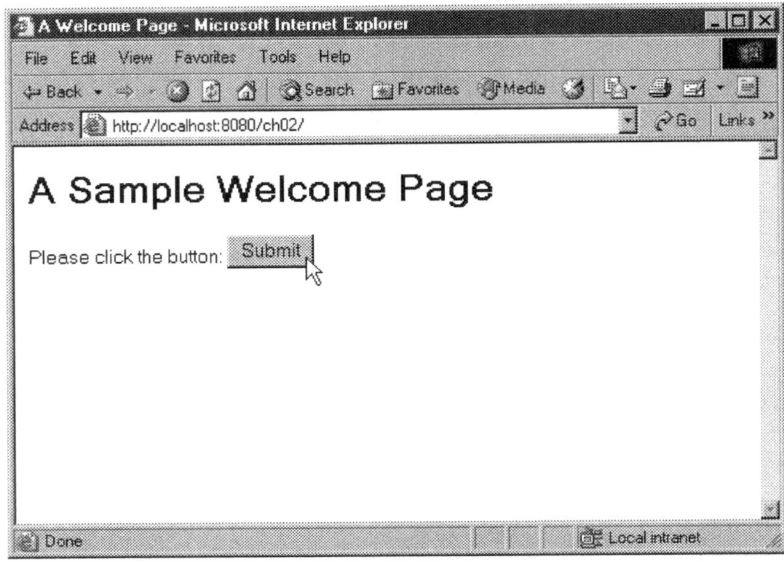

Figure 2-2 A Struts application's Welcome page with a Submit button

There's a Submit button in this page that will cause the action servlet to execute an action called **Data**, which will forward control to the results page shown in Figure 2-3.

This application is designed to get us started, so to keep things simple, this example intentionally does not send any data from HTML controls to the application. We'll see how to modify the application in the next Module.

Because we've just gone over the struts-blank application skeleton, we can use struts-blank as the backbone of this new application. Either rename the Tomcat webapps/struts-blank directory to webapps/ch02, or copy struts-blank.war to ch02.war, drop it into the Tomcat webapps directory, and restart Tomcat to create webapps/ch02.

The first step is to create the web page you see in Figure 2-2. We won't forward to a Welcome page in this application as the struts-blank application does; we'll get right to work without any forwards. To create the web page you see in Figure 2-2, copy the Welcome page, webapps/ch02/pages/Welcome.jsp, over to default page for this application, webapps/ch02/index.jsp.

Open the new index.jsp page. We'll execute an action named Data when the user clicks the Submit button, so make these changes in this new version of index.jsp:

```
<%@ taglib uri="/tags/struts-html" prefix="html" %>
<%@ taglib uri="/tags/struts-logic" prefix="logic" %>

<html:html locale="true">
<head>
<title>A Welcome Page</title>
<html:base/>
</head>
<body bgcolor="white">

<h1>A Sample Welcome Page</h1>

<logic:notPresent name="org.apache.struts.action.MESSAGE" scope="application">
  <font color="red">
    ERROR:  Application resources not loaded -- check servlet container
    logs for error messages.
  </font>
</logic:notPresent>

    <html:form action="Data">
          Please click the button:
          <html:submit />
    </html:form>

</body>
</html:html>
```

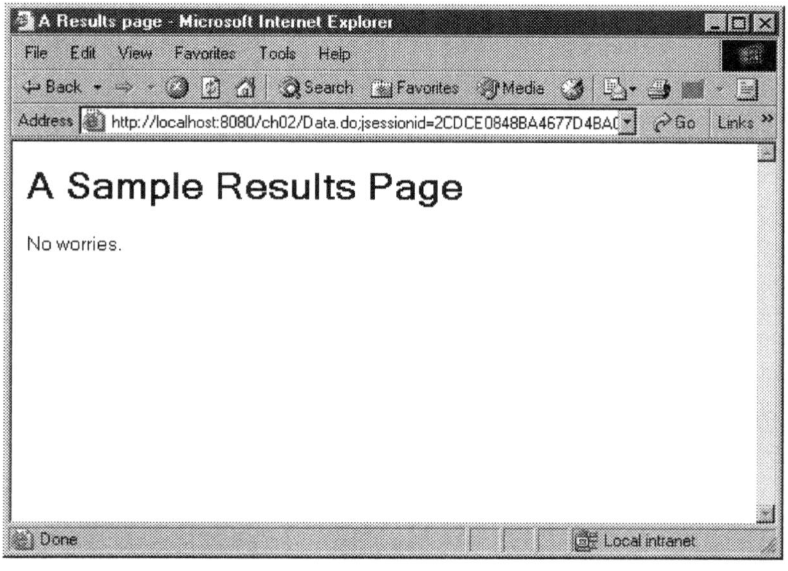

Figure 2-3 A Struts application's results page

When the user clicks the Submit button, we'll execute an action named **Data**. To connect that action to Java code, **ch02.DataAction**, add this **<action>** element to WEB-INF/struts-config.xml:

```
<action-mappings>
        .
        .
        .
    <action
      path="/Data"
      type="ch02.DataAction"
      input="/index.jsp">
    </action>
        .
        .
        .
</action-mappings>
```

We'll also define two forwards that the action can direct the action servlet to, a **success** forward to a results page named results.jsp (which you saw in Figure 2-3), and a **failure** forward that sends the user back to the Welcome page, index.jsp:

```
<action-mappings>
        .
        .
        .
    <action
      path="/Data"
      type="ch02.DataAction"
      name="dataForm"
      input="/index.jsp">
      <forward name="success" path="/results.jsp"/>
      <forward name="failure" path="/index.jsp"/>
    </action>
        .
        .
        .
</action-mappings>
```

Now that we're using an action, we'll also need an action form. Call the action form **dataForm**, even though it won't do anything because there's no data in the HTML form that we want to send to the action. Here's how to add that action form to the action:

```
<action-mappings>
        .
        .
        .
    <action
      path="/Data"
      type="ch02.DataAction"
      name="dataForm"
      input="/index.jsp">
      <forward name="success" path="/results.jsp"/>
      <forward name="failure" path="/index.jsp"/>
    </action>
        .
        .
        .
</action-mappings>
```

We can connect the **dataForm** bean to a Java class, **ch02.DataForm**, by adding a **<form-bean>** element to the **<form-beans>** element in struts-config.xml:

```
    <form-beans>
        .
        .
        .
    <form-bean name="dataForm"
      type="ch02.DataForm"/>
        .
        .
        .
    <form-beans>
```

In this simple example, the form bean will only be a placeholder and won't actually hold any data. In this case, we'll just add an empty **validate** method to our form bean. This method checks if the data from the HTML form meets your validity conditions (which we'll learn more about in the next module), but we won't do anything with it here:

```
package ch02;

import javax.servlet.http.HttpServletRequest;
import org.apache.struts.action.*;

public class DataForm extends ActionForm {

  public ActionErrors validate(ActionMapping mapping,
    HttpServletRequest request) {
```

```
      return new ActionErrors();
    }
}
```

In the action class, **DataAction**, you'll implement the **execute** method that will be called when the action is executed:

```
package ch02;

import java.io.IOException;
import javax.servlet.*;
import javax.servlet.http.*;
import org.apache.struts.action.*;

public class DataAction extends Action {

  public ActionForward execute(ActionMapping mapping,
    ActionForm form,
    HttpServletRequest request,
    HttpServletResponse response)
    throws IOException, ServletException {
          .
          .
          .
  }
}
```

In this action, we'll forward some text, "No worries.", to the results page. Because we haven't started creating form beans that can hold data yet, we'll store that data in a **request** object attribute named **DATA**:

```
package ch02;
          .
          .
          .
public class DataAction extends Action {

  public ActionForward execute(ActionMapping mapping,
    ActionForm form,
    HttpServletRequest request,
    HttpServletResponse response)
    throws IOException, ServletException {

    String text = "No worries.";
```

```
    String target = new String("success");
    request.setAttribute("DATA", text);
        .
        .
        .
  }
}
```

We will also forward on to the **success** forward, which corresponds to the results.jsp page this way:

```
package ch02;
        .
        .
        .
public class DataAction extends Action {

  public ActionForward execute(ActionMapping mapping,
    ActionForm form,
    HttpServletRequest request,
    HttpServletResponse response)
    throws IOException, ServletException {

    String text = "No worries.";
    String target = new String("success");
    request.setAttribute("DATA", text);
    return (mapping.findForward(target));
  }
}
```

Progress Check

1. What method is called to execute an action in Struts 1.1?

2. How do you forward to a target in an action?

---

1. The **execute** method.

2. **mapping.findForward(target)**.

Finally, in the results.jsp page, we'll recover the data stored in the servlet context **DATA** attribute with the request object's **getAttribute()** method this way:

```
<html>
  <head>
    <title>A Results page</title>
  </head>
  <body>
  <h1>A Sample Results Page</h1>

<%= request.getAttribute("DATA") %>

  </body>
</html>
```

That completes the code. To compile this code, make sure struts.jar from the Struts download is in your classpath, as well as servlet-api.jar (servlet-api.jar was called servlet.jar in Tomcat 4.*x*). Note that if struts.jar and servlet-api.jar are not in the current directory, you should preface their names with the correct path (the period [.] at the end also adds the current directory and its subdirectories to the classpath):

```
%set classpath=servlet-api.jar;struts.jar;.
```

Next, compile DataForm.java and DataAction.java. If your Java installation's bin directory isn't in your computer's path, preface javac with the path to the Java bin directory (such as C:\jdk1.4\bin\javac):

```
%javac DataForm.java
%javac DataAction.java
```

TIP

When we start working with form classes that hold data, our action class will need to import those classes. In such a case, because the code in DataForm.java is in the ch02 package, the Java compiler will search for a directory named ch02 that holds DataForm.class. To make sure it finds that file, add a ch02 subdirectory to the current directory and put DataForm.class in it.

This creates DataForm.class and DataAction.class. Because we've put these classes in a package named **ch02**, these files should be copied to the WEB-INF/classes/ch02 directory. Here's where to put all the new and changed files in this application:

```
tomcat
 |__jakarta-tomcat-5.0.19
     |__webapps
         |__ch02
             |__index.jsp
             |__results.jsp
             |
             |__META-INF
             |   |__MANIFEST.MF
             |
             |__pages
             |
             |__WEB-INF
                 |__struts-bean.tld
                 |__struts-config.xml
                 |__struts-html.tld
                 |__struts-logic.tld
                 |__struts-nested.tld
                 |__struts-template.tld
                 |__struts-tiles.tld
                 |__tiles-defs.xml
                 |__validation.xml
                 |__validator-rules.xml
                 |__web.xml
                 |__classes
                 |      |__resources
                 |      |   |__application.properties
                 |      |
                 |      |__ch02
                 |          |__DataForm.class
                 |          |__DataAction.class
                 |
                 |__lib
                 |   |__commons-beanutils.jar
                 |   |__commons-collections.jar
                 |   |__commons-digester.jar
                 |   |__commons-fileupload.jar
                 |   |__commons-lang.jar
                 |   |__commons-logging.jar
                 |   |__commons-validator.jar
                 |   |__jakarta-oro.jar
                 |   |__struts.jar
                 |
                 |__src
                     |__build.xml
                     |__README.txt
```

```
|__java
   |__resources
      |__application.properties
```

That completes the example. When the user clicks the Submit button, the Data action will now be executed and forward data to the results.jsp view, which will recover and display it. Not bad! In the next module, we'll elaborate this example further to read data from the user.

Use Struts 1.2

This example used the Struts 1.1 download and libraries, but Struts 1.2 is on the horizon as well. As of this writing, there is an early edition of Struts 1.2 available, and we'll be mentioning the differences between these versions throughout the book. The example we just completed works unchanged with either the Struts 1.1 or 1.2 .jar files.

Module 2 Mastery Check

1. What does the acronym MVC stand for?

   A. Method, View, Controller

   B. Method, View, Control

   C. Model, View, Controller

   D. Model, View, Control

2. In MVC architecture, the view is often implemented using:

   A. JSPs

   B. Servlets

   C. JavaBeans

   D. HTML

3. How does an action servlet find an action's code?

   A. Using an ActionForm

   B. Using an ActionServlet

   C. Using an ActionConnect

   D. Using an ActionMapping

4. How many custom JSP tag libraries come with Struts?

A. 4

B. 6

C. 8

D. 10

5. What JSP directive do you use to add support for a Struts tag library in a JSP file?

A. A JSP **<%@taglibrary%>** directive

B. A JSP **<%@taglib%>** directive

C. A JSP **<%@tlib%>** directive

D. A JSP **<%@library%>** directive

6. What custom JSP tag can you use to create an HTML form that connects to a Struts action named Data?

A. **<html:form method="DataAction">**

B. **<form method="DataAction">**

C. **<html:form action="Data">**

D. **<form action="Data">**

7. What two elements in web.xml set up the action servlet?

A. **<servlets>** and **<struts>**

B. **<servlet>** and **<struts>**

C. **<servlet>** and **<servlet-mappings>**

D. **<servlet>** and **<servlet-mapping>**

8. In <action> elements in struts-config.xml, what attribute do you use to indicate what form bean an action should use?

A. <bean>

B. <name>

C. <formBean>

D. <form>

9. In the **<form-beans>** element in struts-config.xml, what attribute do you use to specify the name of the Java class for the form bean?

   A. class

   B. form

   C. bean

   D. type

10. What objects are passed to the **execute** method of an action?

   A. **ActionForm**, **HttpServletRequest**, and **HttpServletResponse** objects

   B. **ActionMapping**, **HttpServletRequest**, and **HttpServletResponse** objects

   C. **ActionMapping**, **ActionForm**, **HttpServletRequest**, and **HttpServletResponse** objects

   D. **ActionMapping**, **ActionForm**, **ActionForward**, **HttpServletRequest**, and **HttpServletResponse** objects

Module 3

Handling User Input

CRITICAL SKILLS

3.1 Read User Input

3.2 Create a Full Struts Example

In this module, we'll start by learning how to accept and deal with user input. After we've done that, we'll be ready to tackle a full-scale Struts application, complete with your own custom tags and various HTML controls.

CRITICAL SKILL 3.1

Read User Input

In the previous module, we created an application that displayed a Submit button that the user could click to see a message, "No worries." In this module, we'll extend that example to accept user input and use a form bean to hold that data. You can see this application by navigating to http://localhost:8080/ch03/, as shown in Figure 3-1. The application asks the user to enter their name, as you see in the figure.

When the user enters their name and clicks the Submit button, that name is sent to our action via a form bean. The action reads it and forwards it on to the Results page, which displays the name as shown in Figure 3-2.

The example we created in the previous module was a good start. Now it's time to extend that example to handle data using a form bean. Let's take a look at how this works. If you want to follow along, copy over the webapps/ch02 folder to webapps/ch03; we'll be renaming the **ch02** package as **ch03**.

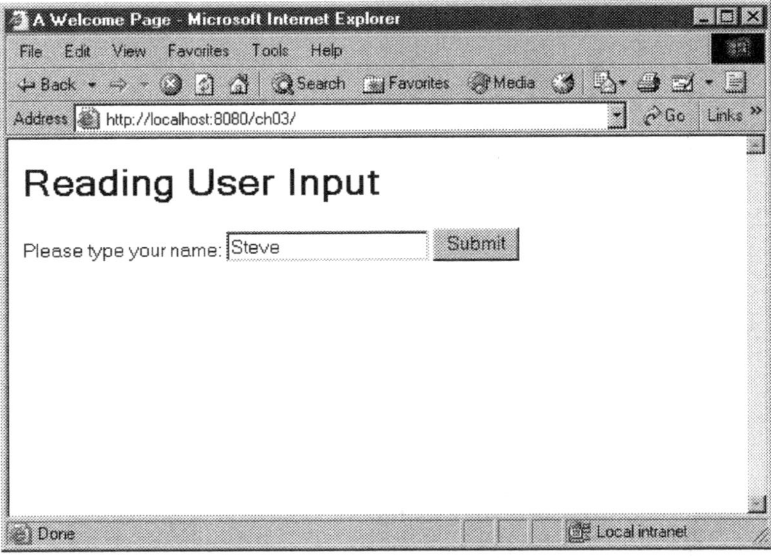

Figure 3-1 Reading user input

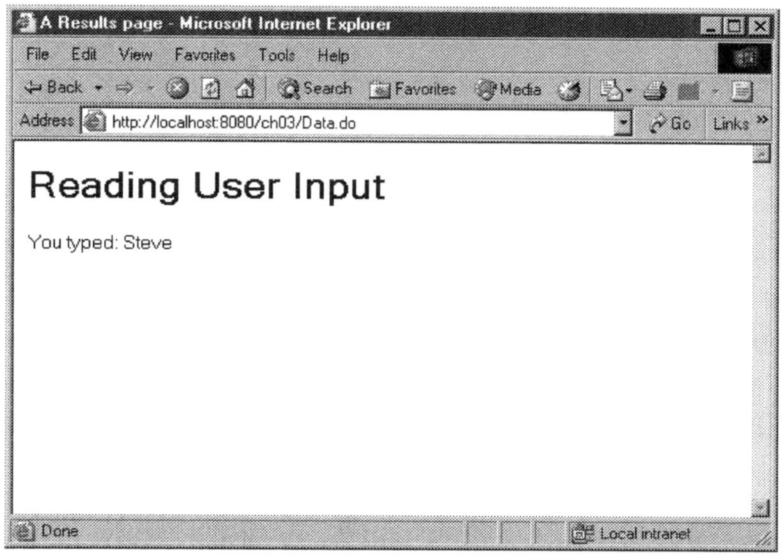

Figure 3-2 Displaying what the user entered

The Welcome Page

To start, we'll modify the Welcome page from what it was in the previous module. There, we had only a Submit button, but in this case we'll need to add an HTML text field. You can create that text field with the Struts **<html:text>** custom tag. You can also give a name to the bean property that will store the text from this text field; call it **text** in index.jsp:

```
<%@ taglib uri="/tags/struts-html" prefix="html" %>
<%@ taglib uri="/tags/struts-logic" prefix="logic" %>

<html:html locale="true">
<head>
<title>A Welcome Page</title>
<html:base/>
</head>
<body bgcolor="white">

<logic:notPresent name="org.apache.struts.action.MESSAGE" scope="application">
  <font color="red">
    ERROR:  Application resources not loaded -- check servlet container
```

```
    logs for error messages.
  </font>
</logic:notPresent>
    <h1>Reading User Input</h1>

    <html:form action="Data">
          Please type your name: <html:text property="text" />
          <html:submit />
    </html:form>

</body>
</html:html>
```

The Action Form

Our data form, **DataForm**, will have to be able to deal with this **text** property. To implement that property, we'll add these methods to DataForm.java:

```
package ch03;

import javax.servlet.http.HttpServletRequest;
import org.apache.struts.action.ActionForm;
import org.apache.struts.action.ActionMapping;
import org.apache.struts.action.ActionError;
import org.apache.struts.action.ActionErrors;

public class DataForm extends ActionForm {

  private String text = null;

  public String getText() {

    return (text);
  }

  public void setText(String text) {

    this.text = text;
  }

  public void reset(ActionMapping mapping,
    HttpServletRequest request) {

    this.text = null;
  }
}
```

When the Struts framework makes bean objects from this class, each bean object will now support the **text** property so we can access the text from the HTML text field in index.jsp. We've already set up the application to use this bean, **dataForm**, in this application, as you can see in struts-config.xml, where we connect this bean to the **Data** action:

```
<action-mappings>
 <action
   path="/Data"
   type="ch03.DataAction"
   name="dataForm"
   input="/index.jsp">
   <forward name="success" path="/results.jsp"/>
   <forward name="failure" path="/index.jsp"/>
 </action>
</action-mappings>
```

In the **<form-beans>** element, we connected the bean name **dataForm** to the correct Java class, **ch03.DataForm**:

```
<form-beans>
<form-bean name="dataForm"
  type="ch03.DataForm"/>
</form-beans>
```

The new bean, complete with the **text** property, is ready to go. When the user enters their name in index.jsp and clicks Submit, the action servlet will store the text from the text field in the **text** property of this bean, and it'll pass the bean object on to the action's **execute** method.

The Action

In the action for this application, **ch03.DataAction**, we can recover the text from the form bean because that bean is passed to the action in the **execute** method:

```
public ActionForward execute(ActionMapping mapping,
  ActionForm form,
  HttpServletRequest request,
  HttpServletResponse response)
  throws IOException, ServletException {
      .
      .
      .
}
```

To use this new bean in DataAction.java, we'll start by importing its class so Java knows about the bean's **text** property.

```
package ch03;

import ch03.DataForm;
import java.io.IOException;
import javax.servlet.*;
import javax.servlet.http.*;
import org.apache.struts.action.*;

        .
        .
        .
```

If the **form** variable passed to us in the **execute** method is not **null**, we'll cast it to the **DataForm** type so the Java compiler won't complain when we refer to the **text** property, which doesn't exist in the **ActionForm** base class:

```
package ch03;
        .
        .
        .
public class DataAction extends Action {

  public ActionForward execute(ActionMapping mapping,
    ActionForm form,
    HttpServletRequest request,
    HttpServletResponse response)
    throws IOException, ServletException {

    if ( form != null ) {
      DataForm dataForm = (DataForm)form;
        .
        .
        .
    }
        .
        .
        .
}
```

You can access the text from the HTML text field using the **form** variable's **getText** method like this:

```
package ch03;
        .
        .
        .
public class DataAction extends Action {

  public ActionForward execute(ActionMapping mapping,
    ActionForm form,
    HttpServletRequest request,
    HttpServletResponse response)
    throws IOException, ServletException {

    String text = null;

    if ( form != null ) {
      DataForm dataForm = (DataForm)form;
      text = dataForm.getText();
    }
        .
        .
        .
}
```

At this point, you've recovered the text from the HTML text field. We want to pass that text on to the Results page, but because the text is already in the **dataForm** bean, all we have to do is to forward on to the Results page. The JSP code in the Results page will have access to the **dataForm** bean and can recover the text there. Here's how we indicate to the action servlet that we want to forward on to the Results page:

```
package ch03;
        .
        .
        .
public class DataAction extends Action {

  public ActionForward execute(ActionMapping mapping,
    ActionForm form,
    HttpServletRequest request,
    HttpServletResponse response)
    throws IOException, ServletException {

    String text = null;
    String target = new String("success");
```

```
    if ( form != null ) {
      DataForm dataForm = (DataForm)form;
      text = dataForm.getText();
    }

    return (mapping.findForward(target));
  }
}
```

The Results Page

When we pass control to the **success** forward in the action's **execute** method, the action servlet checks the action's mapping to find that the **success** forward corresponds to results.jsp:

```
<action-mappings>
 <action
   path="/Data"
   type="ch03.DataAction"
   name="dataForm"
   input="/index.jsp">
   <forward name="success" path="/results.jsp"/>
   <forward name="failure" path="/index.jsp"/>
 </action>
</action-mappings>
```

In results.jsp, we want to recover the value of the text property from the **dataForm** bean, which means using the **<bean:write>** custom Struts JSP tag. To use that tag, you start by adding support for the **bean** tag library, which we didn't need in the Results page in Module 2:

```
<%@ taglib uri="/tags/struts-bean" prefix="bean" %>
<html>
  <head>
    <title>A Results page</title>
  </head>
  <body>

        .
        .
        .
```

Ask the Expert

Q: Is there any other way to pass data from a web page to an action besides relying on the form bean?

A: There sure is. Because you passed a **request** object in the action's **execute** method, you can use that object's **getParameter** method to read data from the web page (like this: **text = request.getParameter("text");**). However, because Struts is set up to pass beans back and forth between the various components of an application, it usually makes sense to stick with the bean's way of containing data.

Now you can access the text property in the **dataForm** bean and write that **text** to the Results page, like this:

```
<%@ taglib uri="/tags/struts-bean" prefix="bean" %>
<html>
  <head>
    <title>A Results page</title>
  </head>
  <body>

    <h1>Reading User Input</h1>
    You typed: <bean:write name="dataForm" property="text"/>
  </body>
</html>
```

That's it. When the user enters their name and clicks Submit, that name appears in the Results page.

We've completed the basics of Struts programming with examples that built gradually from the ground up, and you're now prepared to tackle a full Struts application. We'll do that next.

Progress Check

1. What do you need to do to the **form** variable passed to the **execute** method before accessing your data?
2. What do you have to do to pass a form bean from an action to a Results page?

---

1. You first cast it to the type of your form bean rather than the generic **ActionForm** class.
2. Nothing; the form bean will be accessible from the Results page already. All you have to do is to forward to that page.

CRITICAL SKILL 3.2

Create a Full Struts Example

The remainder of this module is all about a full-scale Struts example. This example is the one we saw at work in the beginning of Module 1—the Struts Café that lets the user choose their lunch. You can see this application at work by navigating to http://localhost:8080/ch03/ch03_01.jsp, where users can order various items, as shown in Figure 3-3.

When a user clicks the Place Your Order! button, their order is summarized, as shown in Figure 3-4.

You can base this example on the struts-blank application if you like, but there's no need to do that since we'll develop the code from scratch. Up to this point, we've used the struts-blank application as a skeleton for our work, which meant that the Struts files were already installed in the directories we needed them in. To create an application from scratch, copy the Struts files like this:

- Copy the Struts files commons-*.jar from the Struts distribution into the WEB-INF/lib directory of your web application.
- Copy the Struts file struts.jar from the Struts distribution into the WEB-INF/lib directory of your web application.
- Copy all of the Struts files struts-*.tld from the Struts distribution into the WEB-INF directory of your web application.

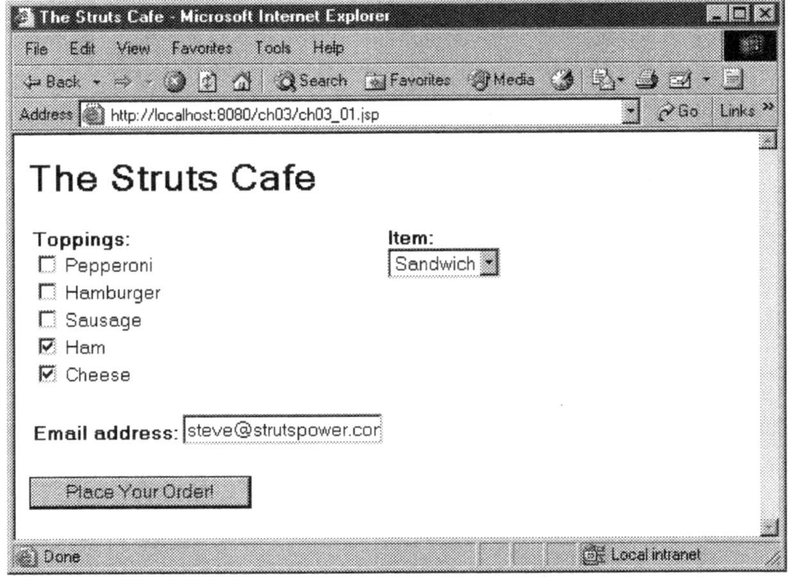

Figure 3-3 The Struts Café Welcome page

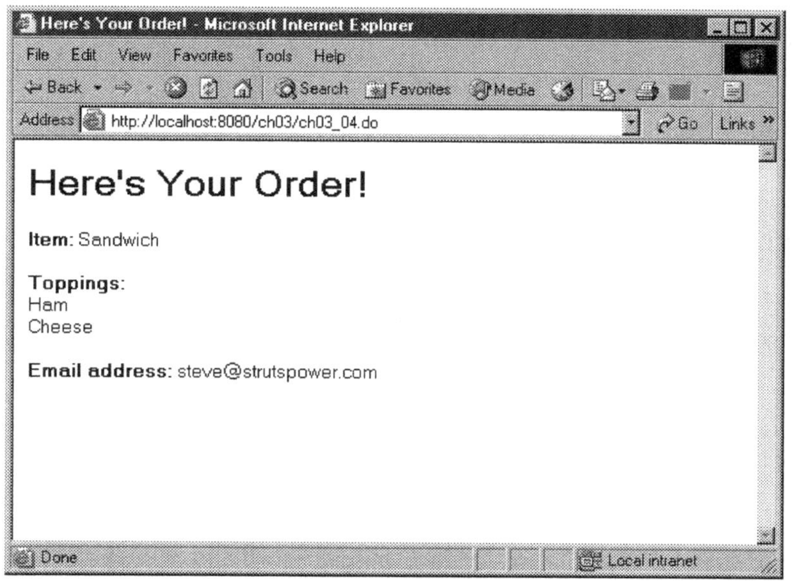

Figure 3-4 The Struts Café Results page

Note that this is the recommended way of doing things. Your web server may have a folder for files common to all web applications, as Tomcat does, and you may want to store the Struts files there. But the Struts group issues this warning on that technique:

"WARNING—If you are going to be hosting multiple Struts based applications on the same servlet container, you will be tempted to place the struts.jar file into the shared repository supported by your container. Be advised that this will likely cause you to encounter ClassNotFoundException problems unless all of your application classes are stored in the shared repository."

In this case, we'll be using the same ch03 folder we used earlier in this chapter, so struts-blank.war has already stored the Struts files as needed for us. We'll begin with the support code with the Welcome page.

The Custom JSP Tags

The Welcome page, ch03_01.jsp, displays a selection of toppings (ham, cheese, etc.) and lets the user select an item to put those toppings on (pizza, sandwich, etc.). We'll use the Struts **<html>** custom JSP tags to create the HTML controls shown in Figure 3-3, such as the list of check boxes on the left and the Item drop-down select control on the right. To supply the text these controls will need, we'll create our own custom JSP tags. These tags will store the needed text data in Java objects and store them in the application's page context where the code in the Welcome page can access that data. Using custom JSP tags like this is a standard way of making data available to the Struts **<html>** tags.

Let's take a look at how this works. We start by creating a custom JSP tag, ch03_02.java, that will supply the possible items the user can select (pizza, sandwich, etc.). We'll create a custom tag, **<ch03:items/>**, that will insert an object named **items**, which is an array of strings holding the available items, into the page context where the Welcome page can get at them. We'll do that by making the **ch03_02** class extend the **TagSupport** class that you create custom JSP tags with and overriding the **doStartTag** method, which is called when the **<ch03:items/>** tag is first encountered in the Welcome page:

```
package ch03;

import java.util.*;
import javax.servlet.jsp.tagext.TagSupport;

public class ch03_02 extends TagSupport
{
    public int doStartTag()
      {
          .
          .
          .
    }
}
```

Ask the Expert

Q: I don't know how to create a custom tag library. Do you need to use custom JSP tags to interact with the Struts <html> tags?

A: You don't have to use your own custom JSP tags to supply data to the Struts **<html>** tags, although this is a standard way to do things. You can use the action form instead, as we'll see when we discuss the **<html>** tags in more depth. If you don't know how to create custom JSP tags, don't despair. However, creating custom tag libraries isn't as hard as you might think; take a look at the following text.

In **doStartTag**, we'll create an array named **itemsArray** that will include the possible items the user can order, and we'll store this array in a page context called **items**:

```
package ch03;

import java.util.*;
import javax.servlet.jsp.tagext.TagSupport;

public class ch03_02 extends TagSupport
{
    public int doStartTag()
      {

        String[] itemsArray = {"", "Pizza", "Calzone", "Sandwich"};

        pageContext.setAttribute("items", itemsArray);

        return SKIP_BODY;
    }
}
```

Now when the **<ch03:items/>** tag is encountered in the Welcome page, it'll store the array of items the user can order in a page attribute named **items**. Similarly, in ch03_03.java, we'll create a new custom JSP tag, **<ch03:toppings/>**, that will store the toppings the user can order (pepperoni, cheese, etc.) in a page context attribute named **toppings**:

```
package ch03;

import java.util.*;
import javax.servlet.jsp.tagext.TagSupport;

public class ch03_03 extends TagSupport
{
    public int doStartTag()
      {
        String[] toppingsArray = {"Pepperoni", "Hamburger", "Sausage",
            "Ham", "Cheese"};

        pageContext.setAttribute("toppings", toppingsArray);

        return SKIP_BODY;
    }
}
```

Progress Check

1. What method do you override to handle the case when the beginning of a JSP custom tag is encountered by the web server?
2. What Java class do you extend to write your own custom JSP tags?

Like the other compiled class files in this example, ch03_02.class and ch03_03.class are in the **ch03** package and go into the WEB-INF/classes/ch03 directory. To compile them, we need to pick up the Java support for the **TagSupport** class. In Tomcat 4.*x*, that support was in servlet.jar, but in Tomcat 5.*x* the support for servlets was broken out into servlet-api.jar, and the support for tag libraries went into jsp-api.jar (which you can find in the Tomcat common/lib directory, along with servlet-api). If you're using Tomcat 5.*x*, set your classpath to something like this before compiling ch03_02.java and ch03_03.java:

```
%set classpath=servlet-api.jar;jsp-api.jar;struts.jar;.
```

Now we'll connect the **ch03_02** and **ch03_03** classes to the tags **<ch03:items/>** and **<ch03:toppings/>**, as far as the application itself is concerned. You do that in a tag library definition TLD file, which goes in the WEB-INF directory. In this case, that file will be named ch03.tld, and it starts in the standard way for a TLD file:

```
<?xml version="1.0"?>
<!DOCTYPE taglib PUBLIC "-//Sun Microsystems, Inc.//DTD JSP Tag Library 1.1//EN"
    "http://java.sun.com/j2ee/dtds/web-jsptaglibrary_1_1.dtd">

<taglib>
    <tlibversion>1.0</tlibversion>
    <jspversion>1.2</jspversion>
    <shortname>StrutsCafeExample</shortname>
    <info>
        Supports the Struts Cafe
    </info>
        .
        .
        .
```

1. The **doStartTag()** method.
2. The **TagSupport** class.

You declare tags with the **<tag>** element in a TLD file. To connect the **ch03_02** and **ch03_03** classes to the tags **<ch03:items/>** and **<ch03:toppings/>**, here's how the **<tag>** elements look:

```
<?xml version="1.0"?>
<!DOCTYPE taglib PUBLIC "-//Sun Microsystems, Inc.//DTD JSP Tag
Library 1.1//EN"
    "http://java.sun.com/j2ee/dtds/web-jsptaglibrary_1_1.dtd">

<taglib>
    <tlibversion>1.0</tlibversion>
    <jspversion>1.2</jspversion>
    <shortname>StrutsCafeExample</shortname>
    <info>
        Supports the Struts Cafe
    </info>

    <tag>
        <name>items</name>
        <tagclass>ch03.ch03_02</tagclass>
        <bodycontent>empty</bodycontent>
   </tag>

    <tag>
        <name>toppings</name>
        <tagclass>ch03.ch03_03</tagclass>
        <bodycontent>empty</bodycontent>
    </tag>
</taglib>
```

That's all for the ch03.tld file, but we must still install our new set of custom JSP tags in web.xml to make Tomcat aware of them. You do that with a **<taglib>** element in web.xml, so add that element now at the very end of the **<web-app>** element in web.xml like this:

```
        .
        .
        .
  <taglib>
    <taglib-uri>/ch03</taglib-uri>
    <taglib-location>/WEB-INF/ch03.tld</taglib-location>
  </taglib>

</web-app>
```

Now we're ready to supply the Struts **<html>** tags the data they need. As in the struts-blank application, we'll also use application.properties file (that is, WEB-INF/classes/resources/application.properties) to store text used in our JSP pages. This text can be retrieved with the Struts **<bean>** JSP tag. In this case, we'll store the prompts shown in Figure 3-3 in application.properties. To do this, add these messages to application.properties (which already exists because the struts-blank application, as used earlier in this module, created it):

```
email=<b>Email address:</b>
items=<b>Item:</b>
toppings=<b>Toppings:</b>

errors.header=<font color="red">Please correct the following error(s):<ul>
errors.footer=</ul>
# -- standard errors --
        .
        .
        .
```

In addition to these messages, we'll also take a look at how to handle errors in Struts applications in this example. To do this, add the error messages error.noemail, error.noitems, and error.notoppings in case the user didn't enter an e-mail address or select an item or any toppings. Here's what those messages look like in application.properties:

```
email=<b>Email address:</b>
items=<b>Item:</b>
toppings=<b>Toppings:</b>

errors.header=<font color="red">Please correct the following error(s):</font><ul>
errors.footer=</ul>
# -- standard errors --
errors.header=<UL>
errors.prefix=<LI><font color="red">
errors.suffix=</font></LI>
errors.footer=</UL>
# -- validator --
errors.invalid={0} is invalid.
errors.maxlength={0} can not be greater than {1} characters.
errors.minlength={0} can not be less than {1} characters.
errors.range={0} is not in the range {1} through {2}.
errors.required={0} is required.
errors.byte={0} must be an byte.
errors.date={0} is not a date.
errors.double={0} must be an double.
errors.float={0} must be an float.
errors.integer={0} must be an integer.
errors.long={0} must be an long.
errors.short={0} must be an short.
errors.creditcard={0} is not a valid credit card number.
errors.email={0} is an invalid e-mail address.
```

```
error.noemail=Please enter your email address.
error.noitems=Please select an item.
error.notoppings=Please select at least one topping.
        .
        .
        .
You didn't close your <font> tag in errors.header.[fixed]
```

That completes the support we'll need for the Welcome page, which we'll build next.

The Welcome Page

We begin the Welcome page by setting up the tag libraries we'll use—including our own ch03 tag library, which we'll give the prefix ch03 to, allowing us to use the custom JSP tags **<ch03:items/>** and **<ch03:toppings/>**:

```
<%@ taglib uri="/tags/struts-bean" prefix="bean" %>
<%@ taglib uri="/tags/struts-html" prefix="html" %>
<%@ taglib uri="/tags/struts-logic" prefix="logic" %>
<%@ taglib uri="/ch03" prefix="ch03" %>
        .
        .
        .
```

We'll use our custom tags to fill the items and toppings page context attributes, as well as the Struts **<html:errors/>** custom JSP tag, which will display a list of errors for the user to fix if we indicate that there are any:

```
<%@ taglib uri="/tags/struts-bean" prefix="bean" %>
<%@ taglib uri="/tags/struts-html" prefix="html" %>
<%@ taglib uri="/tags/struts-logic" prefix="logic" %>
<%@ taglib uri="/ch03" prefix="ch03" %>

<HTML>
    <HEAD>
        <TITLE>The Struts Cafe</TITLE>
    </HEAD>

    <BODY>
        <H1>The Struts Cafe</H1>
        <html:errors/>
        <ch03:items/>
        <ch03:toppings/>
        .
        .
        .
```

To arrange the controls in the Welcome page shown in Figure 3-3, we'll use an HTML table. We'll start with the toppings you see in the figure, beginning with the message "Toppings:", which you access from application.properties as **<bean:message key="toppings"/>**. To create the list of check boxes shown in Figure 3-1 for the toppings, we'll use a Struts **<logic:iterate>** tag. (We'll see how tags like <logic> and <html> work in more detail throughout the book; this will give us an overview of what they do.) This **<logic:iterate>** tag lets you loop over the items in an array of strings, which is what we need here. Here's how you set this loop up to iterate over the items in the array of toppings, which is installed in the **toppings** attribute, and which we'll refer to as **toppings1** in this tag:

```
<logic:iterate id="toppings1" name="toppings">
    .
    .
    .
    <%= toppings1 %>
    <BR>
</logic:iterate>
```

To produce the multiple check boxes shown in Figure 3-3, you can use the Struts **<html:multibox>** element. Here's how that works, where we're using the **toppings1** object to supply the captions of the check boxes (note also that the **<html:form>** tag's action attribute is set to the name of the action we'll be using in this example, **ch03_04**):

```
<BODY>
    <H1>The Struts Cafe</H1>
    <html:errors/>
    <ch03:items/>
    <ch03:toppings/>
    <html:form action="ch03_04.do">
        <TABLE>
            <TR>
                <TD ALIGN="LEFT" VALIGN="TOP">
                    <bean:message key="toppings"/>
                    <BR>
                    <logic:iterate id="toppings1" name="toppings">
                        <html:multibox property="toppings">
                            <%= toppings1 %>
                        </html:multibox>
                        <%= toppings1 %>
                        <BR>
                    </logic:iterate>
                </TD>
                .
                .
                .
```

That creates the list of check boxes shown in Figure 3-1. We can also stock the drop-down select control that displays the possible items (pizza, sandwich, and so on) the user can order. To do that, we'll use a Struts **<html:select/>** custom JSP tag, placing **<html:option/>** tags inside it to add the items the select control should display. The object **items** we've created with our custom JSP tag **<ch03:items/>** will supply the needed data. Here's what the code looks like:

```
<BODY>
    <H1>The Struts Cafe</H1>
    <html:errors/>
    <ch03:items/>
    <ch03:toppings/>
    <html:form action="ch03_04.do">
        <TABLE>
            <TR>
                <TD ALIGN="LEFT" VALIGN="TOP">
                    .
                    .
                    .
                </TD>
                <TD ALIGN="LEFT" VALIGN="TOP">
                    <bean:message key="items"/>
                    <BR>
                    <html:select property="items">
                        <html:options name="items"/>
                    </html:select>
                </TD>
    .
    .
    .
```

Finally, we'll use an **<html:text>** custom JSP tag to create a text field, as we did earlier in this module, to handle the user's e-mail:

```
<BODY>
    <H1>The Struts Cafe</H1>
    <html:errors/>
    <ch03:items/>
    <ch03:toppings/>
    <html:form action="ch03_04.do">
        <TABLE>
            <TR>
                <TD ALIGN="LEFT" VALIGN="TOP">
                    .
                    .
                    .
```

```
                        </TD>
                        <TD ALIGN="LEFT" VALIGN="TOP">
                            .
                            .
                            .
                        </TD>
                    </TR>
                    <TR>
                        <TD ALIGN="LEFT">
                                        <BR>
                            <bean:message key="email"/>
                            <html:text property="email"/>
                        </TD>
                    <TR>
                </TABLE>
                      <BR>
                <html:submit value="Place Your Order!"/>
            </html:form>
        </BODY>
</HTML>
```

That completes the Welcome page. Coming up next is the action form, which holds the data from the Welcome page.

Progress Check

1. What Struts custom tag do you use to loop over an array of strings?
2. What Struts custom tag do you use to create multiple check boxes?
3. What two Struts custom tags do you use to create a drop-down list control?

The Action Form

The action form is supported by the class **ch03_06** in this example and will hold the data the user entered in the Welcome page. We'll need to store various strings here, corresponding to

1. The **<logic:iterate>** tag.
2. The **<html:multibox>** tag.
3. The **<html:select>** and **<html:option>** tags.

the properties we want our form bean to have—**email** for the user's e-mail address, **items** to hold their item selection, and an array of strings named **toppings**:

```
package ch03;
import org.apache.struts.action.ActionForm;

public class ch03_06 extends ActionForm
{

    private String email = "";
    private String items = "";
    private String[] toppings;
        .
        .
        .
```

Set up a Java property for each of these data items:

```
package ch03;
import org.apache.struts.action.ActionForm;

public class ch03_06 extends ActionForm
{

    private String email = "";
    private String items = "";
    private String[] toppings;

    public String getEmail()
      {
        return email;
    }

    public void setEmail(String email)
      {
        this.email = email;
    }

    public String getItems()
      {
        return items;
    }

    public void setItems(String items)
      {
        this.items = items;
```

```
    }

    public String[] getToppings() {
        return toppings;
    }

    public void setToppings(String[] toppings) {
        this.toppings = toppings;
    }
}
```

That creates the form bean we'll use in this example, **ch03_06**. You add it to the **<form-beans>** element in struts-config.xml this way:

```
<form-beans>
        .
        .
        .
        <form-bean name="ch03_06" type="ch03.ch03_06"/>
        .
        .
        .
</form-beans>
```

The Action

Next, we'll set up the action this example uses, ch03_04 (as given by the action attribute of the **<html:form>** tag in the Welcome page), starting with an action mapping element in struts-config.xml. Note that we're also creating a forward named "OK" here that will forward to the Results page, ch03_05.jsp:

```
<action-mappings>
        .
        .
        .
    <action path="/ch03_04"
      type="ch03.ch03_04"
      name="ch03_06"
      scope="request"
      input="/ch03_01.jsp">
      <forward name="OK" path="/ch03_05.jsp"/>
        .
        .
        .
    </action>
</action-mappings>
```

In the action, we'll check to make sure the user has entered a value for each item we require. We start in the **execute** method by casting the bean passed to our bean class, **ch03_06**:

```
package ch03;

import java.io.*;
import java.util.*;
import ch03.ch03_06;
import javax.servlet.http.HttpServletRequest;
import javax.servlet.http.HttpServletResponse;
import javax.servlet.ServletException;
import org.apache.struts.action.*;

public class ch03_04 extends Action
{
  public ActionForward execute(ActionMapping mapping,
    ActionForm form,
    HttpServletRequest request,
    HttpServletResponse response)
    throws IOException, ServletException {

        ch03_06 orderForm = (ch03_06)form;
        .
        .
        .
```

In Struts 1.1, errors are handled with the **ActionErrors** class (but not in Struts 1.2, as we'll discuss at the end of this module). Here's how it works: we'll create a new **ActionErrors** object and check the size of the strings passed for the user's selections. If any of those strings are empty, we'll use the **ActionErrors** object's **add** method to add a new error to the list that should be displayed by the **<html:errors/>** custom tag in the Welcome page. We do that with a call to the **add** method like this, where we're checking the user's e-mail:

```
        ActionErrors actionerrors = new ActionErrors();

        String email = orderForm.getEmail();
        if(email.trim().equals("")) {
            actionerrors.add(ActionErrors.GLOBAL_ERROR, new
                ActionError("error.noemail"));
        }
```

If the **email** string is empty, we indicate that there's been an error and that we want to display the message **error.noemail**. Here's how you can handle the various errors in case the user omitted any of the data we're requiring:

```
package ch03;

import java.io.*;
import java.util.*;
import ch03.ch03_06;
import javax.servlet.http.HttpServletRequest;
import javax.servlet.http.HttpServletResponse;
import javax.servlet.ServletException;
import org.apache.struts.action.*;

public class ch03_04 extends Action
{
  public ActionForward execute(ActionMapping mapping,
    ActionForm form,
    HttpServletRequest request,
    HttpServletResponse response)
    throws IOException, ServletException {

        ch03_06 orderForm = (ch03_06)form;

        ActionErrors actionerrors = new ActionErrors();

        String email = orderForm.getEmail();
        if(email.trim().equals("")) {
            actionerrors.add(ActionErrors.GLOBAL_ERROR, new
                ActionError("error.noemail"));
        }

        String items = orderForm.getItems();
        if(items.trim().equals("")) {
            actionerrors.add("ActionErrors.GLOBAL_ERROR", new
                ActionError("error.noitems"));
        }

        String[] toppings = orderForm.getToppings();
        if(toppings == null) {
            actionerrors.add("ActionErrors.GLOBAL_ERROR", new
                ActionError("error.notoppings"));
        }

        if(actionerrors.size() != 0) {
            saveErrors(request, actionerrors);
```

```
            return new ActionForward(mapping.getInput());
        }
        return mapping.findForward("OK");
    }
}
```

At the end of the **execute** method, you can check if there have been any errors with the **size** method of the **ActionErrors** object. If it's nonzero, you have errors to report. You can do that by saving the errors with the **ActionForm saveErrors()** method and then forward back to the input page (i.e., the Welcome page), which you can find with the **mapping.getInput** method:

```
package ch03;

import java.io.*;
import java.util.*;
import ch03.ch03_06;
import javax.servlet.http.HttpServletRequest;
import javax.servlet.http.HttpServletResponse;
import javax.servlet.ServletException;
import org.apache.struts.action.*;

public class ch03_04 extends Action
{
  public ActionForward execute(ActionMapping mapping,
    ActionForm form,
    HttpServletRequest request,
    HttpServletResponse response)
    throws IOException, ServletException {
        .
        .
        .

        String[] toppings = orderForm.getToppings();
        if(toppings == null) {
            actionerrors.add("ActionErrors.GLOBAL_ERROR", new
                ActionError("error.notoppings"));
        }

        if(actionerrors.size() != 0) {
            saveErrors(request, actionerrors);
            return new ActionForward(mapping.getInput());
        }
        return mapping.findForward("OK");
    }
}
```

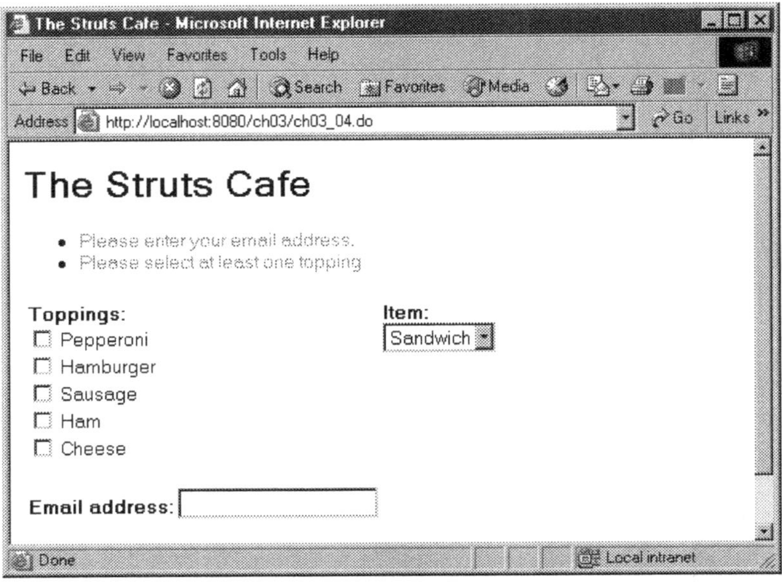

Figure 3-5 Handling errors

You can see how these errors appear when we return to the Welcome page in Figure 3-5, where the user has omitted their e-mail address and has not selected any toppings.

If there are no errors, however, forward on to the Results page (with the code **return mapping.findForward("OK");** that's the last line in the **execute()** method). We'll take a look at the Results page next.

The Results Page

The Results page is ch03_05.jsp, and we'll use the **ch03_06** bean to display the user's selections, interacting with that bean with the Struts **<bean:write>** JSP tag. Recall that the toppings are stored in an array of strings, so we'll use the **<logic:iterate>** tag to display them all, adding a **
** element to place the toppings on different lines:

```
<%@ taglib uri="/tags/struts-bean" prefix="bean" %>
<%@ taglib uri="/tags/struts-logic" prefix="logic" %>

<HTML>
    <HEAD>
        <TITLE>Here's Your Order!</TITLE>
    </HEAD>

    <BODY>
```

```
        <H1>Here's Your Order!</H1>
        <bean:message key="items"/>
        <bean:write name="ch03_06" property="items"/>
        <BR>
        <BR>
        <bean:message key="toppings"/>
        <BR>
        <logic:iterate id="toppings1" name="ch03_06" property="toppings">
            <%= toppings1 %>
            <BR>
        </logic:iterate>
        <BR>
        <bean:message key="email"/>
        <bean:write name="ch03_06" property="email"/>
        <BR>
    </BODY>
</HTML>
```

That completes the Results page, and that completes the code for this project. You're ready to roll.

Installing the Files

To install the files, compile the .java class files first, setting the classpath something like this if you're using Tomcat 5.*x* (as usual, if the .jar files aren't in the current directory, qualify each .jar file's name with the correct path):

```
%set classpath=servlet-api.jar;jsp-api.jar;struts.jar;.
```

Compile each .java file with javac as before (and as usual, if the Java compiler, javac, is not in your machine's path, qualify it with the appropriate path, such as c:\jdk1.4\bin\javac):

```
%javac ch03_06.java
```

Bear in mind that **ch03.ch03_04** (the action) imports **ch03.ch03_06** (the action form). You'll need to compile **ch03.ch03_06** first and copy it into a subdirectory named **ch03** of your current directory so Java can find it when you compile **ch03.ch03_04**.

Here's how to install the project files in Tomcat's webapps/ch03 directory:

```
webapps
|
|__ch03
   |    ch03_01.jsp [View: Start Page]
```

```
|   ch03_05.jsp [View: Results Page]
|
|__WEB-INF
    |   struts-config.xml [Struts Configuration File]
    |   ch03.tld  [Custom Tag Definitions]
    |   Struts TLD files [Struts Tag Definitions]
    |   web.xml  [Application Descriptor File]
    |
    |__lib
    |       struts.jar  [Java Archive of Struts Classes]
    |
    |__classes
        |__resources
        |   application.properties [Contains Property Values]
        |
        |__ch03
              ch03_02.class  [Custom Tag 1 Implementation]
              ch03_03.class  [Custom Tag 2 Implementation]
              ch03_04.class  [Action Form]
              ch03_06.class  [Action]
```

After installing the project's files, start Tomcat and navigate to http://localhost:8080/ch03/ch03_01.jsp to get the application started. That's all you need.

Use Struts 1.2

This project used the Struts 1.1 download and libraries, but Struts 1.2 is on the horizon. You can convert this project to use the early release of Struts 1.2 if you make one change: instead of the **ActionErrors** collection and **ActionError** objects, which have been deprecated in Struts 1.2, use the **ActionMessages** collection and **ActionMessage** objects. This change only affects the action ch03_04.java. Here are the changes to make:

```
package ch03;

import java.io.*;
import java.util.*;
import ch03.ch03_06;
import javax.servlet.http.HttpServletRequest;
import javax.servlet.http.HttpServletResponse;
import javax.servlet.ServletException;
import org.apache.struts.action.*;

public class ch03_04 extends Action
```

```
{
  public ActionForward execute(ActionMapping mapping,
    ActionForm form,
    HttpServletRequest request,
    HttpServletResponse response)
    throws IOException, ServletException {

        ActionMessages actionmessages = new ActionMessages();

        ch03_06 orderForm = (ch03_06)form;

        String email = orderForm.getEmail();
        if(email.trim().equals("")) {
            actionmessages.add(ActionMessages.GLOBAL_MESSAGE,
                new ActionMessage("error.noemail"));
        }

        String items = orderForm.getItems();
        if(items.trim().equals("")) {
            actionmessages.add("ActionMessages.GLOBAL_MESSAGE",
                new ActionMessage("error.notype"));
        }

        String[] toppings = orderForm.getToppings();
        if(toppings == null) {
            actionmessages.add("ActionMessages.GLOBAL_MESSAGE",
                new ActionMessage("error.noitems"));
        }

        if(actionmessages.size() != 0) {
            saveErrors(request, actionmessages);
            return new ActionForward(mapping.getInput());
        }
        return mapping.findForward("OK");
    }
}
```

After making this change, you can compile with the early release Struts 1.2 .jar files and run the project as before (although this might have changed by the time you read this, as new beta versions of Struts 1.2 come out). We'll refer to this change—using the **ActionMessages** collection and **ActionMessage** objects instead of the **ActionErrors** collection and **ActionError** objects in upcoming modules—when talking about Struts 1.2.

Module 3 Mastery Check

1. What custom Struts JSP tag can you use to create an HTML text field?

   A. **<text>**

   B. **<textfield>**

   C. **<html:text>**

   D. **<html:textfield>**

2. To implement a String property named **Data**, what methods should you implement in the action form?

   A. **data**

   B. **dataIn**, **dataOut**

   C. **getData**, **setData**

   D. **getData**, **setData**, **reset**

3. Which JSP directive should you use to connect to a form bean in a Results page?

   A. **<%@ taglibrary uri="/tags/struts" prefix="bean" %>**

   B. **<%@ taglibrary uri="/tags/bean" prefix="bean" %>**

   C. **<%@ taglib uri="/tags/struts-bean" prefix="bean" %>**

   D. **<%@ taglib uri="/tags/bean" prefix="bean" %>**

4. What custom Struts JSP tag do you use to insert bean data to a JSP page?

   A. **<bean:insert>**

   B. **<bean:message>**

   C. **<bean:bean>**

   D. **<bean:write>**

5. When you're writing your own custom JSP tag, what Java class do you typically extend?

   A. **Tag**

   B. **TagSupport**

   C. **TagLib**

   D. **TagLibrary**

6. How do you access data under the name text and insert it in a JSP page using Struts?

   A. **<bean:write name="dataForm" property="text"/>**

   B. **<bean:write name="dataForm" data="text"/>**

   C. **<bean:write name="dataForm" value="text"/>**

   D. **<bean:write name="dataForm" name="text"/>**

7. What method do you override in code for a custom JSP tag to handle the beginning of a tag?

   A. **BeginTag**

   B. **doBeginTag**

   C. **doStartTag**

   D. **BeginOpenTag**

8. What Struts custom JSP tag do you use to insert in a JSP page to display errors, if there are any?

   A. **<html:error>**

   B. **<html:errors>**

   C. **<html:displayError>**

   D. **<html:errorDiv>**

9. What Struts custom JSP tag do you use to loop over arrays of strings?

   A. **<logic:iterate>**

   B. **<logic:loop>**

   C. **<logic:again>**

   D. **<logic:iteration>**

10. What Struts custom JSP tag do you use to display a number of check boxes?

    A. **<html:checkboxes>**

    B. **<html:multibox>**

    C. **<html:checkbox>**

    D. **<html:multiboxes>**

Module 4

Working with Models and ActionForms

CRITICAL SKILLS

4.1 Work with Models

4.2 Work with Action Forms

This module is about working with models and action forms. Up to this point, the projects we've developed haven't used a model to handle any data crunching, but we're going to change that now.

We'll also look at working with action forms in this module. We've already used action forms to hold the data used by actions, but there's more to action forms than we've seen so far. In this module, we'll learn how to fill HTML controls with data from an action form, even the first time a web page is displayed, meaning we won't have to create our own custom JSP tags to stock HTML controls with data, as we did in Module 3.

We'll also see how to use the action form **validate** method to validate data. Up to this point, we've performed data validation in the action itself, but one of the jobs of action forms is to validate the data they're sent, using the **validate** method. In this way, we'll be able to move the task of validating data from the action to the action form, and since the action form's task is to handle data, that's appropriate.

Some applications use dozens of properties in action forms, and sometimes developers rebel against having to set up all those property methods in a Java action form class. For that reason, it's possible now to set up an action form entirely in struts-config.xml—no Java code needed—using the Struts **DynaActionForm** class. We'll learn how to use that class in this module. As long as we just want to set up a simple property for each data item in a form and don't try to do anything too complex, the **DynaActionForm** class can save a great deal of time. We'll see how to work with this class and convert an action to handle dynamic forms in this module as well.

We'll begin by adding a model to our applications for some behind-the-scenes data crunching.

CRITICAL SKILL

4.1 Work with Models

As you recall, Struts applications closely mirror the MVC (Model-View-Controller) architecture. We've discussed the view and the controller aspects of Struts applications in some depth; it's time to add the model. As an example, we'll use a model to do a little data crunching—nothing too involved, just converting a string to uppercase.

We can see our application in Figure 4-1.

After the user enters text to capitalize and clicks the Convert button, the application passes that text to its model, which returns the capitalized text. The resulting capitalized text is displayed in the Results page, as shown in Figure 4-2.

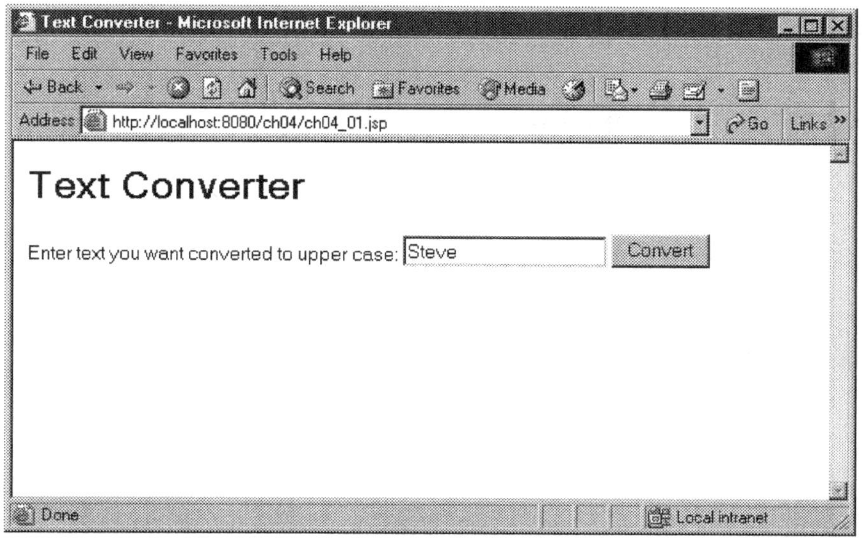

Figure 4-1 Accepting text to capitalize

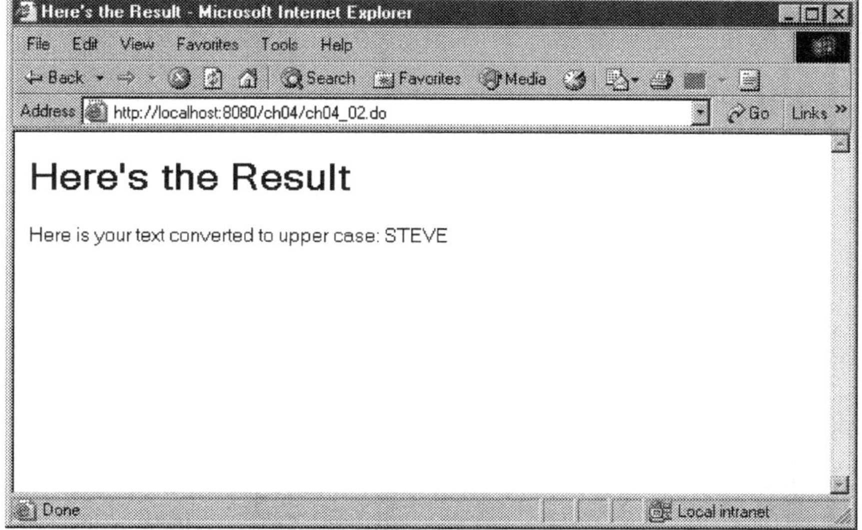

Figure 4-2 The resulting capitalized text

As with all Struts applications, this application uses multiple files. Here are the central ones for our purposes:

- ch04_01.jsp: The Welcome page
- ch04_02.java: The Action
- ch04_03.java: The Action Form
- ch04_04.java: The Model
- ch04_05.jsp: The Results page

The Welcome page, ch04_01.jsp, is standard. Here, we're displaying any possible errors with **<html:errors/>**, setting up a form with the action **ch04_02**, displaying a prompt retrieved from application.properties, and adding a text field that corresponds to the action form property **text**:

```
<%@ taglib uri="/tags/struts-bean" prefix="bean" %>
<%@ taglib uri="/tags/struts-html" prefix="html" %>

<HTML>
    <HEAD>
        <TITLE>Text Converter</TITLE>
    </HEAD>

    <BODY>
        <H1>Text Converter</H1>
        <html:errors/>
        <html:form action="ch04_02.do">
            <bean:message key="prompt"/>
            <html:text property="text"/>
            <html:submit value="Convert"/>
        </html:form>
    </BODY>
</HTML>
```

Here are the messages we'll add to application.properties for this application:

```
prompt=Enter text you want converted to upper case:
tocaps=Here is your text converted to upper case:

errors.header=<font color="red">Please correct the following
error(s):<ul>
```

```
errors.footer=</ul>
errors.header=<UL>
errors.prefix=<LI><font color="red">
errors.suffix=</LI></font>
errors.footer=</UL>

error.notext=Please enter some text.
```

In the **<action>** element in struts-config.xml, we connect the action for this application to an action form, **ch04_03**:

```
<action path="/ch04_02"
  type="ch04.ch04_02"
  name="ch04_03"
  input="/ch04_01.jsp">
  <forward name="success" path="/ch04_05.jsp"/>
</action>
```

The **ch04_03** action form is connected to the class **ch04.ch04_03**:

```
<form-bean name="ch04_03"
  type="ch04.ch04_03"/>
```

In the action form's code, ch04_03.java, we'll add the code support for the **text** property:

```
package ch04;
import org.apache.struts.action.ActionForm;

public class ch04_03 extends ActionForm
{
    private String text = "";

    public String getText()
      {
        return text;
    }

    public void setText(String text)
      {
        this.text = text;
    }
}
```

In the action's code, ch04_02.java, we can cast the action form object passed to the class we're using in this project, **ch04_03**, and recover the text the user entered from the **text** property:

```
package ch04;

import java.io.*;
import java.util.*;
import ch04.ch04_03;
import ch04.ch04_04;
import javax.servlet.http.HttpServletRequest;
import javax.servlet.http.HttpServletResponse;
import javax.servlet.ServletException;
import org.apache.struts.action.*;

public class ch04_02 extends Action
{
  public ActionForward execute(ActionMapping mapping,
    ActionForm form,
    HttpServletRequest request,
    HttpServletResponse response)
    throws IOException, ServletException {

        ch04_03 textForm = (ch04_03)form;

        String text = textForm.getText();
        .
        .
        .
```

Now we have the data the user entered. It's time for the model to come into play. After the usual error checking in the action, we'll create an object of the model's class, **ch04_04**. This class has a method, **process**, to handle the work the model will do in this case, which is to capitalize the text we send to it. To use the model, we create a new object of the **ch04_04** class in the action:

```
package ch04;

import java.io.*;
import java.util.*;
import ch04.ch04_03;
import ch04.ch04_04;
import javax.servlet.http.HttpServletRequest;
import javax.servlet.http.HttpServletResponse;
import javax.servlet.ServletException;
import org.apache.struts.action.*;

public class ch04_02 extends Action
```

```
{
  public ActionForward execute(ActionMapping mapping,
    ActionForm form,
    HttpServletRequest request,
    HttpServletResponse response)
    throws IOException, ServletException {

        ActionErrors actionerrors = new ActionErrors();

        ch04_03 textForm = (ch04_03)form;

        String text = textForm.getText();

        if(text.trim().equals("")) {
            actionerrors.add(ActionErrors.GLOBAL_ERROR, new
            ActionError("error.notext"));
        }

        if(actionerrors.size() != 0) {
            saveErrors(request, actionerrors);
            return new ActionForward(mapping.getInput());
        }

        ch04_04 model = new ch04_04();
        .
        .
        .
```

To use the model, pass the text we read from the Welcome page to the **process** method and get the capitalized version back:

```
        ch04_04 model = new ch04_04();

        text = model.process(text);
        .
        .
        .
```

After getting the capitalized text back, we put that text into the action form and forward it to the Results page:

```
        ch04_04 model = new ch04_04();

        text = model.process(text);

        textForm.setText(text);

        return mapping.findForward("success");
```

Creating the Model

In Struts applications, the code for the model is up to us; there's no Struts **ActionModel** class or anything like that to base our model's class on. When writing the model, we just write the utility methods we want to call. For example, the model in this project, ch04_04.java, has a **process** method, which takes a string, capitalizes it, and returns the result. Here's the code:

```
package ch04;

public class ch04_04
{
    public String process(String text)
    {
        return text.toUpperCase();
    }
}
```

That's all we need for the model in this project. After the model capitalizes the text, that text is stored in the action form. The Results page reads the newly capitalized text and displays it:

```
<%@ taglib uri="/tags/struts-bean" prefix="bean" %>

<HTML>
    <HEAD>
        <TITLE>Here's the Result</TITLE>
    </HEAD>

    <BODY>
        <H1>Here's the Result</H1>
        <bean:message key="tocaps"/>
        <bean:write name="ch04_03" property="text"/>
    </BODY>
</HTML>
```

Now when the user enters text to be capitalized, that text is passed to the model, which does the work. The text is re-inserted into the form bean and displayed in the Results page.

Although this example was a simple one because we don't need anything special to create a model in a Struts application, it does let us add a model to a Struts application.

Ask the Expert

Q: Does a Struts application need a model?

A: No, but in larger applications, it's hard to avoid it. The controller is made up of the action servlet and the action(s), and its function is, as its name implies, to control the flow of the application. The actual work that the application does—the guts of the program—shouldn't go into the controller, except in relatively simple applications. The model is for behind-the-scenes work, applying business rules, looking up data, launching worker threads to perform involved calculations, and more.

Struts came about in the first place to handle larger web applications by providing a framework for those applications. It's easy to write programs in an ad hoc manner, but when it comes to trying to track down errors, you'll be out of luck if the presentation logic is mixed in with the program's logic. For anything more substantial, move the application's logic to the model.

Use Struts 1.2

Because we developed the code for the model ourselves, there's very little that has to be upgraded to work with Struts 1.2 in this project. The only changes to make are in the action, where we need to replace **ActionError** and **ActionErrors** with **ActionMessage** and **ActionMessages**:

```
package ch04;

import java.io.*;
import java.util.*;
import ch04.ch04_03;
import ch04.ch04_04;
import javax.servlet.http.HttpServletRequest;
import javax.servlet.http.HttpServletResponse;
import javax.servlet.ServletException;
import org.apache.struts.action.*;

public class ch04_02 extends Action
{
  public ActionForward execute(ActionMapping mapping,
    ActionForm form,
```

```
        HttpServletRequest request,
        HttpServletResponse response)
        throws IOException, ServletException {

            ActionMessages actionmessages = new ActionMessages();

            ch04_03 textForm = (ch04_03)form;

            String text = textForm.getText();
            if(text.trim().equals("")) {
                actionmessages.add(ActionMessages.GLOBAL_MESSAGE, new
                    ActionMessage("error.notext"));
            }

            if(actionmessages.size() != 0) {
                saveErrors(request, actionmessages);
                return new ActionForward(mapping.getInput());
            }

            ch04_04 model = new ch04_04();

            text = model.process(text);

            textForm.setText(text);

            return mapping.findForward("success");
        }
    }
```

Passing Action Forms to the Model

This project demonstrated where the model fits into the Struts architecture, and we extracted the data we wanted to work on and passed it explicitly to the model. Some applications, however, will use dozens of properties, and passing each data item individually gets to be a chore. For that reason, it often makes sense to simply pass the action form itself to the model because the single action form object holds all the data the model needs.

In this project, we'd pass the action form to the model's **process** method, and that method would return the action form with the new data installed. Here's how it would work:

```
import java.util.*;
import ch04.ch04_03;
import ch04.ch04_04;
import javax.servlet.http.HttpServletRequest;
import javax.servlet.http.HttpServletResponse;
import javax.servlet.ServletException;
import org.apache.struts.action.*;
```

```
public class ch04_02 extends Action
{
  public ActionForward execute(ActionMapping mapping,
    ActionForm form,
    HttpServletRequest request,
    HttpServletResponse response)
    throws IOException, ServletException {

        ActionErrors actionerrors = new ActionErrors();

        ch04_03 textForm = (ch04_03)form;
        .
        .
        .
        ch04_04 model = new ch04_04();

        textForm = model.process(textForm);

        return mapping.findForward("success");
    }
}
```

To make this work in the model, we import the action form class:

```
package ch04;

import ch04.ch04_03;

        .
        .
        .
```

We can work on the data in the passed action form directly:

```
package ch04;

import ch04.ch04_03;

public class ch04_04
{
    public ch04_03 process(ch04_03 form)
    {
        form.setText(form.getText().toUpperCase());
        return form;
    }
}
```

Note that we can also send **request** objects or even the entire servlet context object and all its attributes (use the method **getServletContext** to get the servlet context) to the model as well. In modern web applications, the model itself can be very involved, acting as a middle tier for a database application, perhaps connecting to remote data objects on other servers. Separating the model out from the rest of the code so it can do its thing without overlapping the rest of the application's code is good programming practice.

CRITICAL SKILL 4.2

Work with Action Forms

We've used action forms to get our Struts code working already, but there's more to discuss, starting with the question of why action forms exist at all—why aren't they just simple beans that hold the data exactly as passed to us from an HTML form?

There are a number of answers to this question. First, action forms are not just transfer objects designed to shuttle data back and forth between the browser and Struts actions. When the data the user entered into an HTML form is passed to the action servlet, that data is stored in the action form and passed to an action. If, however, we use check boxes in the HTML form and leave one or more unchecked, the browser won't send any data back for the unchecked check boxes, which means that a faithful representation of what the browser sends us in a bean would omit anything for those check boxes. The action servlet, however, does better than that, setting the properties corresponding to the unchecked check boxes to **false**.

There's also a **validate** method built into action forms that the action servlet will call automatically to check the data sent from the browser. If it doesn't validate, the action servlet loads the requisite error messages and sends them back to the user automatically.

In addition, the data sent back from the browser is simply in string form because it's sent using the HTTP protocol. The action servlet does somewhat better than that: it can assign both string and Boolean values to action form properties. We can also add methods to the action form to convert properties to other types besides strings and Booleans ourselves.

For example, if the text the user entered in the previous project was an integer, we can use the action form as a type converter to get and set that value in numerical format. Here's what that looks like, where we're adding **getNumber** and **setNumber** properties to the action form:

```
package ch04;
import org.apache.struts.action.ActionForm;

public class ch04_03 extends ActionForm
{

    private String text = "";

    public String getText()
    {
```

```
        return text;
    }

    public void setText(String text)
    {
        this.text = text;
    }

    public Integer getNumber()
    {
        return Integer.parseInt(text);
    }

    public void setNumber(Integer value)
    {
        this.text = String.valueOf(value);
    }

}
```

Action forms can also contain helper methods; beans that function as simple data transfer objects can't do this. For example, to retrieve the text in the action form in uppercase, we can add a helper method such as **getTextUpperCase**:

```
package ch04;
import org.apache.struts.action.ActionForm;

public class ch04_03 extends ActionForm
{

    private String text = "";

    public String getText()
    {
        return text;
    }

    public void setText(String text)
    {
        this.text = text;
    }

    public String getTextUpperCase()
    {
        return text.toUpperCase();
    }
}
```

Another use for action forms is to populate HTML forms with data, even the first time the controls in an HTML form appear. In Module 3, we passed data to the HTML controls in the Welcome page by creating custom JSP tags to create data objects which could then be used by Struts tags such as **<logic:iterate/>**. However, we can also stock controls with data using action controls. Let's look at that now in a new project.

Populating HTML Controls with Data from the Action Form

Take a look at the Welcome page in Figure 4-3. This is the first time the user has seen this page, and the text in the text field Enter Your Text Here is coming from the action form.

To see how to stock HTML controls with data like this, we'll create a new project. Here are the project files:

- ch04_06.jsp: The Welcome page
- ch04_07.java: The action
- ch04_08.java: The action form
- ch04_09.jsp: The Results page

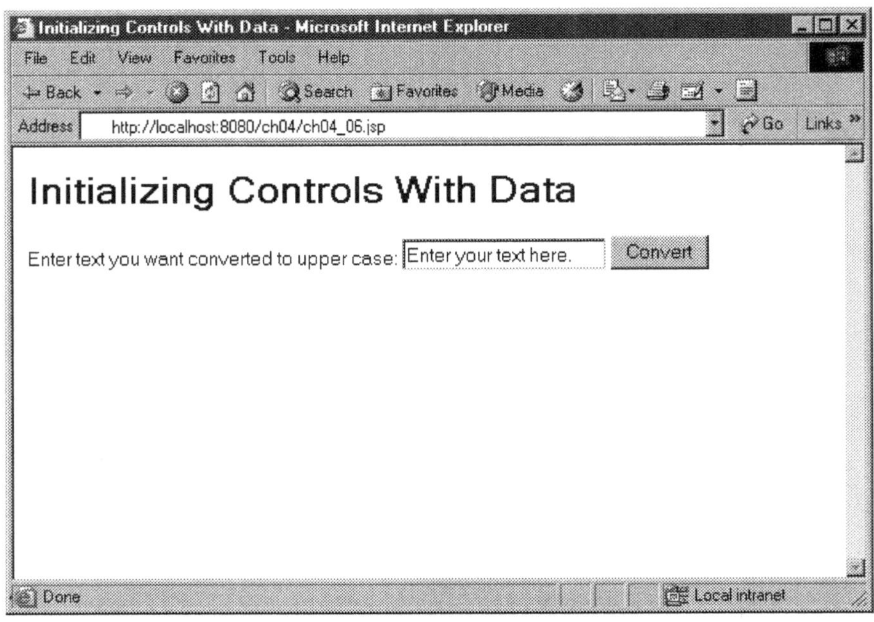

Figure 4-3 Filling HTML controls with data

In the Welcome page, the HTML form is connected to the action **ch04_07.do**, and the text field is connected to the property **text**:

```
<%@ taglib uri="/tags/struts-bean" prefix="bean" %>
<%@ taglib uri="/tags/struts-html" prefix="html" %>

<HTML>
    <HEAD>
        <TITLE>Initializing Controls With Data</TITLE>
    </HEAD>

    <BODY>
        <H1>Initializing Controls With Data</H1>
        <html:errors/>
        <html:form action="ch04_07.do">
            <bean:message key="prompt"/>
            <html:text property="text"/>
            <html:submit value="Convert"/>
        </html:form>
    </BODY>
</HTML>
```

In the **<action>** element for this action in struts-config.xml, we connect this action to the form bean **ch04_08**:

```
<action path="/ch04_07"
  type="ch04.ch04_07"
  name="ch04_08"
  scope="request"
  validate="true"
  input="/ch04_06.jsp">
  <forward name="success" path="/ch04_09.jsp"/>
</action>
```

We connect the form bean **ch04_08** to the Java class **ch04.ch04_08**:

```
<form-bean name="ch04_08"
  type="ch04.ch04_08"/>
```

In the form bean's code, ch04_08.java, we set up the **text** property:

```
package ch04;
import org.apache.struts.action.*;
import javax.servlet.http.HttpServletRequest;
import javax.servlet.http.HttpServletResponse;
```

```
public class ch04_08 extends ActionForm
{

    private String text = "";

    public String getText()
    {
        return text;
    }

    public void setText(String text)
    {
        this.text = text;
    }
        .
        .
        .
```

This action form is connected to the text that will be shown in the text field. To initialize that text to "Enter your text here.", we can use the action form's **reset** method, which is called before anything else in the action form. In this case, we will initialize the **text** property like this in the **reset** method in the action form's code, ch04_08.java:

```
package ch04;
import org.apache.struts.action.*;
import javax.servlet.http.HttpServletRequest;
import javax.servlet.http.HttpServletResponse;

public class ch04_08 extends ActionForm
{

    private String text = "";

    public String getText()
    {
        return text;
    }

    public void setText(String text)
    {
        this.text = text;
    }

    public void reset(ActionMapping mapping, HttpServletRequest request)
```

```
        {
            this.text = "Enter your text here.";
        }
}
```

That completes the action form. Here's what the action looks like that handles the task of capitalizing the entered text:

```
package ch04;

import java.io.*;
import java.util.*;
import ch04.ch04_08;
import javax.servlet.http.HttpServletRequest;
import javax.servlet.http.HttpServletResponse;
import javax.servlet.ServletException;
import org.apache.struts.action.*;

public class ch04_07 extends Action
{
  public ActionForward execute(ActionMapping mapping,
    ActionForm form,
    HttpServletRequest request,
    HttpServletResponse response)
    throws IOException, ServletException {
        ActionErrors actionerrors = new ActionErrors();

        ch04_08 textForm = (ch04_08)form;

        String text = textForm.getText();
        if(text.trim().equals("")) {
            actionerrors.add(ActionErrors.GLOBAL_ERROR, new
            ActionError("error.notext"));
        }

        if(actionerrors.size() != 0) {
            saveErrors(request, actionerrors);
            return new ActionForward(mapping.getInput());
        }

        ch04_08 textForm = (ch04_08)form;

        String text = textForm.getText();

        textForm.setText(text.toUpperCase());
```

```
            return mapping.findForward("success");
        }
    }
```

Finally, the results are displayed in the Results page, ch04_09.java:

```
<%@ taglib uri="/tags/struts-bean" prefix="bean" %>

<HTML>
    <HEAD>
        <TITLE>Here's the Result</TITLE>
    </HEAD>

    <BODY>
        <H1>Here's the Result</H1>
        <bean:message key="tocaps"/>
        <bean:write name="ch04_08" property="text"/>
    </BODY>
</HTML>
```

That's all it takes; now we can store data in HTML controls as soon as they appear. The **reset** method can also be called when the data in the action form should be reset back to its default values.

The **reset** method can also assign the Java value **null** to the properties of an action form, but if we're working with check boxes, the Struts convention is to assign a value of **false** to the corresponding properties, not **null**.

Progress Check

1. What method do you use to initialize the data in an action form?

2. What are the only datatypes in an action to store data passed from an HTML form?

---

1. The **validate** method.

2. String and Boolean datatypes.

Another common task for action forms is to validate data. We've been letting the action do that so far, but it often makes more sense for the action form, which is in charge of holding that data, to check the user's data instead.

Validating Data with the Action Form

Up to now, we've validated the data the user entered in the action ourselves. If there were errors, we saved them and forwarded them on to the input page (which we've been setting to the Welcome page in the action mapping):

```
String text = textForm.getText();

if(text.trim().equals("")) {
    actionerrors.add(ActionErrors.GLOBAL_ERROR, new
    ActionError("error.notext"));
}

if(actionerrors.size() != 0) {
    saveErrors(request, actionerrors);
    return new ActionForward(mapping.getInput());
}
.
.
.
```

However, action forms are also set up to handle this task, and we don't need to perform any explicit forwarding ourselves if we let our action form validate our data. To implement validation in our action form, override the **validate** method. The action servlet will call our action form's **validate** method, and if there are errors, it'll display them in our input page automatically (if we've used the **<html:errors/>** Struts element)—the action isn't even called.

Here's how to set up this method. It's passed the action mapping and the request object and returns an **ActionErrors** collection (**ActionMessages** in Struts 1.2):

```
public ActionErrors validate(ActionMapping mapping, HttpServletRequest
    request)
{
    .
    .
    .
}
```

In this method, we check the data entered by the user and add an **ActionError** object (**ActionMessage** object in Struts 1.2) to an **ActionErrors** collection for each error. We can also access error messages from the application.properties file from inside the action form's code as we see here, where we're using the message **error.notext**:

```
public ActionErrors validate(ActionMapping mapping, HttpServletRequest
    request)
{
    ActionErrors actionerrors = new ActionErrors();

    if(text.trim().equals("")) {
        actionerrors.add(ActionErrors.GLOBAL_ERROR, new
            ActionError("error.notext"));
    }
    .
    .
    .
}
```

Then we return the **ActionErrors** collection from this method. If this collection contains any **ActionError** objects, the action servlet will send the corresponding error messages back to the browser. Here's how the **validate** method works in this project's action form:

```
package ch04;
import org.apache.struts.action.*;
import javax.servlet.http.HttpServletRequest;
import javax.servlet.http.HttpServletResponse;

public class ch04_08 extends ActionForm
{

    private String text = "";

    public String getText()
    {
        return text;
    }

    public void setText(String text)
    {
        this.text = text;
    }

    public void reset(ActionMapping mapping, HttpServletRequest request)
    {
        this.text = "Enter your text here.";
    }
```

```
    public ActionErrors validate(ActionMapping mapping, HttpServletRequest
        request)
    {
        ActionErrors actionerrors = new ActionErrors();

        if(text.trim().equals("")) {
            actionerrors.add(ActionErrors.GLOBAL_ERROR, new
                ActionError("error.notext"));
        }
        return actionerrors;
    }
}
```

We'll also remove the error-checking code from action ch04_07.java, which no longer needs it:

```
package ch04;

import java.io.*;
import java.util.*;
import ch04.ch04_08;
import javax.servlet.http.HttpServletRequest;
import javax.servlet.http.HttpServletResponse;
import javax.servlet.ServletException;
import org.apache.struts.action.*;

public class ch04_07 extends Action
{
  public ActionForward execute(ActionMapping mapping,
    ActionForm form,
    HttpServletRequest request,
    HttpServletResponse response)
    throws IOException, ServletException {

        ch04_08 textForm = (ch04_08)form;

        String text = textForm.getText();

        textForm.setText(text.toUpperCase());

        return mapping.findForward("success");
    }
}
```

As we can see in Figure 4-4, this new version of the project uses the action form's **validate** method to catch errors.

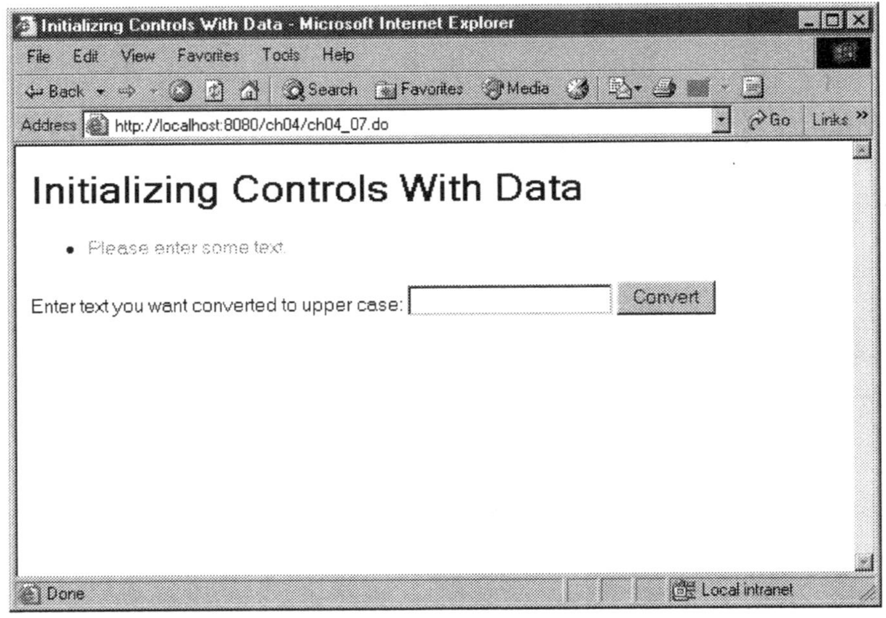

Figure 4-4 Catching errors

Progress Check

1. What method do you use to check data stored in an action form?
2. What do you pass back to the action servlet from this method?

There's something else we can do with the Java code that supports an action form: we can omit it altogether. See the next topic for details on this.

Using DynaActionForms

If all we need an action form to do is to pass on the data from an HTML form, we may be able to get away without writing any Java code for an action form. The **DynaActionForm** class was

1. The **validate** method.

2. You pass back an **ActionErrors** collection with an **ActionError** object corresponding to each error, or with no ActionError object if there were no errors.

a recent innovation in Struts, and it lets us set up an action form entirely in struts-config.xml—no Java code needed. However, the **DynaActionForm** class will only provide us with properties corresponding to the input HTML form, nothing beyond that.

We're going to rewrite this module's project to use the **DynaActionForm** class. Here are the new project files:

- ch04_10.jsp: The Welcome page
- ch04_11.java: The action
- ch04_12: The DynaActionForm
- ch04_13.jsp: The Results page

We can see the new version of the project in Figure 4-5.

When we enter text to be capitalized and click the Convert button, the text is stored in the **DynaActionForm**, which the action can treat much as a standard action form. The text is retrieved from the action form and capitalized, as shown in Figure 4-6, the Results page.

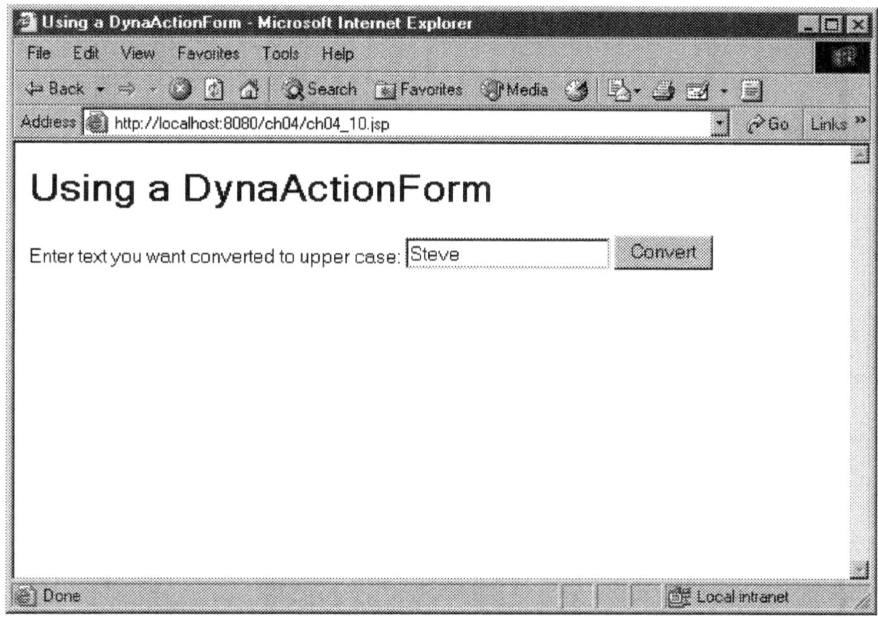

Figure 4-5 Using a DynaActionForm

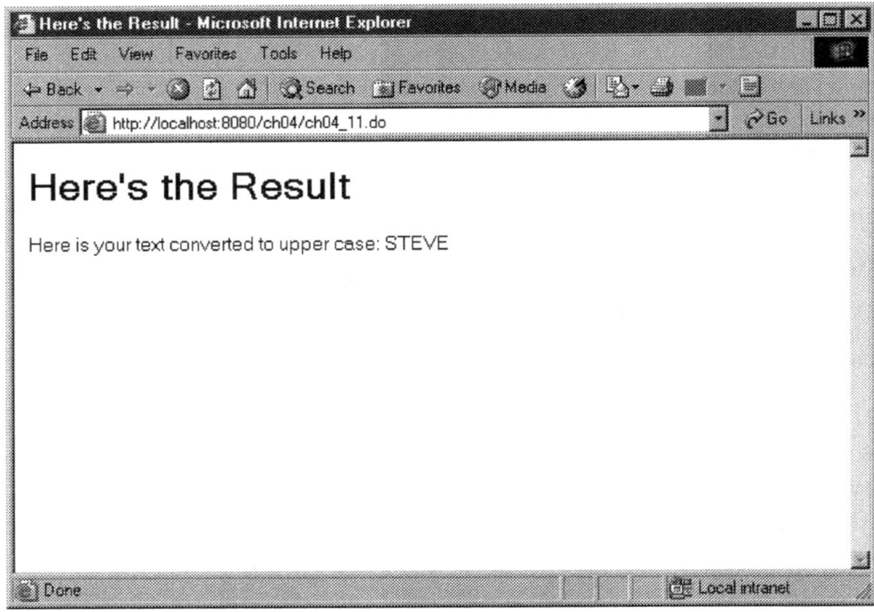

Figure 4-6 The Results page

The Welcome page, ch04_10.jsp, displays the text field and Convert button to the user that we see in Figure 4-5; note that the HTML form here is connected to the action **ch04_11.do**:

```
<%@ taglib uri="/tags/struts-bean" prefix="bean" %>
<%@ taglib uri="/tags/struts-html" prefix="html" %>

<HTML>
    <HEAD>
        <TITLE>Using a DynaActionForm</TITLE>
    </HEAD>

    <BODY>
        <H1>Using a DynaActionForm</H1>
        <html:errors/>
        <html:form action="ch04_11.do">
            <bean:message key="prompt"/>
            <html:text property="text"/>
            <html:submit value="Convert"/>
        </html:form>
    </BODY>
</HTML>
```

The action **ch04_11** is connected to an action form named **ch04_12** in the **<action>** element:

```
<action path="/ch04_11"
  type="ch04.ch04_11"
  name="ch04_12"
  input="/ch04_10.jsp">
  <forward name="success" path="/ch04_13.jsp"/>
</action>
```

So how do we set up the action form to use the **DynaActionForm** class? We do that by specifying the **org.apache.struts.action.DynaActionForm** class as the type of our action form. Here's how that works in struts-config.xml as we create the **ch04_12** action form:

```
<form-bean
    name="ch04_12"
    type="org.apache.struts.action.DynaActionForm">
    .
    .
    .
</form-bean>
```

We also include a **<form-property>** element for each property we want to recover from the HTML form, which is the **text** property here:

```
<form-bean
    name="ch04_12"
    type="org.apache.struts.action.DynaActionForm">
    <form-property
        name="text"
        type="java.lang.String"/>
</form-bean>
```

That's all we need to create the action form. We use this action form a little differently than we would a Java-based one, however. When the form is passed to the action, we cast it as a **DynaActionForm** object. Then we can use the object's **get** method to recover properties from it by name. For example, here's how we'd recover the value of the **text** property:

```
DynaActionForm textForm = (DynaActionForm)form;

String text = (String) textForm.get("text");
.
.
.
```

To set the value of a property, we can call a **DynaActionForm** object's **set** method. Here's how that works in this project's action, ch04_11.java, where we recover the text the user wants to capitalize, convert it to uppercase, store it in the action form again, and forward to the Results page:

```
package ch04;

import java.io.*;
import java.util.*;
import javax.servlet.http.HttpServletRequest;
import javax.servlet.http.HttpServletResponse;
import javax.servlet.ServletException;
import org.apache.struts.action.*;

public class ch04_11 extends Action
{
  public ActionForward execute(ActionMapping mapping,
    ActionForm form,
    HttpServletRequest request,
    HttpServletResponse response)
    throws IOException, ServletException {

        DynaActionForm textForm = (DynaActionForm)form;

        String text = (String) textForm.get("text");

        textForm.set("text", text.toUpperCase());

        return mapping.findForward("success");
    }
}
```

That's all we need; now we can recover the value of the **text** property in the Results page, ch04_13.jsp, and display that value:

```
<%@ taglib uri="/tags/struts-bean" prefix="bean" %>

<HTML>
    <HEAD>
        <TITLE>Here's the Result</TITLE>
    </HEAD>

    <BODY>
```

```
        <H1>Here's the Result</H1>
        <bean:message key="tocaps"/>
        <bean:write name="ch04_12" property="text"/>
    </BODY>
</HTML>
```

That completes the project. As shown in Figures 4-5 and 4-6, the **DynaActionForm** object is able to pass the project's data to the action as well as a Java-based action form. No Java needed for the action form at all—not bad.

Progress Check

1. What element do you use inside a **<form-bean>** element to set up a property in a **DynaActionForm**?
2. How do you get the value of a property in an action when you're using a **DynaActionForm**?

Ask the Expert

Q: Can you initialize the values of properties set up in a DynaActionForm **in struts-config.xml?**

A: As of Struts 1.1, the **DynaActionForm reset** method does not initialize property values as specified in **<form-property>** elements in struts-config.xml. If we want to initialize our properties, we must subclass the **DynaActionForm** class and write our own **reset** method. We can also override the **initialize** method inside the subclassed class to do the same thing. However, now that we're writing our action form in Java again, we've lost most of the advantages of using a **DynaActionForm**.

Use Struts 1.2

Using a DynaActionForm is completely compatible with Struts 1.2 (at least at this point in the Struts 1.2 beta cycle). This project compiles and works just fine using Struts 1.2.

---

1. You use a **<form-property>** element to specify property names and types.
2. You use the **get** method like this, where you're getting the value of a property named **data**: **form.get("data")**.

✓ Module 4 Mastery Check

1. On what class do you base the model in a Struts application?

   A. **ActionModel**

   B. **Model**

   C. **ModelFactory**

   D. Your own class

2. What **ActionForm** method do you use to set properties to default values?

   A. **reset**

   B. **default**

   C. **init**

   D. **start**

3. Can an action servlet store data from an HTML form in an action form using the Java **int** datatype?

   A. Yes, **int** datatypes are no problem.

   B. No, an action servlet can only store String and Boolean values in an action form.

4. What **ActionForm** method do you use to check data the user entered?

   A. **check**

   B. **validate**

   C. **dataValidate**

   D. **validation**

5. What two objects are passed to the method used in an action form to validate data?

   A. **ActionForm** and **HttpServletResponse**

   B. **ActionForm** and **HttpServletRequest**

   C. **HttpServletRequest** and **HttpServletResponse**

   D. **ActionMapping** and **HttpServletRequest**

6. What class do you assign to the **<form-bean>** element's **type** attribute when you want to use a **DynaActionForm**?

   A. **org.apache.struts.DynaActionForm**

   B. **javax.servlet.DynaActionForm**

   C. **org.apache.struts.action.DynaActionForm**

   D. **javax.servlet.struts.DynaActionForm**

7. What element do you use to set up a custom property in the **<form-bean>** element when you're setting up a **DynaActionForm**?

   A. **<property>**

   B. **<form-property>**

   C. **<custom-property>**

   D. **<property-data>**

8. What two attributes do you use to set up a custom property when using a **DynaActionForm**?

   A. **name** and **size**

   B. **property** and **type**

   C. **type** and **size**

   D. **name** and **type**

9. What **DynaActionForm** method do you use to assign a new value to a property?

   A. **assign**

   B. **change**

   C. **setProperty**

   D. **set**

10. One of the reasons that action forms have their own Struts class and are not just simple beans is that:

    A. Beans don't support text properties.

    B. Unselected check boxes aren't reported by HTML browsers.

    C. Beans can't be serialized.

    D. HTML browsers don't interface to simple beans.

Module 5

Using Actions

CRITICAL SKILLS

5.1 Use the <action> Element

5.2 Use ForwardAction

5.3 Use IncludeAction

5.4 Use DispatchAction

5.5 Use LookupDispatchAction

5.6 Use SwitchAction

In this module, we're going to get control of Struts actions. The action is part of the controller in a Struts application, along with the action servlet. We've already seen actions at work, but there's a lot more to the story. We're going to look not only at standard actions in this module, but also at other action types available, such as **ForwardAction**, **IncludeAction**, **DispatchAction**, **LookupDispatchAction**, and **SwitchAction**. Actions are the customizable part of the controller in a Struts application. Writing them means you don't have to subclass the action servlet to make your application do what you want. Instead, you extend an action class such as **org.apache.struts.action.Action** to create your own action.

Actions let you validate your data, extract data from an action form, call and interact with business logic in the model, and forward results to the view. There are two components to actions: the **<action>** element in struts-config.xml and the Java class that supports the action in code. We'll look at the **<action>** element first.

CRITICAL SKILL 5.1

Use the <action> Element

We've used the **<action>** element extensively already; here's an example:

```
<action path="/ch04_02"
  type="ch04.ch04_02"
  name="ch04_03"
  input="/ch04_01.jsp">
  <forward name="success" path="/ch04_05.jsp"/>
</action>
```

You've gotten familiar with the **<action>** element's attributes in this case, but there are some you haven't seen yet. All the **<action>** element's attributes appear in Table 5-1.

For example, the **<action>** element's **scope** attribute, which can be set to **request** or **session**, indicates the scope where Struts will find the action form for the action. If true (the default), the **validate** attribute tells the action servlet to call the action form's **validate** method before passing data on to the action:

```
<action
    path="/ch05_02"
    type=ch05.ch05_02"
    name="ch05_03"
    validate="true"
</action>
```

attribute	Name of the request-scope or session-scope attribute that is used to access the **ActionForm** bean if it is other than the bean's specified **name**.
className	The fully qualified Java class name of the **ActionMapping** subclass to use for this action mapping object. Defaults to the type specified by the enclosing **<action-mappings>** element or to **org.apache.struts.action.ActionMapping** if not specified.
forward	Path of the resource that will process this request, instead of the **Action** class specified by **type**. Exactly one of **forward**, **include**, or **type** must be specified.
include	Indicates the resource that will process this request, instead of the **Action** class specified by **type**. Exactly one of **forward**, **include**, or **type** must be specified.
input	Path of the action or other resource to which control should be returned if a validation error is encountered. Valid only when **name** is specified.
name	Name of the form bean, if any, that is associated with this action mapping.
path	The path of the submitted request, starting with a backward slash (/).
parameter	General-purpose parameter that can be used to pass extra information to the **Action** object selected by this action mapping.
prefix	Prefix used to match **request** parameter names to **ActionForm** property names, if any.
roles	List of security role names that are allowed access to this **ActionMapping** object.
scope	The context (**request** or **session**) that is used to access the **ActionForm** bean, if any.
suffix	Suffix used to match **request** parameter names to **ActionForm** bean property names, if any.
type	Fully qualified Java class name of the **Action** subclass that will process requests for this action mapping. Exactly one of **forward**, **include**, or **type** must be specified.
unknown	Set to "true" if this object should be configured as the default action mapping for this module.
validate	Set to **true** if the **validate** method of the **ActionForm** bean should be called prior to calling the **Action** object for this action mapping. Set to **false** if you do not want the **validate** method called.

Table 5-1 The <action> Attributes

We'll also see other attributes of the **<action>** element, such as **include** and **forward**, at work in this module. In addition to attributes, the **<action>** element can contain six different child element types, such as the **<forward>** elements you have already worked with, and the **<exception>** element you'll see in a few pages. You can see all the possibilities in Table 5-2.

Progress Check

1. What element do you use in the **<action>** element to pass control to another resource?
2. What **<action>** element attribute do you use to specify security permissions?

Element	What It Does	Attributes
<icon>	Specifies an icon	ID
<display-name>	Sets the display name of the action	ID
<description>	Gives a description of the action	ID
<set-property>	Sets a property	ID, property, value
<exception>	Specifies an exception handler	ID, bundle, className, handler, key, path, scope, type
<forward>	Defines a forward	ID, className, contextRelative, name, path, redirect

Table 5-2 The Legal <action> Child Elements

1. The **<forward>** element
2. The **roles** attribute

Using Action Classes

By now, we're familiar with the basics of using actions in Struts applications. Such applications start with some kind of Welcome page, such as this one that asks the user to enter some data in a text field named **text**. The form in the page names an action—in this case, **Process**:

```
<%@ taglib uri="/tags/struts-html" prefix="html" %>
<html:html>
<head>
<title>Enter the data</title>
</head>
<body>
    <html:form action="Process">
          Please enter the data: <html:text property="text" />
          <html:submit />
    </html:form>
</body>
</html:html>
```

In an **<action>** element, the **Process** action might be tied to the **dataForm** action form:

```
<action-mappings>
 <action
   path="/Process"
   type="ProcessAction"
   name="dataForm"
   input="/index.jsp">
   <forward name="success" path="/results.jsp"/>
   <forward name="failure" path="/index.jsp"/>
 </action>
</action-mappings>
```

The **dataForm** action form is tied to a Java class in a **<form-beans>** element:

```
<form-beans>
<form-bean name="dataForm"
  type="DataForm"/>
</form-beans>
```

The action form just implements the **text** property:

```
import javax.servlet.http.HttpServletRequest;
import org.apache.struts.action.*;

public class DataForm extends ActionForm {
  private String text = null;

  public String getText() {
    return (text);
  }

  public void setText(String text) {
    this.text = text;
  }
}
```

We'll take a look at the action in code next. In struts-config.xml, we tied the **Process** action to the class **ProcessAction**:

```
<action-mappings>
 <action
   path="/Process"
   type="ProcessAction"
   name="dataForm"
   input="/index.jsp">
   <forward name="success" path="/results.jsp"/>
   <forward name="failure" path="/index.jsp"/>
 </action>
</action-mappings>
```

This class, **ProcessAction**, is the action in the example, and it extends the **org.apache .struts.action.Action** class. We've based classes on the **Action** class before and used a number of **Action** methods, but there are additional methods in this class you should know about. You can see them all in Table 5-3.

Method	Description
ActionForward **execute**(ActionMapping mapping, ActionForm form, javax.servlet.http.HttpServletRequest request, javax.servlet.http.HttpServletResponse response)	Process the specified HTTP request and create the corresponding HTTP response.
ActionForward **execute**(ActionMapping mapping, ActionForm form, javax.servlet.ServletRequest request, javax.servlet.ServletResponse response)	Process the specified non-HTTP request and create the corresponding non-HTTP response.

Table 5-3 The Action Class's Methods

Method	Description
protected java.lang.String **generateToken**(javax.servlet.http.HttpServletRequest request)	Generate a new transaction token, which is used in creating and forcing a single request for a transaction.
protected javax.sql.DataSource **getDataSource**(javax.servlet.http.HttpServletRequest request)	Return the default data source for the current module.
protected javax.sql.DataSource **getDataSource**(javax.servlet.http.HttpServletRequest request, java.lang.String key)	Return the specified data source for the current module.
protected java.util.Locale **getLocale**(javax.servlet.http.HttpServletRequest request)	Return the user's currently selected locale.
protected MessageResources **getResources**	Deprecated. Return the resources for the default module.
protected MessageResources **getResources**(javax.servlet.http.HttpServletRequest request)	Return the default message resources for the current module.
protected MessageResources **getResources**(javax.servlet.http.HttpServletRequest request, java.lang.String key)	Return the specified message resources for the current module.
ActionServlet **getServlet**	Return the controller servlet instance.
protected boolean **isCancelled**(javax.servlet.http.HttpServletRequest request)	Return true if the current form's Cancel button was pressed.
protected boolean **isTokenValid**(javax.servlet.http.HttpServletRequest request)	Return true if there is a token stored in the user's current session, and the value matches the **request** parameter.
ActionForward **perform**(ActionMapping mapping, ActionForm form, javax.servlet.http.HttpServletRequest request, javax.servlet.http.HttpServletResponse response)	Deprecated. Use the **execute** method instead.
ActionForward **perform**(ActionMapping mapping, ActionForm form, javax.servlet.ServletRequest request, javax.servlet.ServletResponse response)	Deprecated. Use the **execute** method instead.
protected void **resetToken**(javax.servlet.http.HttpServletRequest request)	Reset the saved transaction token in the user's session.
protected void **saveErrors**(javax.servlet.http.HttpServletRequest request, ActionErrors errors)	Save the specified error messages keys into the appropriate **request** attribute for use by the <html:errors> tag.
protected void **saveMessages**(javax.servlet.http.HttpServletRequest request, ActionMessages messages)	Save the specified messages keys into the appropriate **request** attribute for use by the <html:messages> tag.
protected void **saveToken**(javax.servlet.http.HttpServletRequest request)	Save a new transaction token in the user's current session, creating a new session if necessary.
protected void **setLocale**(javax.servlet.http.HttpServletRequest request, java.util.Locale locale)	Set the user's currently selected locale.

Table 5-3 The Action Class's Methods *(continued)*

Method	Description
void **setServlet**(ActionServlet servlet)	Set the controller servlet instance.
protected java.lang.String **toHex**(byte[] buffer)	Deprecated. This method will be removed in a release after Struts 1.1.

Table 5-3 The Action Class's Methods *(continued)*

The most significant method is the **execute** method, which we'll now look at in detail.

The execute Method

The **execute** method is passed these objects:

```
public ActionForward execute(ActionMapping mapping,
    ActionForm form,
    HttpServletRequest request,
    HttpServletResponse response)
    throws java.lang.Exception {
        .
        .
        .
}
```

You've seen the **ActionMapping** object before and used its **findForward** method to determine where to find the view. As listed here, **ActionMapping** objects actually have four methods, including the useful **getInputForward**, which forwards to the page given in the action mapping as the input page:

- **ExceptionConfig findException(java.lang.Class type)** Finds and returns the **ExceptionConfig** instance defining how exceptions of the specified type should be handled.
- **ActionForward findForward(java.lang.String name)** Finds and returns the **ForwardConfig** instance defining how forwarding to the specified logical name should be handled.
- **java.lang.String[] findForwards** Returns the logical names of all locally defined forwards for this mapping.
- **ActionForward getInputForward** Creates (if necessary) and returns an **ActionForward** that corresponds to the input property of this **Action**.

Note also that you can get a **String** array of all forwards in this action's mapping using the **getForwards** method.

Usually, the form passed to you in the **execute** method is an object you create yourself, so its methods and fields are up to you. On the other hand, the **HttpServletRequest** and **HttpServletResponse** objects passed to this method are the standard **request** and **response** objects passed to you from the browser (handled in servlet code with the **doGet**, **doPut** and/or **service** methods). That means you can access the data the user entered into the HTML form with the **request** object's **getParameter** method. In this example, you could read the text from the text field you've named text, like this:

```
String text = request.getParameter("text");
```

The **request** and **response** objects can give you all that you'd normally get from these objects in servlet code. For example, you can get access to the current session in an action, like this:

```
HttpSession session = request.getSession();
```

If you wanted to, you could even recover the current action mapping, which is stored in a **request** attribute named **MAPPING_KEY**, like this:

```
ActionMapping mapping = (ActionMapping) request.getAttribute(MAPPING_KEY);
```

For that matter, you could even recover the action form from the **request** object because the action form is stored as a **request** attribute as well, making it easy to pass between the components of a Struts application. Action forms are stored in attributes of the same name, so here's how you could recover the action form from the **request** object if you wanted to:

```
ActionForm form = request.getAttribute(mapping.getName());
```

Progress Check

1. How do you get the input page from the **ActionMapping** argument passed to the **execute** method?
2. How can you access data from a web page without using the action form?

---

1. You can use its **getInputForward** method.
2. You can use the **request** object's **getParameter** method (this object is passed to the **execute** method).

What About Exceptions?

Note that the **execute** method can throw exceptions:

```
public ActionForward execute(ActionMapping mapping,
    ActionForm form,
    HttpServletRequest request,
    HttpServletResponse response)
    throws java.lang.Exception {
        .
        .
        .
}
```

In struts-config.xml, you can have global and local exception handlers to handle the thrown exceptions. For example, say you wanted to catch an application-defined exception named **app.BadPassword**, which extends the **java.lang.Exception** class. You could define a global exception handler for this exception in the **<global-exceptions>** element in struts-config.xml. Like other elements we're already familiar with, such as **<action-mappings>** or **<form-beans>** in struts-config.xml, the **<global-exceptions>** element is a child of the **<struts-config>** element.

Here's what that would look like, where we're indicating that the page that should handle this exception is login.jsp, and the message that should be displayed is stored with the key **error.BadPassword** in application.properties:

```
<struts-config>
        .
        .
        .
    <global-exceptions>

        <exception
           key="error.BadPassword"
           type="app.BadPassword"
           path="/login.jsp"/>

    </global-exceptions>
        .
        .
        .
</struts-config>
```

In login.jsp, you can use **<html:errors />** or **<html:messages />** to display the message corresponding to the key **error.BadPassword**. You also have direct access to the JSP **exception** object in your JSP code in that page, which will hold the **app.BadPassword** object.

You can also make this a local exception—that is, local to the current action. You do that simply by using the **<exception>** element inside the **<action>** element, like this:

```
<action path="/ch04_02"
  type="ch04.ch04_02"
  name="ch04_03"
  input="/ch04_01.jsp">

  <exception key="error.BadPassword"
      type="app.BadPassword"
      path="/login.jsp" />
  <forward name="success" path="/ch04_05.jsp"/>
</action>
```

You can also use your own exception handler instead of the standard **org.apache.struts.action.ExceptionHandler** class. You specify your own exception handler using the **<exception>** element's **className** attribute:

```
<action path="/ch04_02"
  type="ch04.ch04_02"
  name="ch04_03"
  input="/ch04_01.jsp">

  <exception key="error.BadPassword"
      type="app.BadPassword"
      path="/login.jsp"
      className="ch05.ExceptionHandler" />
  <forward name="success" path="/ch04_05.jsp"/>
</action>
```

Progress Check

1. How do you set up a global exception handler?
2. What **<exception>** attribute do you use to set the URL control should be transferred to if an exception has been thrown?

---

1. You use an **<exception>** element in a **<global-exceptions>** element.
2. You use the **path** attribute.

To complete the **execute** method in this example's **ProcessAction** class, we'll read the **text** property of the action form sent to you and pass it on to the Success page. Here's what that looks like:

```
public class ProcessAction extends Action {
  public ActionForward execute(ActionMapping mapping,
    ActionForm form,
    HttpServletRequest request,
    HttpServletResponse response)
    throws java.lang.Exception {

    String text = null;
    String target = new String("success");

    if ( form != null ) {
      DataForm dataForm = (DataForm)form;
      text = dataForm.getText();
    }

    return (mapping.findForward(target));
}
}
```

Passing control to the **success** forward in the action's **execute** method makes the action servlet check the action's mapping to find that the **success** forward corresponds to results.jsp. You can access the **text** property in the **dataForm** bean and write that **text** to the Results page, like this:

```
<%@ taglib uri="/tags/struts-bean" prefix="bean" %>
<html>
  <head>
    <title>A Results page</title>
  </head>
  <body>

    <h1>Reading User Input</h1>
    You typed: <bean:write name="dataForm" property="text"/>
  </body>
</html>
```

That's it for working with a standard action. There are other types of actions available that we'll also take a look at in this module: **ForwardAction**, **IncludeAction**, **DispatchAction**, **LookupDispatchAction**, and **SwitchAction**. Just as standard actions are based on the **org.apache.struts.action.Action** class, each of these actions is a subclass of the Struts **Action** class.

CRITICAL SKILL 5.2

Use ForwardAction

The **org.apache.struts.actions.ForwardAction** class lets you set up an action that forwards to a new URL automatically. In other words, instead of passing control to a Java action class that you've written, actions that use the **ForwardAction** class are simply designed to let you forward to a new URL.

We've already seen an example of the **ForwardAction** class at work in the struts-blank application in Module 2 (not to be confused with the **ActionForward** class, objects that you return from the **execute** method). In that application, the Welcome page, index.jsp, was designed to forward the user on immediately to the application's actual Welcome page, Welcome.jsp. The index.jsp file did that with a forward named **welcome**:

```
<%@ taglib uri="/tags/struts-logic" prefix="logic" %>
<logic:redirect forward="welcome"/>
```

In struts-config.xml, you can define local forwards for each action with **<forward>** elements inside **<action>** elements. You can also define global forwards with **<forward>** elements inside the **<global-forwards>** element (which is a child element of the **<struts-config>** element, like **<action-mappings>** and **<global-exceptions>**), and that's how the struts-blank application connects the **welcome** forward to an action named **Welcome.do**:

```
<global-forwards>
    <!-- Default forward to "Welcome" action -->
    <!-- Demonstrates using index.jsp to forward -->
    <forward
        name="welcome"
        path="/Welcome.do"/>
</global-forwards>
```

The **Welcome.do** action is actually a **ForwardAction** to the real Welcome page, Welcome.jsp. Here's how that works in the **<action>** element:

```
<action-mappings>
        <!-- Default "Welcome" action -->
        <!-- Forwards to Welcome.jsp -->
    <action
        path="/Welcome"
        type="org.apache.struts.actions.ForwardAction"
        parameter="/pages/Welcome.jsp"/>
</action-mappings>
```

If you set up an action with the **org.apache.struts.actions.ForwardAction** class, that action will forward control to the URL given by the **<action>** element's **parameter** attribute.

Ask the Expert

Q: Didn't I see in Table 5-1 that the <action> **element has a** forward **attribute? Does that do the same thing as using the** org.apache.struts.actions.ForwardAction **class?**

A: Yes indeed, you can use the **forward** attribute of the **<action>** element instead of the **ForwardAction** class to create an action that will forward control to a new URL. Here's what that might look like:

```
<action
    path="/ch05_02"
    type=ch05.ch05_02"
    forward="ch05_03"
</action>
```

Progress Check

1. How do you set up a global forward accessible from any action in struts-config.xml?
2. What Struts class do you use to create a forward action?

Before leaving the topic of forwarding, it's also worth mentioning that the **redirect** attribute of the **<forward>** element redirects the browser rather than simply forwarding the request to a new URL:

```
<forward name="success" path="/results.jsp" redirect="true"/>
```

So what's the difference between a forward and a redirect? A forward simply forwards the current **request** object from the browser on to a new URL, but a redirect creates an entirely new **request** object before transferring to the new URL.

---

1. You use an **<forward>** element inside a **<global-forwards>** element.
2. **org.apache.struts.actions.ForwardAction**

CRITICAL SKILL 5.3

Use IncludeAction

Another popular action class is the **org.apache.struts.actions.IncludeAction** class. This action class was designed to let you work with legacy code, including older documents in Struts applications.

Here's an example. Say that you have some legacy code you want to incorporate in a Struts application, such as ch05_01.jsp, which uses the JSP tag **<jsp:getProperty>** to read the property named **text** of a bean named **ch05_02**:

```
<HTML>
    <HEAD>
        <TITLE>Using a Bean</TITLE>
    </HEAD>

    <BODY>
        <H1>Using a Bean</H1>

     The bean says: <jsp:getProperty name="ch05_02" property="text" />


    </BODY>
</HTML>
```

This JSP doesn't use any Struts support, but you can still include it in a Struts application. We'll start by creating the ch05_02 action form, connecting it to the **ch05.ch05_02** class:

```
    <form-bean name="ch05_02"
      type="ch05.ch05_02"/>
```

And the **ch05.ch05_02** class will support the **text** property, like this:

```
package ch05;
import org.apache.struts.action.ActionForm;

public class ch05_02 extends ActionForm
{

    private String text = "";

    public String getText()
    {
        return text;
    }
```

```
    public void setText(String text)
    {
        this.text = text;
    }
}
```

In this Struts application, we'll use an action named **ch05_04** and a Welcome page named ch05_03.jsp. Here's what the **<action>** element for this action looks like (note that we're using **org.apache.struts.actions.IncludeAction** as the type of action, which means we won't have to write the action ourselves):

```
<action path="/ch05_04"
      type="org.apache.struts.actions.IncludeAction"
      parameter="/ch05_01.jsp"
      scope="request"
      name="ch05_02"
      input="/ch05_03.jsp">
    </action>
```

The URL you give in the **parameter** attribute is the resource that will be included by **org.apache.struts.actions.IncludeAction**; in this case, that's our legacy code, ch05_01.jsp. Here's the Welcome page this Struts application uses, ch05_03.jsp, asking the user to enter some text:

```
<%@ taglib uri="/tags/struts-bean" prefix="bean" %>
<%@ taglib uri="/tags/struts-html" prefix="html" %>

<HTML>
    <HEAD>
        <TITLE>Using Include Actions</TITLE>
    </HEAD>

    <BODY>
        <H1>Using Include Actions</H1>
        <html:form action="ch05_04.do">
            Enter some text
            <html:text property="text"/>
            <html:submit value="Submit"/>
        </html:form>
    </BODY>
</HTML>
```

That completes the application. The Welcome page, ch05_03.jsp, appears in Figure 5-1.

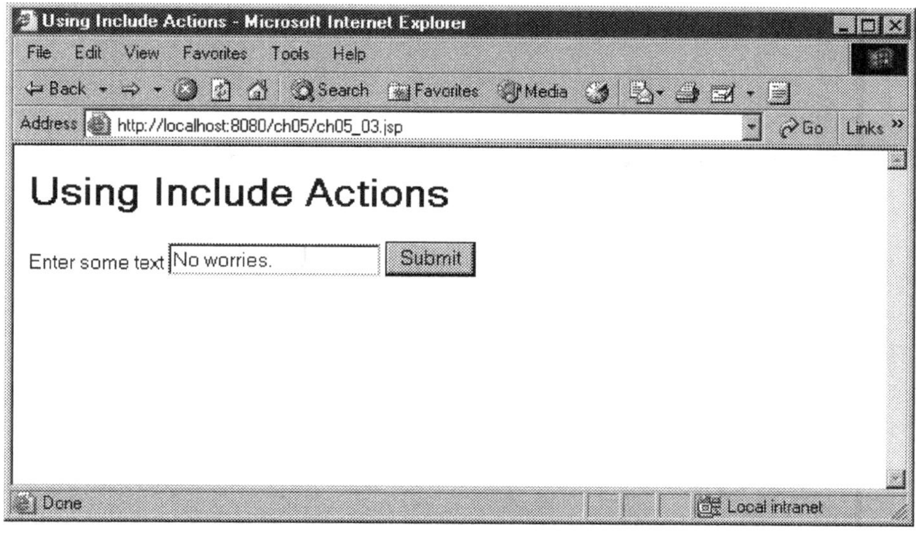

Figure 5-1 A Welcome page for an include action

When the user enters some text and clicks Submit, that text is stored in an action form of the **ch05_02** class. The legacy code, ch05_01.jsp, expects a bean with that name, and it uses the **<jsp:getProperty>** tag to read the **text** property from that bean. The output from the legacy JSP page is included in the output from your application. You can see this when the user clicks the Submit button, and the output from ch05_01.jsp appears, as shown in Figure 5-2.

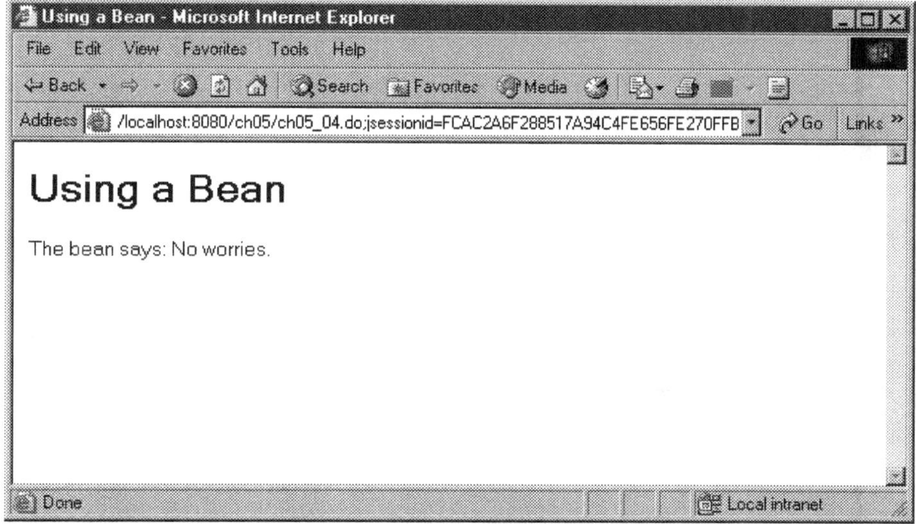

Figure 5-2 Using legacy code

In this way, you can use **include** actions to include the output of legacy, non-Struts code.

There's also an **include** attribute in the **<action>** element that you can use to include the output from other resources.

Progress Check

1. How do you specify the URL of the resource to be included?

CRITICAL SKILL 5.4

Use DispatchAction

The **org.apache.struts.actions.DispatchAction** class lets you group multiple actions into the same class. That's useful if you have many actions and don't want to spread the support for those actions over many files. Here's an example; in this case, we'll have three actions, **red**, **yellow**, and **green**, which the user can select by name, as shown in Figure 5-3.

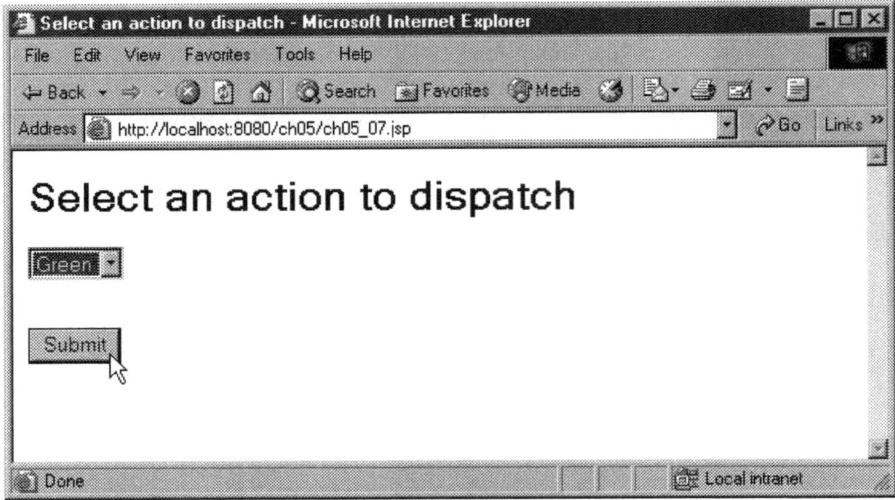

Figure 5-3 Dispatching actions

1. You use the **<action>** element's **parameter** attribute.

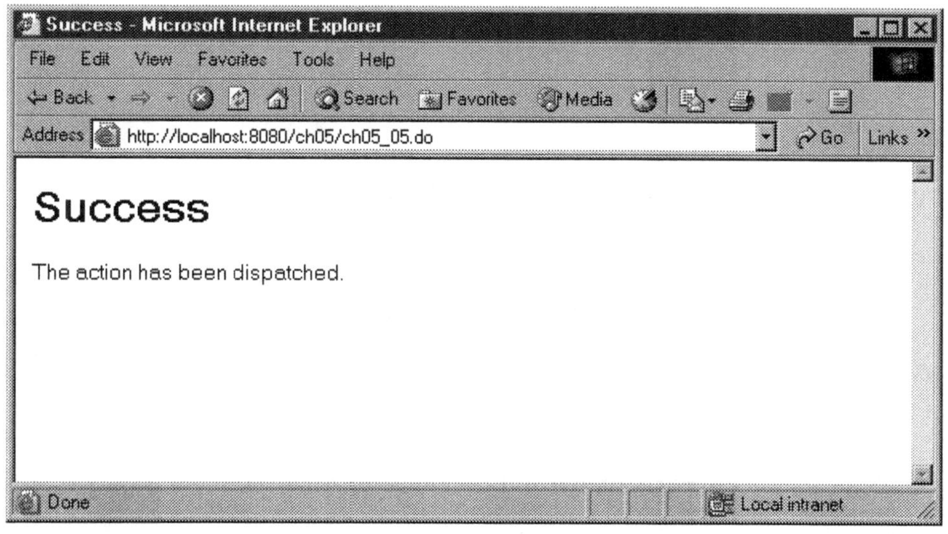

Figure 5-4 Handling a dispatched action

When the user selects an action, that action will print "stop", "caution", or "go" to the console, depending on whether the user selected **red**, **yellow**, or **green**, and it will display the Results page shown in Figure 5-4.

Here's how this works. In the action class, **ch05_05**, which we base on the **org.apache.struts.actions.DispatchAction** class, we'll set up three methods—**red**, **yellow**, and **green**, one for each action we want to support. Each method is passed the same arguments as the **execute** method would be passed in a standard action class:

```
package ch05;

import java.io.*;
import java.util.*;
import javax.servlet.http.HttpServletRequest;
import javax.servlet.http.HttpServletResponse;
import javax.servlet.ServletException;
import org.apache.struts.actions.DispatchAction;

public class ch05_05 extends DispatchAction
{
  public ActionForward red(ActionMapping mapping,
    ActionForm form,
    HttpServletRequest request,
    HttpServletResponse response)
```

```
    throws IOException, ServletException {
         .
         .
         .
    }

  public ActionForward yellow(ActionMapping mapping,
    ActionForm form,
    HttpServletRequest request,
    HttpServletResponse response)
    throws IOException, ServletException {
         .
         .
         .
    }

  public ActionForward green(ActionMapping mapping,
    ActionForm form,
    HttpServletRequest request,
    HttpServletResponse response)
    throws IOException, ServletException {
         .
         .
         .
    }
}
```

In this case, we'll have each method print out the text "stop", "caution", or "go" to the console and forward to the Success page:

```
  public ActionForward red(ActionMapping mapping,
    ActionForm form,
    HttpServletRequest request,
    HttpServletResponse response)
    throws IOException, ServletException {
         System.out.println("Stop.");
         return mapping.findForward("success");
    }

  public ActionForward yellow(ActionMapping mapping,
    ActionForm form,
    HttpServletRequest request,
    HttpServletResponse response)
    throws IOException, ServletException {
         System.out.println("Caution.");
         return mapping.findForward("success");
    }
```

```
  public ActionForward green(ActionMapping mapping,
    ActionForm form,
    HttpServletRequest request,
    HttpServletResponse response)
    throws IOException, ServletException {
        System.out.println("Go.");
        return mapping.findForward("success");
    }
}
```

How does Struts know which method to call? In the **<action>** element, we declare a parameter named **method**:

```
<action path="/ch05_05"
  type="ch05.ch05_05"
  name="ch05_06"
  parameter="method"
  input="/ch05_05.jsp">
  <forward name="success" path="/ch05_08.jsp"/>
</action>
```

We connect this action to an action form named **ch05.ch05_06**:

```
<form-bean name="ch05_06"
  type="ch05.ch05_06"/>
```

The **method** property of the action form will hold the name of the method that Struts is supposed to call in the action class. Here's what the code for the action form, **ch05_06**, looks like:

```
package ch05;
import org.apache.struts.action.ActionForm;

public class ch05_06 extends ActionForm
{

    private String method = "";

    public String getmethod()
    {
        return method;
    }

    public void setMethod(String method)
    {
        this.method = method;
    }
}
```

In the Welcome page, ch05_07.jsp, we'll set up the **<html:select>** control that displays the actions that may be chosen and store them in the action form's **method** property, like this:

```
<%@ taglib uri="/tags/struts-bean" prefix="bean" %>
<%@ taglib uri="/tags/struts-html" prefix="html" %>

<HTML>
    <HEAD>
        <TITLE>Select an action to dispatch</TITLE>
    </HEAD>

    <BODY>
        <H1>Select an action to dispatch</H1>
        <html:form action="ch05_05.do">
            <html:select property="method">
                <html:option value="red">Red</html:option>
                <html:option value="yellow">Yellow</html:option>
                <html:option value="green">Green</html:option>
            </html:select>
            <BR>
            <BR>
            <BR>
            <html:submit />
        </html:form>
    </BODY>
</HTML>
```

Struts is able to determine which method to call using the **method** property. When the user selects the Green option, as shown in Figures 5-3 and 5-4, the **green** method in your action class is called, which prints "Go." to the console (i.e., the window in which Tomcat is running) and displays the Results page, ch05_08.jsp:

```
<HTML>
    <HEAD>
        <TITLE>Success</TITLE>
    </HEAD>

    <BODY>
        <H1>Success</H1>
        The action has been dispatched.
    </BODY>
</HTML>
```

That's all there is to it.

Progress Check

1. How do you specify the method you want to dispatch control to?
2. What's the full name of the class that supports dispatch actions?

CRITICAL SKILL 5.5

Use LookupDispatchAction

The **org.apache.struts.actions.LookupDispatchAction** class is much like the **DispatchAction** class, except that **LookupDispatchAction** uses a Java map to dispatch methods.

In this example, we'll use the same **red**, **yellow**, and **green** methods as in the previous project, but this time you'll also include a new method, **getKeyMethodMap**, to return a Java **Map** object that connects names in application.properties to the **red**, **yellow**, and **green** methods. Here's how that looks in the new action, ch05_09.java:

```
package ch05;

import java.io.*;
import java.util.*;
import javax.servlet.http.HttpServletRequest;
import javax.servlet.http.HttpServletResponse;
import javax.servlet.ServletException;
import org.apache.struts.actions.LookupDispatchAction;

public class ch05_09 extends LookupDispatchAction
{
  public ActionForward red(ActionMapping mapping,
    ActionForm form,
    HttpServletRequest request,
    HttpServletResponse response)
    throws IOException, ServletException {
        System.out.println("Stop.");
        return mapping.findForward("success");
    }

  public ActionForward yellow(ActionMapping mapping,
    ActionForm form,
    HttpServletRequest request,
```

1. You use the **<action>** element's **parameter** attribute to specify the name of the property that will contain the name of the method to call.

2. **org.apache.struts.actions.DispatchAction**

```
    HttpServletResponse response)
    throws IOException, ServletException {
        System.out.println("Caution.");
        return mapping.findForward("success");
    }

  public ActionForward green(ActionMapping mapping,
    ActionForm form,
    HttpServletRequest request,
    HttpServletResponse response)
    throws IOException, ServletException {
        System.out.println("Go.");
        return mapping.findForward("success");
    }

   protected Map getKeyMethodMap()
   {
       Map map = new HashMap();
       map.put("ch05.red", "red");
       map.put("ch05.yellow", "yellow");
       map.put("ch05.green", "green");
       return map;
   }
}
```

With the **Map** object returned from **getKeyMethodMap**, Struts can connect the method names you specify in application.properties with the methods to call in the action class. Here's how we set the keys that hold the action names in application.properties:

```
ch05.red=red
ch05.yellow=yellow
ch05.green=green
```

The name of the method selected by the user will be stored in a property named **method**, as in the previous project:

```
<action path="/ch05_09"
  type="ch05.ch05_09"
  name="ch05_10"
  parameter="method"
  input="/ch05_11.jsp">
  <forward name="success" path="/ch05_12.jsp"/>
</action>
```

Here's the action form for this project, ch05_10.java, which supports the **method** property:

```
package ch05;
import org.apache.struts.action.ActionForm;

public class ch05_10 extends ActionForm
{
    private String method = "";

    public String getmethod()
    {
        return method;
    }

    public void setMethod(String method)
    {
        this.method = method;
    }
}
```

The Welcome page, ch05_11.jsp, asks the user to select an action:

```
<%@ taglib uri="/tags/struts-bean" prefix="bean" %>
<%@ taglib uri="/tags/struts-html" prefix="html" %>

<HTML>
    <HEAD>
        <TITLE>Using LookupDispatchAction</TITLE>
    </HEAD>

    <BODY>
        <H1>Using LookupDispatchAction</H1>
        <html:form action="ch05_09.do">
            Select an action to dispatch:
            <html:select property="method">
                <html:option value="red">Red</html:option>
                <html:option value="yellow">Yellow</html:option>
                <html:option value="green">Green</html:option>
            </html:select>
            <BR>
            <BR>
            <BR>
            <html:submit />
        </html:form>
    </BODY>
</HTML>
```

After the user selects an action and clicks Submit, the corresponding action is run and the Results page, ch05_12.jsp, appears:

```
<HTML>
    <HEAD>
        <TITLE>Success</TITLE>
    </HEAD>

    <BODY>
        <H1>Success</H1>
        The action has been dispatched.
    </BODY>
</HTML>
```

You can see this project at work in Figure 5-5.

If the user selects the Red action, as shown in Figure 5-5, the application will print "Stop." to the console, and you'll see the Results page, as shown in Figure 5-6.

CRITICAL SKILL 5.6

Use SwitchAction

The **SwitchAction** class is often used when you break your application up into *modules*, which you can do as of Struts 1.1. Dividing applications into modules helps separate code and helps with security issues.

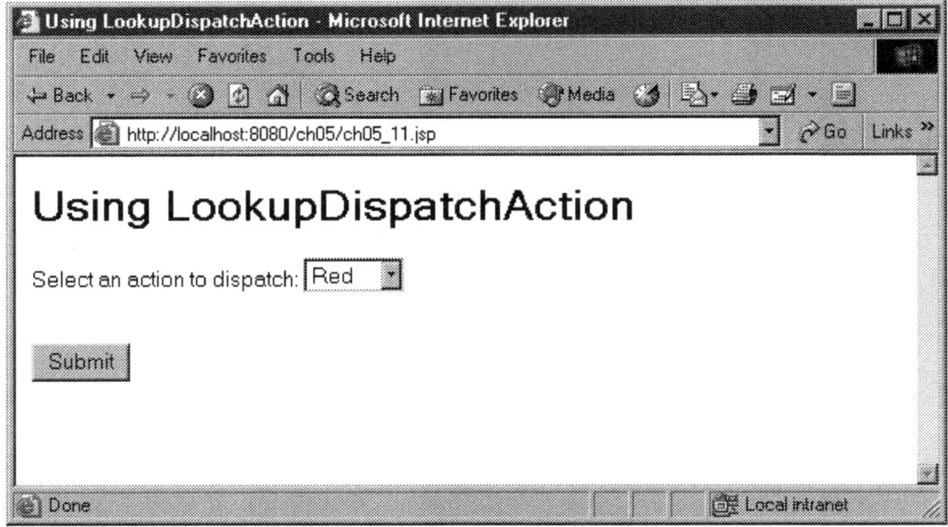

Figure 5-5 Using LookupDispatchAction

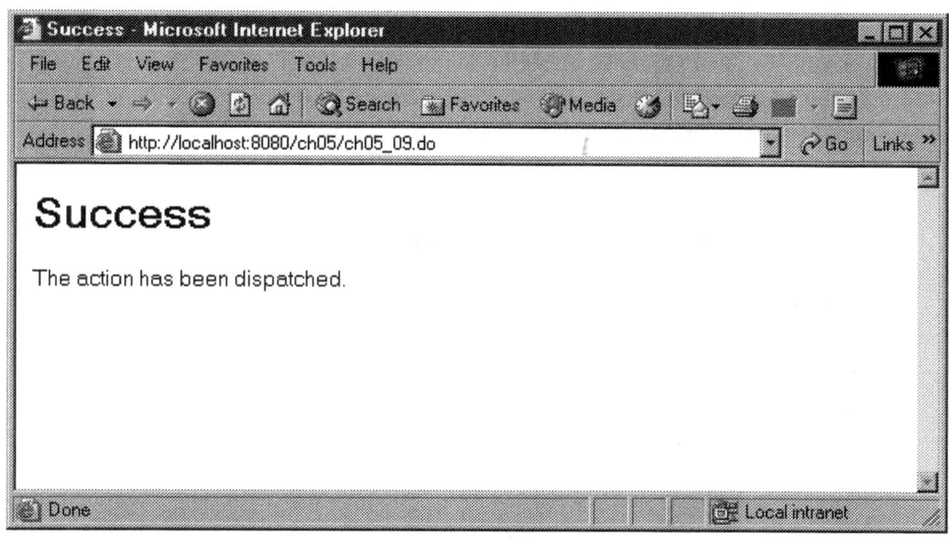

Figure 5-6 Dispatching an action with LookupDispatchAction

For example, if you wanted to create a module named **user**, you could do that in web.xml like this, where you're using a new XML document, struts-config-user.xml, for the new module:

```
<!-- Standard Action Servlet Configuration (with debugging) -->
<servlet>
  <servlet-name>action</servlet-name>
  <servlet-class>org.apache.struts.action.ActionServlet</servlet-class>
  <init-param>
    <param-name>config</param-name>
    <param-value>/WEB-INF/struts-config.xml</param-value>
  </init-param>
  <init-param>
    <param-name>config/user</param-name>
    <param-value>/WEB-INF/struts-config-user.xml</param-value>
  </init-param>
  <init-param>
    <param-name>debug</param-name>
    <param-value>2</param-value>
  </init-param>
  <init-param>
    <param-name>detail</param-name>
    <param-value>2</param-value>
  </init-param>
  <load-on-startup>2</load-on-startup>
</servlet>
```

Now the **user** module operates in its own space, with its own configuration file, struts-config-user.xml. Say that you have an action in the default Struts module that you want to delegate to the **user** module. You could set up an action in the default module like this, using the **org.apache.struts.actions.SwitchAction** class:

```
<action
    path="/result"
    type="org.apache.struts.actions.SwitchAction" />
```

Then you could set up an action, **ch05_13**, like this in the default module:

```
<action path="/ch05_13"
  type="ch05.ch05_13"
  name="ch05_03"
  input="/ch05_01.jsp">
  <forward name="success"
     path="/result.do?page=/ch05_14.do&amp;pref=/user"/>
</action>
```

What is the string "/result.do?page=/ch05_14.do&pref=/user" all about? When the user navigates to the **ch05_13** action, the request is forwarded to the **request** action, with the **page** attribute set to "/ch05_14.do" and the **pref** attribute set to "/user". This causes the request to be switched to ch05_14.do in the **user** module. To make that switching operation work, you have to define the action **ch05_14.do** in the **user** module's configuration file, struts-config-user.xml.

Use Struts 1.2

All the code in this module is up to speed with the early release version of Struts 1.2 as of this writing. Of course, if you start adding validation to your code using **ActionError** and **ActionErrors** objects, it'll be a different story. In that case, switch to **ActionMessage** and **ActionMessages**.

✓ Module 5 Mastery Check

1. What's the full name of the Struts **Action** class?

   A. **javax.servlet.action.Action**

   B. **javax.servlet.struts.action.Action**

   C. **org.struts.action.Action**

   D. **org.apache.struts.action.Action**

2. What **<action>** element attribute specifies the page control should switch to if there's a validation error?

   A. **input**

   B. **error**

   C. **errorHandler**

   D. **exceptionHandler**

3. What values can you set the **<action>** element's **scope** attribute to?

   A. "page" or "session"

   B. "request" or "page"

   C. "request" or "session"

   D. "application" or "session"

4. What **<action>** child element do you use to set up an exception handler?

   A. **<exception>**

   B. **<exceptionHandler>**

   C. **<error>**

   D. **<errorHandler>**

5. What **ActionMapping** method do you use to get all forwards in an action mapping?

   A. **getForward**

   B. **getForwards**

   C. **findForward**

   D. **findForwards**

6. What attribute do you use in an **<exception>** element to specify a custom exception-handling class?

   A. **class**

   B. **className**

   C. **exceptionClass**

   D. **exceptionClassName**

7. When using the **ForwardAction** class, what **<action>** element attribute do you use to specify the URL to forward to?

   A. **url**

   B. **forward**

   C. **attribute**

   D. **parameter**

8. What Struts action class is good to add support for legacy code in a Struts application?

   A. **org.apache.struts.actions.LegacyAction**

   B. **org.apache.struts.actions.IncludeAction**

   C. **org.apache.struts.actions.DispatchAction**

   D. **org.apache.struts.actions.ForwardAction**

9. When you're using the **DispatchAction** class, how do you specify the name of the property you'll use to store the name of the action method you want control dispatched to?

   A. You use the **parameter** attribute of the **<action>** element.

   B. You use the **method** attribute of the **<action>** element.

   C. You use the **dispatch** attribute of the **<action>** element.

   D. You use the **attribute** attribute of the **<action>** element.

10. What method do you use in a **LookupDispatchAction**-based class to return a **Map** object telling Struts which methods it should call to dispatch control?

    A. **getMethodMap**

    B. **getMap**

    C. **getKeyMap**

    D. **getKeyMethodMap**

Module 6

The Struts <html> Tags

CRITICAL SKILLS

6.1 Use the <html:html> Tag

6.2 Use the <html:form> Tag

6.3 Use the <html:submit> Tag

6.4 Use the <html:cancel> Tag

6.5 Use the <html:text> Tag

6.6 Use the <html:errors> Tag

6.7 Use the <html:textarea> Tag

6.8 Use the <html:checkbox> Tag

6.9 Use the <html:radio> Tag

6.10 Use the <html:button> Tag

6.11 Use the <html:link> Tag

6.12 Use the <html:img> Tag

6.13 Use the <html:image> Tag

6.14 Use the <html:select> and <html:option> Tags

6.15 Use the <html:multibox> Tag

6.16 Use the <html:file> Tag

This module is all about using the Struts **<html>** custom JSP tags to create HTML elements in JSP pages. There are many such tags in Struts, as shown in Table 6-1, and we're going to put many of them to work in this module.

Tag Name	Does This
base	Creates an HTML <base> element
button	Creates a Button Input field
cancel	Creates a Cancel button
checkbox	Creates a Checkbox Input field
errors	Displays a set of error messages
file	Creates a File Select Input field
form	Creates an Input form
frame	Creates an HTML frame element
hidden	Creates a hidden field
html	Creates an HTML <html> element
image	Creates an input tag of type "image"
img	Creates an HTML img tag
javascript	Creates JavaScript validation (based on the rules loaded by the **ValidatorPlugIn**)
link	Creates an HTML anchor or hyperlink
messages	Displays a set of messages
multibox	Creates a Checkbox Input field
option	Creates a Select option
options	Creates a collection of Select options
optionsCollection	Creates a collection of Select options
password	Creates a Password Input field
radio	Creates a Radio Button Input field
reset	Creates a Reset Button Input field
rewrite	Creates a URI
select	Creates a select element
submit	Creates a Submit button
text	Creates an input field of Type text
textarea	Creates a text area
xhtml	Creates HTML tags as XHTML

Table 6-1 The Struts <html> Tags

To put the Struts HTML tags to work, you set up the struts-html tag library like this in web.xml:

```
<taglib>
  <taglib-uri>/tags/struts-html</taglib-uri>
  <taglib-location>/WEB-INF/struts-html.tld</taglib-location>
</taglib>
```

You also add struts-html.tld to your WEB-INF directory. Because the Java support for this custom JSP tag library is in struts.jar, all that remains is to use the **<%@taglib%>** JSP directive at the beginning of your JSPs:

```
<%@ taglib uri="/tags/struts-html" prefix="html" %>
```

Now you're free to use the Struts HTML tags like **<html:button>** to create HTML button controls. Each of these tags supports attributes, and we'll list the significant ones for each element in this module. Some attributes are common to all tags that display visible HTML controls (e.g., **<html:button>** but not **<html:form>**), such as the event attributes you see in Table 6-2. For example, you assign the **onclick** attribute the name of the JavaScript event handler that you want to use to handle click events for the control, the **onblur** attribute to handle the case where the control loses the input focus, and so on.

Attribute	Description
onblur	JavaScript event handler to run when this element loses the focus
onchange	JavaScript event handler to run when this element loses the focus and its value has been changed
onclick	JavaScript event handler to run when this element is clicked
ondblclick	JavaScript event handler to run when this element is double-clicked
onfocus	JavaScript event handler to run when this element gets the focus
onkeydown	JavaScript event handler to run when this element has the focus and a key is pressed
onkeypress	JavaScript event handler to run when this element has the focus and a key is pressed and then released
onkeyup	JavaScript event handler to run when this element has the focus and a key is released
onmousedown	JavaScript event handler to run when this element is under the mouse and a mouse button is pressed
onmousemove	JavaScript event handler to run when this element is under the mouse and the pointer is moved
onmouseout	JavaScript event handler to run when the pointer was moved outside the element
onmouseover	JavaScript event handler to run when the pointer is moved inside the element
onmouseup	JavaScript event handler to run when this element is under the mouse pointer and a mouse button is released

Table 6-2 The Struts <html> Tags' Event Attributes

Attribute	Description
style	CSS styles to be applied to this HTML element
styleClass	CSS stylesheet class to be applied to this HTML element; creates a **class**" attribute
styleId	Identifier to be assigned to this HTML element; creates an **id** attribute

Table 6-3 The Struts <html> Tags' Style Attributes

In addition, all visible HTML controls support three style attributes, which you can find in Table 6-3.

To see the Struts **<html>** tags at work, we're going to develop a project in this module, which you can access as http://localhost:8080/ch06/ch06_01.jsp in the code for the book. We'll use HTML controls from simple text fields up through multibox check boxes, clickable image controls, hyperlinks, and file uploading controls in this project.

You can see the first few HTML controls in this project at work in Figure 6-1.

The user can enter data in this page using the HTML controls and click the Submit button, making the project display a Results page as you see in Figure 6-2, summarizing that data.

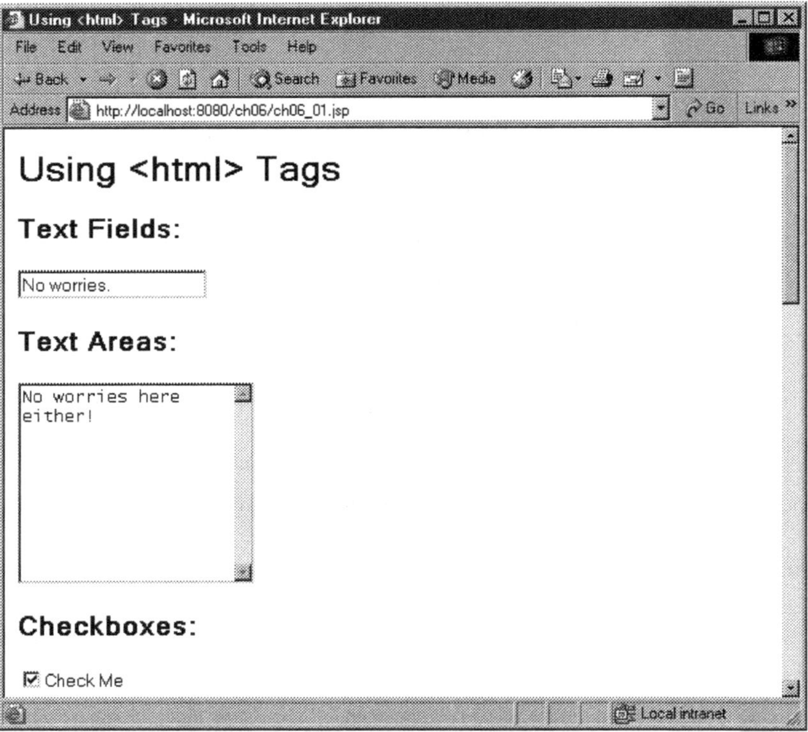

Figure 6-1 The <html> tags project, part 1

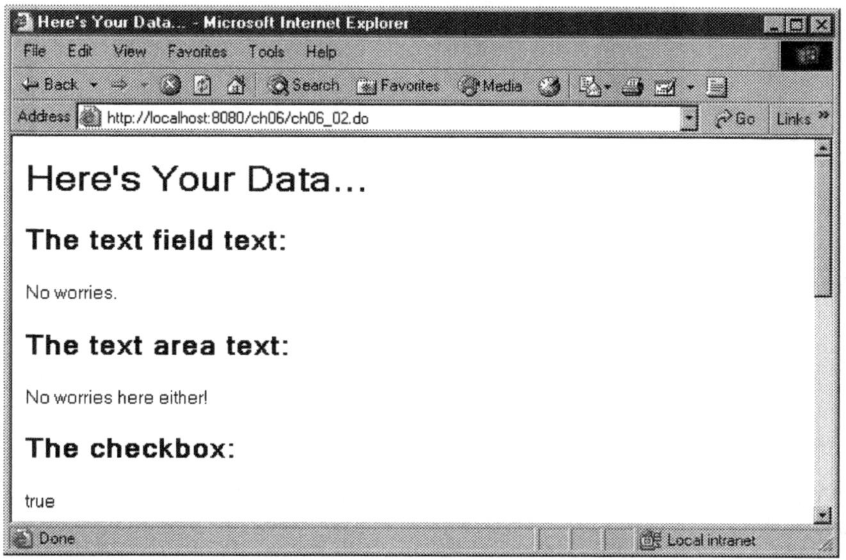

Figure 6-2 The Results page, part 1

Here are the files for this project:

- **ch06_01.jsp** HTML controls page
- **ch06_02.java** The action
- **ch06_03.java** The action form
- **ch06_04.jsp** The Results page

We'll get started creating this project now, starting with the **<html:html>** tag.

CRITICAL SKILL 6.1

Use the <html:html> Tag

You start a JSP page with the **<html:html>** tag, which creates an HTML **<html>** element. The significant attributes of this tag appear in Table 6-4.

Attribute Name	Description
locale	Set to **true** to store a locale in the session based on the current request's Accept-Language header.
xhtml	Set to **true** to make all html tags be written as xhtml.

Table 6-4 The Struts <html:html> Tag's Significant Attributes

Here's how we use this tag in the example project's ch06_01.jsp Welcome page:

```
<%@ taglib uri="/tags/struts-html" prefix="html" %>

<html:html>
    .
    .
    .
```

This is simply translated into:

```
<html>
    .
    .
    .
```

That gets us started with the **<html>** tags; now, how about creating a **<form>** HTML element.

CRITICAL SKILL 6.2

Use the <html:form> Tag

To work with HTML controls, you need to enclose them in an HTML **<form>** element. You can do that with the **<html:form>** custom JSP tag in Struts. The significant attributes of this tag appear in Table 6-5.

Although the **<html:form>** tag is used to support **name**, **type,** and **scope** attributes, they're deprecated now. The preferred usage is to allow the appropriate values to be determined automatically from the corresponding **ActionMapping**.

Attribute Name	Description
action	The URL to which this form will be submitted.
enctype	The content encoding to be used to submit this form, if the method is POST.
focus	The field name to which initial focus will be assigned with a JavaScript function.
method	The HTTP method that will be used to submit this request (GET, POST). Defaults to POST.
name	Deprecated. Formerly held the bean name, but these days, the bean name is determined from the ActionMapping.

Table 6-5 The Struts <html:form> Tag's Significant Attributes

Attribute Name	Description
onreset	JavaScript event handler executed if the form is reset
onsubmit	JavaScript event handler executed if the form is submitted
scope	Deprecated. Formerly held the bean scope, which is now determined from the corresponding ActionMapping
target	Window target to which this form is submitted, such as for use with frames
type	Deprecated. Formerly held the bean type, which is now determined from the corresponding ActionMapping

Table 6-5 The Struts <html:form> Tag's Significant Attributes *(continued)*

Here's how we use this tag in ch06_01.jsp (the **method** and **enctype** attributes are there to handle file uploads later in this module):

```
<html:form action="ch06_02.do" method="POST" enctype="multipart/form-data">
        .
        .
        .
```

This is how this is translated into HTML:

```
<form name="ch06_03" method="POST" action="/ch06/ch06_02.do"
enctype="multipart/form-data">
        .
        .
        .
```

CRITICAL SKILL 6.3

Use the <html:submit> Tag

As you know from prior examples, the **<html:submit>** tag creates a Submit button. The significant attributes of this tag appear in Table 6-6.

Here's how the Submit button is created in the project's ch06_01.jsp:

```
<html:submit value="Submit"/>
```

This is what this is translated into in HTML:

```
<input type="submit" value="Submit">
```

Attribute Name	Description
accesskey	The keyboard character used to move focus to this button.
alt	The alternate text for this button.
altKey	The message resources key of the alternate text for this button.
disabled	Set to **true** if this button should be disabled.
property	Name of the request parameter that will be included with this submission.
tabindex	The tab order for this button.
title	The title for this element.
titleKey	The message resources key for the title for this button.
value	The text of the button label.

Table 6-6 The Struts <html:submit> Tag's Significant Attributes

CRITICAL SKILL 6.4

Use the <html:cancel> Tag

The **<html:cancel>** tag just creates a form Cancel button. In Struts, this control is a Submit button that causes the action servlet to bypass calling the form bean **validate** method. Note that the action is called normally. The significant attributes of this tag appear in Table 6-7.

Attribute Name	Description
accesskey	The keyboard character used to move focus to this button.
alt	The alternate text for this button.
altKey	The message resources key of the alternate text for this button.
disabled	Set to **true** if this button should be disabled.
property	Name of the request parameter that will be included with this submission. If you set this to a nondefault value, Struts won't recognize it as a Cancel button.
tabindex	The tab order for this button.
title	The title for this button.
titleKey	The message resources key for the title for this button.
value	Caption of this button.

Table 6-7 The Struts <html:cancel> Tag's Significant Attributes

Here's how we use this tag in ch06_01.jsp:

```
<html:cancel/>
```

Here's the corresponding HTML:

```
<input type="submit" name="org.apache.struts.taglib.html.CANCEL"
value="Cancel" onclick="bCancel=true;">
```

CRITICAL SKILL 6.5

Use the <html:text> Tag

As you know, the **<html:text>** tag creates a text field. The significant attributes of this tag appear in Table 6-8.

Attribute Name	Description
accesskey	The keyboard character used to transfer the focus to this element.
alt	The alternate text for this text field.
altKey	The message resources key of the alternate text for this text field.
disabled	Set to **true** if this input field should be disabled.
maxlength	Maximum number of characters to accept.
property	Name of the corresponding bean property. This attribute is required.
readonly	Set to **true** if this input field should be read only.
size	Size of the text field.
tabindex	The tab order for this text field.
title	The title for this element.
titleKey	The message resources key for the title for this element.
value	Text to which this text field should be initialized. By default, Struts uses the corresponding bean property value.

Table 6-8 The Struts <html:text> Tag's Significant Attributes

Here's how this module's project creates a text field in ch06_01.jsp:

```
<h2>Text Fields:</h2>
<html:text property="text"/>
<br>
```

Here's the HTML created:

```
<h2>Text Fields:</h2>
<input type="text" name="text" value="">
<br>
```

In the project's form bean, ch06_03, here's how we handle the **text** property:

```
private String text = "";

public String getText()
{
    return text;
}

public void setText(String text)
{
    this.text = text;
}
```

Here's how the **text** property is displayed in the Results page, ch06_04.jsp:

```
<h2>The text field text:</h2>
<bean:write name="ch06_03" property="text"/>
<BR>
```

You can see the text field in Figure 6-1 and the Results page that reports the entered text in Figure 6-2.

CRITICAL SKILL 6.6

Use the <html:errors> Tag

The **<html:errors>** tag is one we've also seen. This tag displays error messages as returned by your code in the input page. The significant attributes of this tag appear in Table 6-9.

Attribute Name	Description
bundle	The servlet context attribute key for the resource bundle to use. Defaults to the application resource bundle used by the action servlet.
name	Name of the request scope bean under which error messages have been stored.
property	Name of the property for which error messages should be displayed.

Table 6-9 The Struts <html:errors> Tag's Significant Attributes

You can access error messages in an application.properties by key, as well as giving (optional) definitions of the following message keys:

- **errors.header** Header text for the error message list. Usually, this text will end with <ul>.
- **errors.footer** Footer text for after the error messages list. Usually, this text will begin with </ul>.
- **errors.prefix** Text that will be added before each error in the list.
- **errors.suffix** Text that will be added after each error in the list.

For example, if you want to make sure the user enters text into the text field, you can use code like this in the action:

```
ActionErrors actionerrors = new ActionErrors();

ch06_03 dataForm = (ch06_03)form;

String text = dataForm.getText();
if(text.trim().equals("")) {
    actionerrors.add(ActionErrors.GLOBAL_ERROR, new
ActionError("error.notext"));
}

if(actionerrors.size() != 0) {
    saveErrors(request, actionerrors);
    return new ActionForward(mapping.getInput());
}
```

We'll add these keys to application.properties:

```
error.notext=Please enter some text.
errors.footer=</ul>
errors.header=<UL>
errors.prefix=<LI><font color="red">
errors.suffix=</LI></font>
errors.footer=</UL>
```

You can see the results in Figure 6-3 if the user didn't enter anything into the text field.

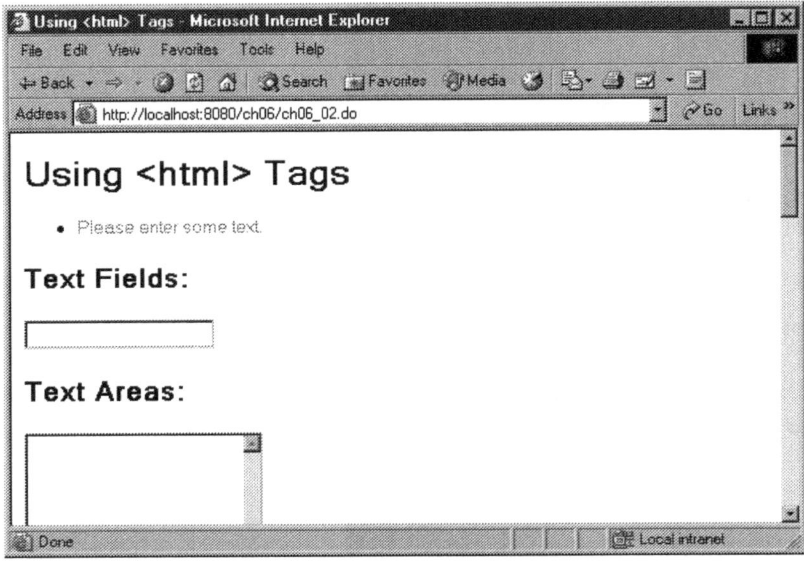

Figure 6-3 Reporting an error

CRITICAL SKILL 6.7

Use the <html:textarea> Tag

The **<html:textarea>** tag creates an HTML text area control, just like a text field, except that it can handle multiple lines of text. The significant attributes of this tag appear in Table 6-10.

In this module's project, we create the text area this way:

```
<h2>Text Areas:</h2>
<html:textarea property="textarea" rows="10"/>
<br>
```

Here's the HTML created:

```
<h2>Text Areas:</h2>
<textarea name="textarea" rows="10"></textarea>
<br>
```

In code, the text area property **textarea** is handled just as the text field **text** property is, with **getTextarea** and **setTextarea** methods in the form bean. You can see the text area at work in Figure 6-1 and the text that was entered into it in Figure 6-2.

Attribute Name	Description
accesskey	The keyboard character used to transfer the focus to this text area.
alt	The alternate text for this text area.
altKey	The message resources key of the alternate text for this text area.
cols	The number of columns.
disabled	Set to **true** if this text area should be disabled.
property	Name of the corresponding bean property. This attribute is required.
readonly	Set to **true** if this text area should be read only.
rows	The number of rows.
tabindex	The tab order for this control.
title	The title for this element.
titleKey	The message resources key for the title for this element.
value	Value to which this control should be initialized. By default, Struts uses the corresponding bean property.

Table 6-10 The Struts <html:textarea> Tag's Significant Attributes

CRITICAL SKILL 6.8

Use the <html:checkbox> Tag

The **<html:checkbox>** tag creates a check box; that is, an HTML **<input>** element of type **checkbox**. The property associated with this field should be of type **boolean**, and any **value** you specify should correspond to one of the strings that indicate a true value (**true**, **yes**, or **on**). The significant attributes of this tag appear in Table 6-11.

In code, check boxes have the values **true** or **false**. Here's how we set up the check box in ch06_01.jsp:

```
<h2>Checkboxes:</h2>
<html:checkbox property="checkbox"/>Check Me
<br>
```

Here's the resulting check box in HTML:

```
<h2>Checkboxes:</h2>
<input type="checkbox" name="checkbox" value="on">Check Me
<br>
```

Attribute Name	Description
accesskey	The keyboard character used to transfer the focus to this element.
alt	The alternate text for this element.
altKey	The message resources key of the alternate text for this element.
disabled	Set to **true** if this input field should be disabled.
property	Name of the bean property for this control. This attribute is required.
tabindex	The tab order for this control.
title	The title for this element.
titleKey	The message resources key for the title for this element.
value	The value to be transmitted if this check box is checked when the form is submitted. By default, the value "on" will be returned.

Table 6-11 The Struts <html:checkbox> Tag's Significant Attributes

Here is what the **checkbox** property looks like in code:

```
private boolean checkbox = false;

public boolean getCheckbox()
{
    return checkbox;
}

public void setCheckbox(boolean checkbox)
{
    this.checkbox = checkbox;
}
```

Here's how this property is used in the Results page:

```
<h2>The checkbox:</h2>
<bean:write name="ch06_03" property="checkbox"/>
<BR>
```

You can see this check box at work in the bottom of Figure 6-1. The user can check or uncheck the control; after clicking Submit, the results appear in the bottom of Figure 6-2, where you see that the check box had been checked.

If you want to create a set of check boxes that acts like a single control, see the multibox control, coming up later in this module.

Progress Check

1. What is the datatype for check box property attributes?
2. How can you specify if a check box should appear checked when it is first displayed?

CRITICAL SKILL 6.9

Use the <html:radio> Tag

The **<html:radio>** tag creates a radio button. If you want to group a number of radio buttons together so they work in concert, give them the same **property** attribute name. The significant attributes of this tag appear in Table 6-12.

Attribute Name	Description
accesskey	The keyboard character used to transfer the focus to this radio button.
alt	The alternate text for this radio button.
altKey	The message resources key of the alternate text for this radio button.
disabled	Set to **true** if this radio button should be disabled.
property	The corresponding bean property for this radio button. This attribute is required.
tabindex	The tab order for this control.
title	The title for this element.
titleKey	The message resources key for the title for this element.
value	The value of the radio button. This attribute is required.

Table 6-12 The Struts <html:radio> Tag's Significant Attributes

1. **boolean**
2. Set its form bean property to **true**.

Here's how we create three radio buttons, only one of which can be selected at once:

```
<h2>Radio Buttons:</h2>
<html:radio property="radio" value="red"/>red
<html:radio property="radio" value="green"/>green
<html:radio property="radio" value="blue"/>blue
<br>
```

Here's the resulting HTML:

```
<h2>Radio Buttons:</h2>
<input type="radio" name="radio" value="red">red
<input type="radio" name="radio" value="green">green
<input type="radio" name="radio" value="blue">blue
<br>
```

The **radio** property will hold a **String** value corresponding to the selected radio button, "red", "green", or "blue". Here's how we handle that property in the form bean:

```
    private String radio = "";

    public String getRadio()
    {
        return radio;
    }

    public void setRadio(String radio)
    {
        this.radio = radio;
    }
```

In the Results page, we just display the selected radio button's value:

```
<h2>The selected radio button:</h2>
<bean:write name="ch06_03" property="radio"/>
<BR>
```

You can see what this looks like in Figure 6-4, where the user has selected the radio button with the value "green".

When the user clicks the Submit button, the selected value is displayed, as shown in Figure 6-5.

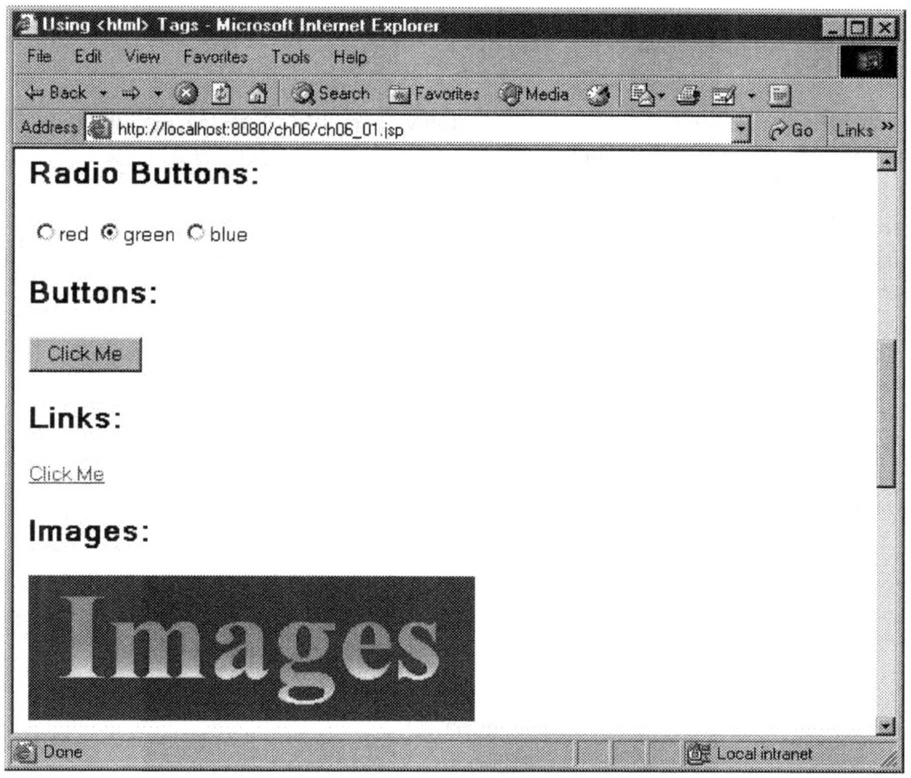

Figure 6-4 The <html> tags project, part 2

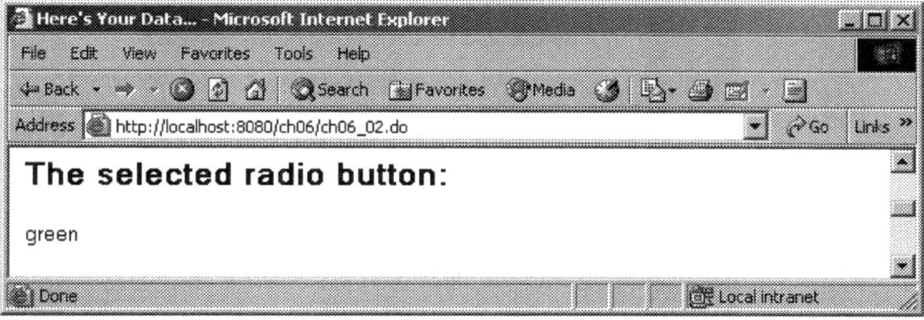

Figure 6-5 The Results page, part 2

CRITICAL SKILL 6.10

Use the <html:button> Tag

The **<html:button>** tag creates an HTML button with the **<button>** tag. Handling this control is a little different from the others in this module, because buttons don't store data in the same way text fields or text areas do. Instead, buttons usually make some action happen, so they're usually connected to JavaScript functions. The significant attributes of this tag appear in Table 6-13.

Here's how we create the button in this project—we're going to use this button with a JavaScript function, so although we'll assign a property to it (as is required), we won't use that property:

```
<h2>Buttons:</h2>
<html:button onclick="clicker()" value="Click Me" property="text"/>
<br>
```

Here's the HTML created:

```
<h2>Buttons:</h2>
<input type="button" name="text" value="Click Me" onclick="clicker()">
<br>
```

Attribute Name	Description
accesskey	The keyboard character used to transfer the focus to this element.
alt	The alternate text for this element.
altKey	The message resources key of the alternate text for this element.
disabled	Set to **true** if this input field should be disabled.
property	Name of the associated bean property. This attribute is required.
tabindex	The tab order for this control.
title	The title for this element.
titleKey	The message resources key for the title for this element.
value	Caption of this button.

Table 6-13 The Struts <html:button> Tag's Significant Attributes

This connects the button click to a JavaScript function named **clicker**, which we can place in the **<head>** section of ch06_01.jsp to display a message:

```
<head>
    <title>Using &lt;html&gt; Tags</title>
    <script language="JavaScript">
        function clicker()
        {
            confirm("You clicked the button.");
        }
    </script>
</head>
```

Now when the user clicks the button, they'll see the JavaScript confirm box that appears in Figure 6-6. In this way, you can use the supported events such as **onclick**, **ondblclick**, and so on to connect your controls to JavaScript code.

CRITICAL SKILL 6.11

Use the <html:link> Tag

The **<html:link>** tag creates an HTML **<a>** tag. The base URL for this hyperlink is calculated based on which of the following attributes you specify (you must specify exactly one of them):

- *forward* Use the value of this attribute as the name of a global ActionForward.
- *action* Use the value of this attribute as the name of an action.
- *href* Use the value of this attribute.
- *page* Generate a server-relative URI by including the context path and application prefix.

The significant attributes of this tag appear in Table 6-14.

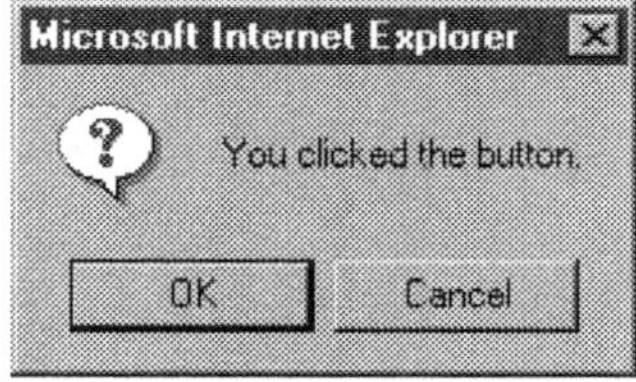

Figure 6-6 Using JavaScript

Attribute Name	Description
accesskey	The keyboard character used to transfer the focus to this element.
action	Name of an action that contains the actual content-relative URI of the destination of this transfer.
anchor	Anchor tag ("#xyz") to be added to the generated hyperlink. (Don't include the "#" character.)
forward	Name of a global ActionForward that contains the actual content-relative URI of the destination of this transfer.
href	URL to which this hyperlink will transfer control if activated.
linkName	This value will create a "name" element in the generated anchor tag.
page	Module-relative path, which should begin with a "/", to which this hyperlink will transfer control.
tabindex	The tab order for this control.
target	The window target in which the resource linked to this hyperlink will be displayed.
title	The title for this hyperlink.
titleKey	The message resources key for the title for this element.

Table 6-14 The Struts <html:link> Tag's Significant Attributes

In our example project, we'll use the **action** attribute to link to the action for this project, **ch06_02**, and give the link the text "Click Me":

```
<h2>Links:</h2>
<html:link action="ch06_02">Click Me</html:link>
<br>
```

This causes Struts to fill in the full name of the project in the generated HTML, as you see here:

```
<h2>Links:</h2>
<a href="/ch06/ch06_02.do">Click Me</a>
<br>
```

Now when the user clicks the link, control will jump to the action immediately.

CRITICAL SKILL 6.12

Use the <html:img> Tag

The **<html:img>** tag creates an HTML **<img>** tag that you can use to display images. The base URL for this image is calculated based on the value specified in the **src** or **page** attributes or by looking up a message resource string based on the **srcKey** or **pageKey** attributes. Note that you must specify exactly one of these attributes.

You can specify the alternate text for this image either directly, through the **alt** attribute, or indirectly from a message resources file, using the **bundle** and **altKey** attributes.

The significant attributes of this tag appear in Table 6-15.

Attribute Name	Description
align	Specifies where the image is aligned to.
alt	Alternative text to be displayed in browsers that don't support graphics.
altKey	The message resources key of the alternate text for this element.
border	The width of the border surrounding the image.
bundle	The resource bundle to use.
height	The height of the image being displayed.
hspace	The amount of horizontal spacing between the image and text.
ismap	The name of the server-side image map this image belongs to.
name	The name of a JSP bean that contains a map representing the query parameters.
page	The module-relative path, starting with a slash, of the image to be displayed. You must specify either the **page** attribute or the **src** attribute.
pageKey	The message key, in the message resources bundle named by the **bundle** attribute, of the string to be used as the module-relative path for this image.
property	The name of the bean property whose return value must be a **java.util.Map** containing the query parameters to be added to the src URL. Specify the **name** attribute if you use this attribute.
src	The URL for this image. You must specify either the **page** attribute or the **src** attribute.
srcKey	The message key in the message resources bundle of the string to be used as the URL of this image.
usemap	The name of the map as defined within this page.
vspace	The amount of vertical spacing between the image and text.
width	The width of the image.

Table 6-15 The Struts <html:img> Tag's Significant Attributes

In this module's project, we'll place an image, image.jpg, in the webapps/ch06 folder. Here's how we reference that image in an **<html:img>** tag:

```
<h2>Images:</h2>
<html:img page="/image.jpg"/>
<br>
```

Here's the generated HTML, where Struts has rewritten the URL:

```
<h2>Images:</h2>
<img src="/ch06/image.jpg">
<br>
```

You can see the image in Figure 6-4, no problem. Note that if you want to create an image button or image map, you should use the **<html:image>** tag instead, which is coming up next.

Progress Check

1. What two attributes must you specify one of to use the **<html:img>** tag?

CRITICAL SKILL 6.13

Use the <html:image> Tag

The **<html:image>** tag creates an **<input>** tag of type **image**—that is, an image map or an image button. As with the **<html:img>** tag, the base URL for this image is calculated based on the value specified in the **src** or **page** attributes or by looking up a message resource string based on the **srcKey** or **pageKey** attributes. The significant attributes of this tag appear in Table 6-16.

Not only can this control function as an image button, it can also be an image map, telling you just where the mouse was clicked. Here's how that works; the x and y coordinates will be passed as ***propertyname*.x** and ***propertyname*.y**, where ***propertyname*** is the name you give to the control's property. In this case, we'll just give the control's **property** attribute the value "":

```
<h2>Image Controls:</h2>
<html:image page="/imagecontrol.jpg" property=""/>
<br>
```

---

1. The **src** or **page** attribute

Attribute Name	Description
accesskey	The keyboard character used to transfer the focus to this element.
align	The alignment for this image.
alt	The alternate text for this image.
altKey	The message resources key of the alternate text for this image.
border	The width of the border of this image, measured in pixels.
bundle	The resource bundle to use.
disabled	Set to **true** if this control should be disabled.
page	The module-relative path of the image for this input tag.
pageKey	The key of the message resources string specifying the module-relative path of the image for this input tag.
property	The property name of this image tag. The parameter names will be ***propertyname.x*** and ***propertyname.y***, for the x and y coordinates of the mouse click in the image.
src	The source URL of the image for this input tag.
srcKey	The key of the message resources string specifying the source URL of the image for this input tag.
tabindex	The tab order for this control.
title	The title for this element.
titleKey	The message resources key for the title for this element.
value	The value that will be submitted by this image button when it is clicked.

Table 6-16 The Struts <html:image> Tag's Significant Attributes

This means we can simply create **x** and **y** string properties in the form bean like this:

```
private String x;
private String y;

public String getX()
{
    return x;
}

public void setX(String x)
{
    this.x = x;
}
```

```
public String getY()
{
    return y;
}

public void setY(String y)
{
    this.y = y;
}
```

We can display the location at which the mouse went down in the Results page like this:

```
<h2>The location of the mouse:</h2>
(<bean:write name="ch06_03" property="x"/>,
<bean:write name="ch06_03" property="y"/>)
<BR>
```

You can see all this in operation in the project for this module in Figure 6-7, where the user is about to click the image control.

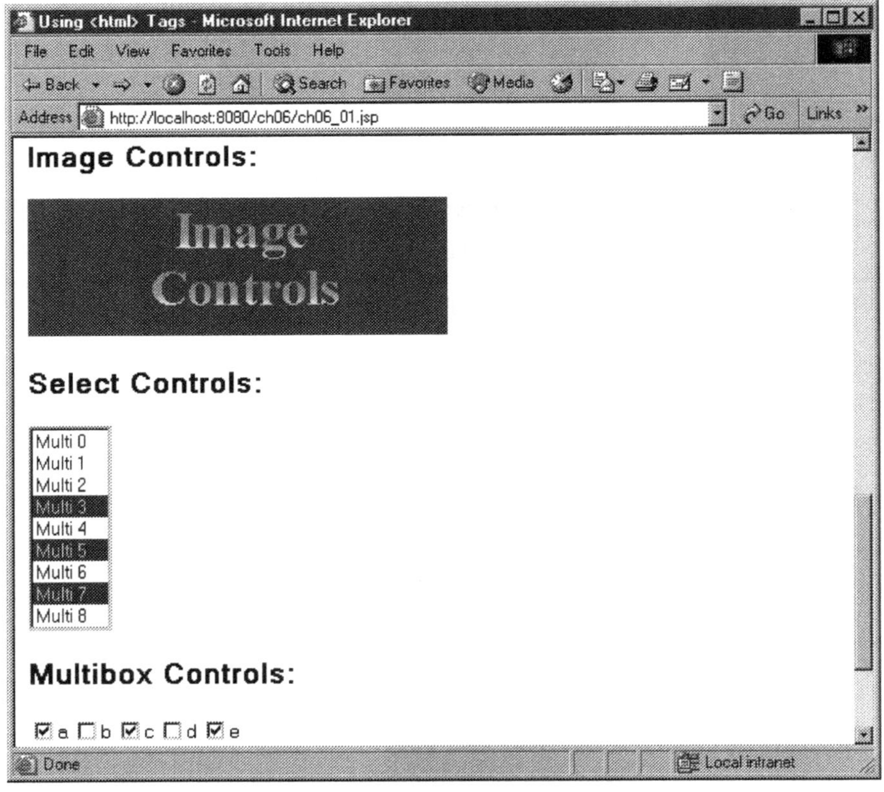

Figure 6-7 The <html> tags project, part 3

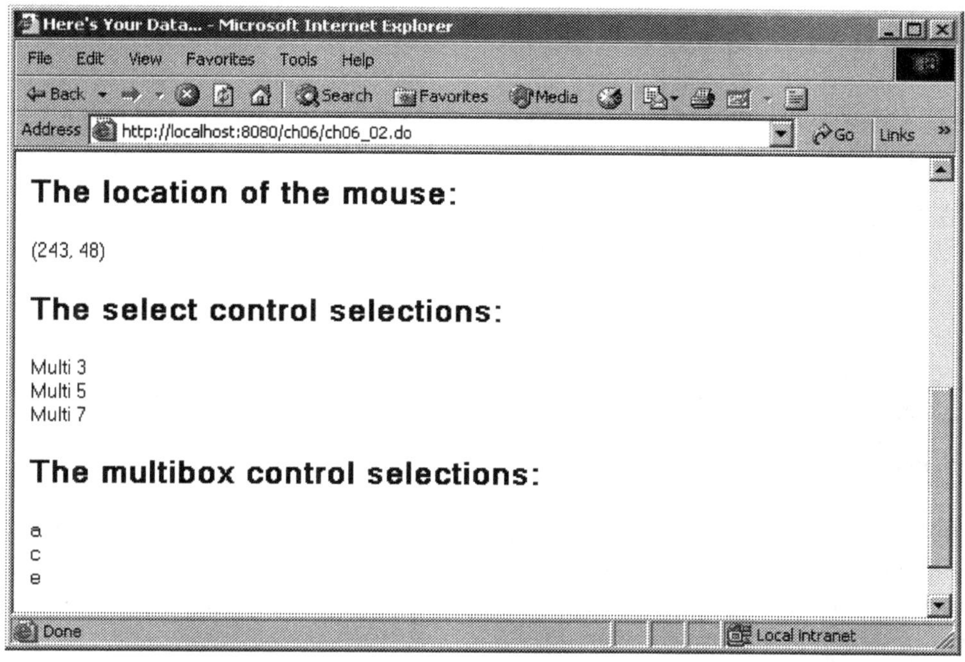

Figure 6-8 The Results page, part 3

The Results page indicates where the user clicked the image control, as shown in Figure 6-8.

Progress Check

1. If you assigned the **<html:image>** tag's **property** attribute the value **data**, what property names would be given to the x and y coordinates of the mouse?
2. Give four ways of specifying the URL of the image for the **<html:image>** tag.

---

1. **data.x** and **data.y**
2. The **page**, **src**, **pageKey**, and **srcKey** attributes

Ask the Expert

Q: The x and y positions of the mouse are passed as String **objects—isn't that a problem when I want to see what area the user clicked in an image map?**

A: If you want to convert the **String** objects passed to you holding the x and y mouse position to an **int**, you can use the **Integer.parseInt** method.

CRITICAL SKILL 6.14

Use the <html:select> and <html:option> Tags

The **<html:select>** and **<html:option>** tags create **<select>** controls and **<option>** elements, respectively. Using these tags, you can create scrollable lists or drop-down list boxes. The significant attributes of the **<html:select>** tag appear in Table 6-17, and the significant attributes of the **<html:option>** tag in Table 6-18.

Attribute Name	Description
alt	The alternate text for this select control.
altKey	The message resources key of the alternate text.
disabled	Set to **true** if this select control should be disabled.
multiple	If present and set to any value, the select element will support multiple selections.
property	Name of the associated bean property. This attribute is required.
size	The number of options displayed at once.
tabindex	The tab order for this control.
title	The title for this element.
titleKey	The message resources key for the title for this element.
value	The value to use for marking an option selected.

Table 6-17 The Struts <html:select> Tag's Significant Attributes

Attribute Name	Description
bundle	The resource bundle.
disabled	Set to **true** if this option should be disabled.
key	If present, defines the message key in the resource bundle specified by bundle for the text displayed for this option.
value	Value to be submitted for this field if this option is selected by the user. This attribute is required.

Table 6-18 The Struts <html:option> Tag's Significant Attributes

In this module's example project, we create a **<select>** control that supports multiple selections, using **<option>** elements like this:

```
<h2>Select Controls:</h2>
<html:select property="multipleSelect" size="9" multiple="true">
    <html:option value="Multi 0">Multi 0</html:option>
    <html:option value="Multi 1">Multi 1</html:option>
    <html:option value="Multi 2">Multi 2</html:option>
    <html:option value="Multi 3">Multi 3</html:option>
    <html:option value="Multi 4">Multi 4</html:option>
    <html:option value="Multi 5">Multi 5</html:option>
    <html:option value="Multi 6">Multi 6</html:option>
    <html:option value="Multi 7">Multi 7</html:option>
    <html:option value="Multi 8">Multi 8</html:option>
</html:select>
```

Here's the generated HTML:

```
<h2>Select Controls:</h2>
<select name="multipleSelect" multiple="multiple" size="9">
    <option value="Multi 0">Multi 0</option>
    <option value="Multi 1">Multi 1</option>
    <option value="Multi 2">Multi 2</option>
    <option value="Multi 3" selected="selected">Multi 3</option>
    <option value="Multi 4">Multi 4</option>
    <option value="Multi 5" selected="selected">Multi 5</option>
    <option value="Multi 6">Multi 6</option>
    <option value="Multi 7" selected="selected">Multi 7</option>
    <option value="Multi 8">Multi 8</option>
</select>
```

The **<select>** control's property is **multipleSelect**, and it holds a **String** array of selected items in the control. We'll start by selecting items 3, 5, and 7:

```
private String[] multipleSelect = {"Multi 3", "Multi 5", "Multi 7"};

    public String[] getMultipleSelect() {
        return (this.multipleSelect);
    }

    public void setMultipleSelect(String multipleSelect[]) {
        this.multipleSelect = multipleSelect;
    }
```

You can see these selections already made in Figure 6-7. When the user clicks the Submit button, we display all the selected items with a **<logic:iterate>** element:

```
<h2>The select control selections:</h2>
<logic:iterate id="select1" name="ch06_03" property="multipleSelect">
<%= select1 %>
<BR>
</logic:iterate>
<BR>
```

You can see all the selected items displayed in the Results page in Figure 6-8. Not bad—now you can use multiple-selection **<select>** controls.

CRITICAL SKILL

6.15 Use the <html:multibox> Tag

The **<html:multibox>** tag creates a group of check boxes that use the same property and that act together. The significant attributes of this tag appear in Table 6-19.

Attribute Name	Description
accesskey	The keyboard character used to transfer the focus to this element.
alt	The alternate text for this element.
altKey	The message resources key of the alternate text for this element.
disabled	Set to **true** if this control should be disabled.
property	Name of the associated bean property. This attribute is required.
tabindex	The tab order for this control.
title	The title for this element.
titleKey	The message resources key for the title for this element.
value	The value to be submitted if this check box is checked.

Table 6-19 The Struts <html:multibox> Tag's Significant Attributes

Here's how we create a set of check boxes with this tag in the project:

```
<h2>Multibox Controls:</h2>
    <html:multibox property="multiBox" value="a" />a
    <html:multibox property="multiBox" value="b" />b
    <html:multibox property="multiBox" value="c" />c
    <html:multibox property="multiBox" value="d" />d
    <html:multibox property="multiBox" value="e" />e
<br>
```

Here's the generated HTML—note that all check boxes have the same **name** attribute value:

```
<h2>Multibox Controls:</h2>
    <input type="checkbox" name="multiBox" value="a">a
    <input type="checkbox" name="multiBox" value="b">b
    <input type="checkbox" name="multiBox" value="c">c
    <input type="checkbox" name="multiBox" value="d">d
    <input type="checkbox" name="multiBox" value="e">e
<br>
```

In code, you handle the **multiBox** property as an array of strings:

```
private String[] multiBox = new String[5];

public String[] getMultiBox()
  {
    return multiBox;
}

public void setMultiBox(String[] multiBox)
{
    this.multiBox = multiBox;
}
```

You can handle this property in the Results page with a **<logic:iterate>** tag:

```
<h2>The multibox control selections:</h2>
<logic:iterate id="multibox1" name="ch06_03" property="multiBox">
    <%= multibox1 %>
    <BR>
</logic:iterate>
<BR>
```

You can see how this works in the bottom of Figure 6-7, where three check boxes have been checked. Those three check boxes are reported in the Results page, as you see in Figure 6-8.

Attribute Name	Description
accept	List of comma-delimited content types that the server knows how to process. Can be used by the browser to limit the file options available for selection.
accesskey	The keyboard character used to transfer the focus to this element.
alt	The alternate text for this element.
altKey	The message resources key of the alternate text for this element.
disabled	Set to **true** if this file control should be disabled.
maxlength	Maximum number of input characters to accept. This is ignored by most browsers.
property	Name of the associated form bean property. This attribute is required.
size	Size of the file selection control.
tabindex	The tab order for this control.
title	The title for this file control.
titleKey	The message resources key for the title for this element.
value	Initial value in the control. Note that for security reasons, this is ignored by most browsers.

Table 6-20 The Struts <html:file> Tag's Significant Attributes

CRITICAL SKILL 6.16

Use the <html:file> Tag

The last **<html>** tag we'll take a look at in this module is **<html:file>**. You use this control to upload files to the server; the significant attributes of this tag appear in Table 6-20.

In this module's project, we'll upload a file and display its text in the Results page. Here's how you create a file control with a property named **file**—note that to upload files, you set the **<html:form>** tag's **method** attribute to POST and **enctype** attribute to "multipart/form-data":

```
<html:form action="ch06_02.do" method="POST" enctype="multipart/form-
data">

<h2>File Controls:</h2>
<html:file property="file" />
```

The file's contents are stored using a **FormFile** object named **file**, so we'll create the **file** property this way in the form bean:

```
private FormFile file;

public FormFile getFile()
{
    return file;
}

public void setFile(FormFile file)
{
    this.file = file;
}
```

To extract the text of the uploaded file from the **file** object, we'll create a helper method **getFileText** in the form bean:

```
public String getFileText() {

    try {
        ByteArrayOutputStream byteStream = new ByteArrayOutputStream();
        InputStream input = file.getInputStream();

        byte[] dataBuffer = new byte[4096];
        int numberBytes = 0;
        while ((numberBytes = input.read(dataBuffer, 0, 4096)) != -1) {
            byteStream.write(dataBuffer, 0, numberBytes);
        }
        fileText = new String(byteStream.toByteArray());
        input.close();
    }
    catch (IOException e) {
        return null;
    }
    return fileText;
}
```

We can display the file's text in the Results page calling this helper method this way:

```
<h2>The file's text:</h2>
<bean:write name="ch06_03" property="fileText"/>
```

You can see how it looks at work in Figure 6-9, where we're using the File control to upload the source for the project's action, ch06_02.java.

The Results page displays the text of ch06_02.jsp, as you see in Figure 6-10.

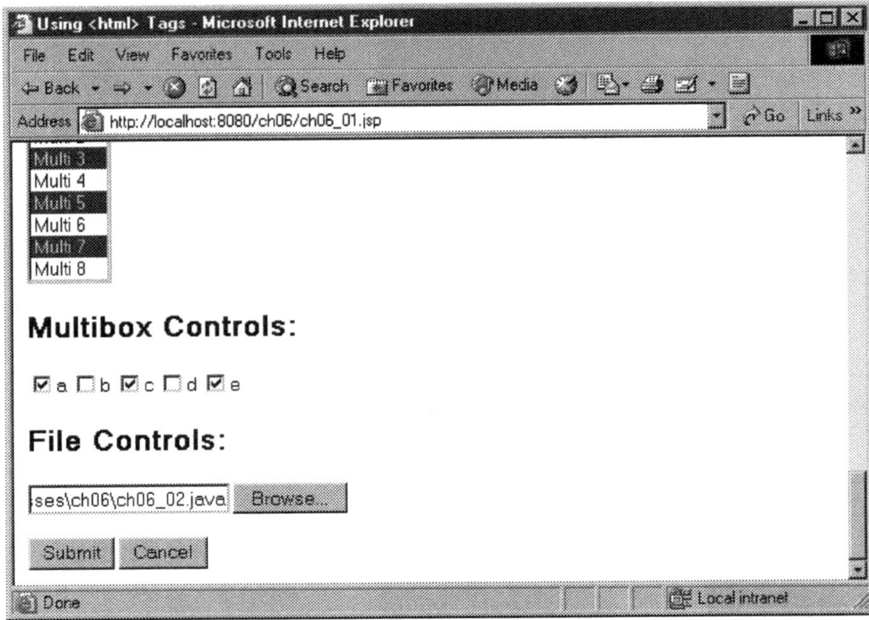

Figure 6-9 The <html> project's File Upload control

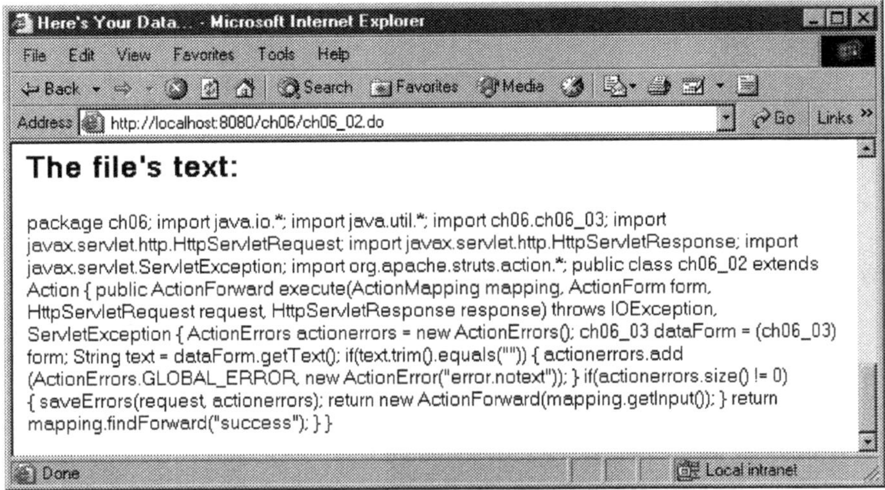

Figure 6-10 Uploading a file

The browser strips out all line breaks in the file. If you want to display the text of a file this way preserving line breaks, replace them all with HTML **
** elements.

Now we're able to upload entire files—very cool.

Progress Check

1. How can you limit the maximum length of the uploaded file?
2. How can you read data from an uploaded file?

Use Struts 1.2

All the code in this module works with the early release version of Struts 1.2 as of this writing; the only issue is that, as before, you'll need to switch to **ActionMessage** and **ActionMessages**.

Module 6 Mastery Check

1. Which of the following JSP directives would add support for the HTML custom Struts JSP tags?

   A. **<%@ taglib uri="/tags/html" attribute="html" %>**

   B. **<%@ taglib uri="/tags/html" prefix="html" %>**

   C. **<%@ taglib uri="/tags/struts-html" prefix="html" %>**

   D. **<%@ taglib uri="/tags/struts-html-taglib" prefix="html" %>**

---

1. You can use the **<html:file>** tag's **maxlength** attribute.

2. You can create an **InputStream** object with the **FormFile** object's **getInputStream** method. Then you can use the **read** method of the **InputStream** object.

2. What Struts HTML tag attribute handles the case where the control loses the input focus?

   A. **focus**

   B. **onfocus**

   C. **ondefocus**

   D. **onblur**

3. What attribute do you use to set the caption of a Submit button using the **<html:submit>** tag?

   A. **caption**

   B. **value**

   C. **name**

   D. **title**

4. What attribute do you use to name a control as far as Struts is concerned so it can retrieve the control's data?

   A. **property**

   B. **name**

   C. **value**

   D. **data**

5. What attributes of the <html:link> tag must you specify exactly one of to set up a link?

   A. **forward** or **action**

   B. **forward**, **href**, or **page**

   C. **action**, **href**, or **page**

   D. **forward**, **action**, **href**, or **page**

6. How do you set the text the hyperlink should display using **<html:link>**?

   A. You use the **value** attribute.

   B. You enclose the text in the body of the **<html:link>** element.

   C. You use a resource bundle key with the prefix **link:**.

   D. It can't be done.

7. What attributes can you use to specify alternate test for an image using **<html:image>**?

   A. **text**

   B. **alt**

   C. **alt** or **bundle** and **altKey**

   D. **alt** or **resource** and **key**

8. What is the datatype of the x and y locations passed to you when handling the mouse location?

   A. **String**

   B. **int**

   C. **long**

   D. **boolean**

9. Which HTML attribute is set to the same value for all multibox check boxes in a group?

   A. **value**

   B. **name**

   C. **property**

   D. **checked**

10. What class holds the data of an uploaded file?

    A. **FormFile**

    B. **File**

    C. **UloadFile**

    D. **StrutsStream**

Module 7

The Struts <logic> and <bean> Tags

CRITICAL SKILLS

7.1 Use the <logic:empty> and <logic:notEmpty> Tags

7.2 Use the <logic:equal> and <logic:notEqual> Tags

7.3 Use the <logic:greaterEqual> and <logic:greaterThan> Tags

7.4 Use the <logic:lessEqual> and <logic:lessThan> Tags

7.5 Use the <logic:match> and <logic:notMatch> Tags

7.6 Use the <logic:present> and <logic:notPresent> Tags

7.7 Use the <logic:iterate> Tag

7.8 Use the <logic:forward> and <logic:redirect> Tags

7.9 Use the <bean:cookie> Tag

7.10 Use the <bean:define> Tag

7.11 Use the <bean:header> Tag

7.12 Use the <bean:message> Tag

7.13 Use the <bean:parameter> Tag

7.14 Use the <bean:struts> Tag

7.15 Use the <bean:write> Tag

This module is all about using the Struts **<logic>** and **<bean>** custom JSP tags in Struts applications. We've already seen a few of these tags throughout the book, but there are many more to come. We'll start with the **<logic>** tags.

The <logic> Tags

You can see the **<logic>** tags in Table 7-1, and we're going to put them to work in this module. Most of them function as tests, conditionally including the contents of the **<logic>** element in the output. For example, you can use the **<logic:equal>** tag to check if a variable (such as a bean property) holds a particular value. If so, the body of the **<logic:equal>** element will be included in the document you're sending to the browser, but if not, the body of the element will not be included. Others let you do such things as loop over a collection of items, such as **<logic:iterate>**.

Tag Name	Description
empty	Include the body content of this element if the indicated variable is either **null** or an empty string.
equal	Include the body content of this element if the indicated variable is equal to the value you specify.
forward	Forward control to the page specified by an ActionForward entry.
greaterEqual	Include the body content of this element if the indicated variable is greater than or equal to the value you specify.
greaterThan	Include the body content of this element if the indicated variable is greater than the value you specify.
iterate	Repeat the nested body content of this tag over a specified collection.
lessEqual	Include the body content of this element if the indicated variable is greater than or equal to the value you specify.
lessThan	Include the body content of this element if the indicated variable is less than the value you specify.
match	Include the body content of this element if the value you specify is an appropriate substring of the indicated variable.
messagesNotPresent	Include the body content of this element if the specified message is not present in this request.
messagesPresent	Include the body content of this element if the specified message is present in this request.
notEmpty	Include the body content of this element if the indicated variable is neither null nor an empty string nor an empty java.util.Collection.

Table 7-1 The Struts <logic> Tags

Tag Name	Description
notEqual	Include the body content of this element if the indicated variable is not equal to the value you specify.
notMatch	Include the body content of this element if the value you specify is not an substring of the indicated variable.
notPresent	Include the body content of this element if the value you specify is not present in this request.
Present	Include the body content of this element if the value you specify is present in this request.
Redirect	Create an HTTP Redirect.

Table 7-1 The Struts <logic> Tags *(continued)*

To see the **<logic>** tags at work, take a look at the first project for this module, which you can load from http://localhost:8080/ch07/ch07_01.jsp in the downloadable code for this book. As you see in Figure 7-1, the Welcome page for this project asks the user to enter some data. In this case, the user is entering a value of 6.

The Results page uses various **<logic>** tags to examine the data the user entered, as you can see in the Results page, part 1, which appears in Figure 7-2. We'll decipher what's going on in this page in this module.

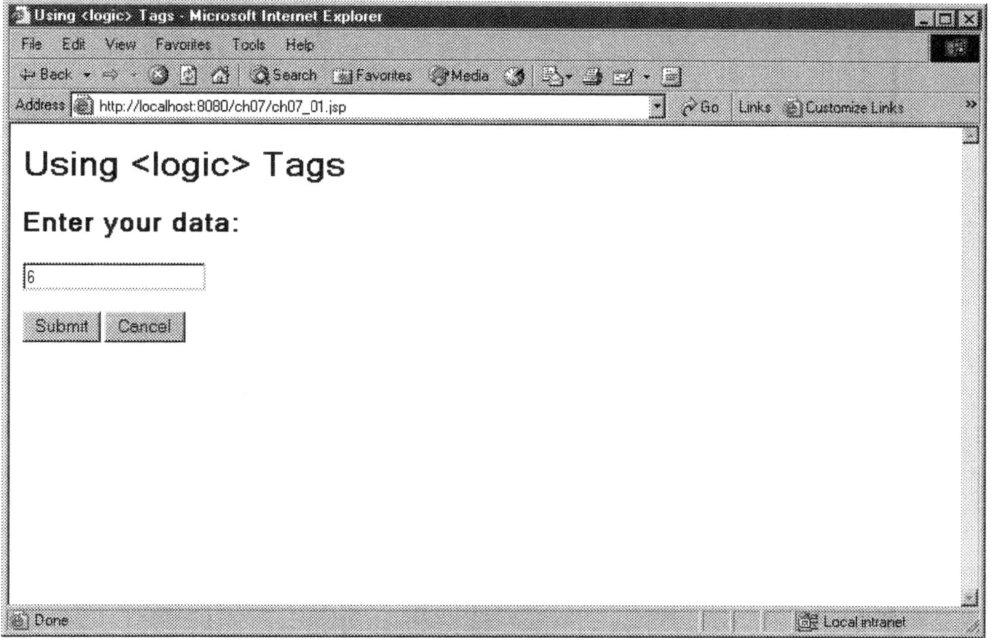

Figure 7-1 The <logic> tags project

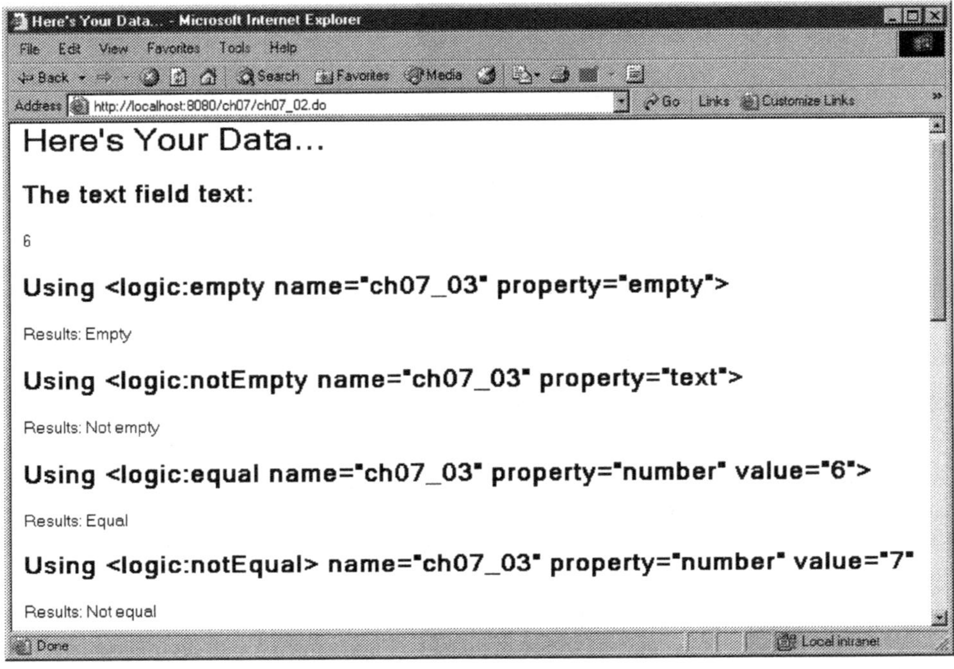

Figure 7-2 The Results page, part 1

Here are the files for this project:

- **ch07_01.jsp** The Welcome page
- **ch07_02.java** The action
- **ch07_03.java** The action form
- **ch07_04.jsp** The Results page

Here's the Welcome page for this project, ch07_01.jsp, which just asks the user to enter some data:

```
<%@ taglib uri="/tags/struts-html" prefix="html" %>
<%@ taglib uri="/tags/struts-logic" prefix="logic" %>

<html:html>
    <head>
        <title>Using &lt;logic&gt; Tags</title>
    </head>
```

```
    <body>
        <h1>Using &lt;logic&gt; Tags</h1>

        <html:form action="ch07_02.do">

            <h2>Enter your data:</h2>
            <html:text property="text"/>

            <br>
            <br>

            <html:submit value="Submit"/>
            <html:cancel/>
        </html:form>
    </body>
</html:html>
```

The action for this project, ch07_02.java, passes the data in the form bean on to the Results page (and we'll construct the Results page's code piece by piece in this module). The form bean, ch07_03.java, defines three properties: **empty**, which is a **String** property holding the empty string; **text**, which holds the text the user entered; and **number**, which holds the text the user entered converted to an **int** (for example, if the user entered the string "6", **number** would hold an **int** value of 6):

```
package ch07;

import org.apache.struts.action.*;
import javax.servlet.http.HttpServletRequest;
import javax.servlet.http.HttpServletResponse;

public class ch07_03 extends ActionForm
{
    private String empty = "";
    private String text = "";
    private int number;

    public String getEmpty()
    {
        return empty;
    }

    public void setEmpty(String text)
    {
    }
```

```
    public String getText()
    {
        return text;
    }

    public void setText(String text)
    {
        this.text = text;
        this.number = Integer.parseInt(text);
    }

    public int getNumber()
    {
        return number;
    }

    public void setNumber(int number)
    {
        this.number = number;
    }
}
```

We're going to put all of these properties to work with the Struts **<logic>** tags now, starting with the **empty** property, which we'll use with the **<logic:empty>** and **<logic:notEmpty>** tags.

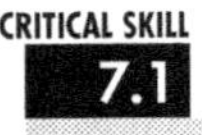

Use the <logic:empty> and <logic:notEmpty> Tags

The **<logic:empty>** and **<logic:notEmpty>** tags lets you check if a variable is empty (holds null) or is an empty string. You can see the significant attributes for these tags in Table 7-2.

Attribute Name	Description
name	If property is not used, this bean is the variable to be compared. If you use property, this is the bean whose property you're comparing.
property	The bean property to check.
scope	The bean scope (defaults to any scope).

Table 7-2 The Struts <logic:empty> and <logic:notEmpty> Tags Attributes

In the form bean for this project, there's a property named **empty** that's set to an empty string:

```
private String empty = "";

public String getEmpty()
{
    return empty;
}

public void setEmpty(String text)
{
}
```

We'll use this property with the **<logic:empty>** tag in the Results page like this—if the **empty** property is indeed empty, the body of the **<logic:empty>** element will be included in the results document:

```
<h2>Using &lt;logic:empty name="ch07_03" property="empty"&gt;</h2>
<logic:empty name="ch07_03" property="empty">
Results: Empty
</logic:empty>
<BR>
```

Here's how we'll test the **<logic:notEmpty>** tag—in this case, we'll check a non-empty property, the **text** property; because it's not empty, the body of this element (the text "Results: Not empty") will be included in the Results page:

```
<h2>Using &lt;logic:notEmpty name="ch07_03" property="text"&gt;</h2>
<logic:notEmpty name="ch07_03" property="text">
Results: Not empty
</logic:notEmpty>
<BR>
```

As you can see in Figure 7-2, the **empty** property is indeed empty, and the **text** property is not empty. Using this tag, you can check which variables hold **null** before using them in code.

CRITICAL SKILL 7.2

Use the <logic:equal> and <logic:notEqual> Tags

The **<logic:equal>** and **<logic:notEqual>** tags let you compare the value in a variable against a constant value. The body of the **<logic:equal>** element is included if the values are equal, and the body of the **<logic:equal>** element is included if the values are not equal. You can see the significant attributes for these tags in Table 7-3. Note that you can use this tag to compare values of cookies and HTTP headers (for HTTP headers, the comparison is case-insensitive).

To test this **<logic>** tag, the form bean for this project supports a property named **number**, which holds the number the user entered, converted from text to an **int** value. In the **<logic>** project for this module, we'll test the value the user entered (6 in Figure 7-1) against the value 6 in a **<logic:equal>** element whose contents should appear in the Results page because the two tested values are equal:

```
        <h2>Using &lt;logic:equal name="ch07_03" property="number"
value="6"&gt;</h2>
        <logic:equal name="ch07_03" property="number" value="6">
        Results: Equal
        </logic:equal>
        <BR>
```

Similarly, we can make sure that the user did not enter 7 by using the **<logic:notEqual>** tag like this in the Results page:

```
        <h2>Using &lt;logic:notEqual&gt; name="ch07_03" property="number"
value="7"</h2>
        <logic:notEqual name="ch07_03" property="number" value="7">
        Results: Not equal
        </logic:notEqual>
        <BR>
```

You can see how this works in Figure 7-2, where the **<logic:equal>** and **<logic:notEqual>** tags are indeed verifying that the user entered a value of 6, not 7. One of the most common uses of these tags are to let you compare collections.

Attribute Name	Description
cookie	The cookie whose value you want to compare.
header	The header whose value you want to compare (in this case, the comparison is case-insensitive).
name	If property is not used, this bean is the variable to be compared. If you use property, this is the bean whose property you're comparing.
parameter	The variable to be compared is the value of the request parameter specified by this attribute (or the first value if there are multiple values).
property	The property of a bean to compare.
scope	The bean scope (defaults to any scope).
value	The constant value to which the variable will be compared. This attribute is required.

Table 7-3 The Struts <logic:equal> and <logic:notEqual> Tag Attributes

Progress Check

1. Which attribute do you use to specify the constant you want to compare against?
2. Which comparison is done in a case-insensitive manner?

CRITICAL SKILL 7.3

Use the <logic:greaterEqual> and <logic:greaterThan> Tags

The **<logic:greaterEqual>** and **<logic:greaterThan>** tags let you compare the value in a variable to a constant text value. You can test whether the value you're testing is greater than or equal to (**<logic:greaterEqual>**) or greater than (**<logic:greaterThan>**) the test value with these two tags. You can see the significant attributes for these tags in Table 7-4.

Attribute Name	Description
cookie	The cookie whose value you want to compare.
header	The header whose value you want to compare (in this case, the comparison is case-insensitive).
name	If **property** is not used, this bean is the variable to be compared. If you use **property**, this is the bean whose property you're comparing.
parameter	The variable to be compared is the value of the request parameter specified by this attribute (or the first value if there are multiple values).
property	The property of a bean to compare.
scope	The bean scope (defaults to any scope).
value	The constant value to which the variable will be compared. This attribute is required.

Table 7-4 The Struts <logic:greaterEqual> and <logic:greaterThan> Tag Attributes

1. **value**
2. Comparisons involving HTTP headers

In the **<logic>** project for this module, we'll test the value the user entered (6 in Figure 7-1) against the values 3 and 4 with **<logic:greaterEqual>** and **<logic:greaterThan>** as you see in this code from the Results page:

```
        <h2>Using &lt;logic:greaterEqual&gt;</h2>
        <logic:greaterEqual name="ch07_03" property="number" value="3">
        Results: Greater than or equal
        </logic:greaterEqual>
        <BR>

        <h2>Using &lt;logic:greaterThan name="ch07_03" property="number"
value="4"&gt;</h2>
        <logic:greaterThan name="ch07_03" property="number" value="4">
        Results: Greater than
        </logic:greaterThan>
        <BR>
```

You can see these tags at work in the Results page in Figure 7-3—as you see, the **<logic:greaterEqual>** and **<logic:greaterThan>** tags are reporting that 6 is greater than or equal to 3, and it's also greater than 4.

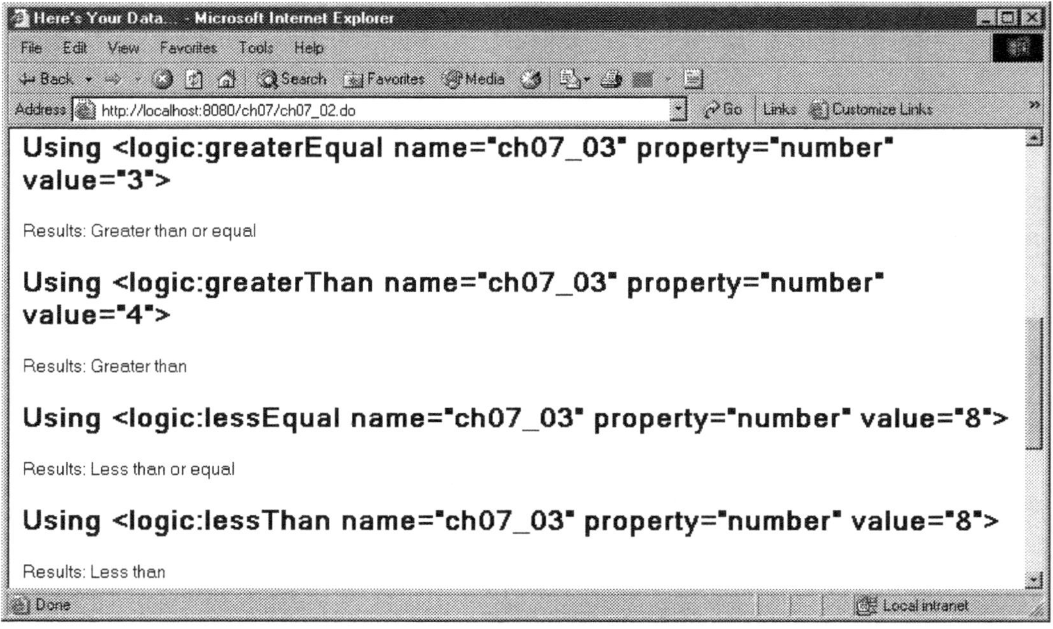

Figure 7-3 The Results page, part 2

CRITICAL SKILL 7.4

Use the <logic:lessEqual> and <logic:lessThan> Tags

The **<logic:lessEqual>** and **<logic:lessThan>** tags also perform comparisons, as their names indicate. The body of the **<logic:lessEqual>** element is included in the output if the value of the variable you're comparing is less than or equal to a constant value, and the body of the **<logic:lessThan>** element is included if the value of the variable you're comparing is less than the constant value. You can see the significant attributes for these tags in Table 7-5.

In the sample project for this module, we'll compare the value the user entered, 6 in this case, to the positive integer 8 using these two tags, like this:

```
        <h2>Using &lt;logic:lessEqual name="ch07_03" property="number"
value="8"&gt;</h2>
        <logic:lessEqual name="ch07_03" property="number" value="8">
        Results: Less than or equal
        </logic:lessEqual>
        <BR>

        <h2>Using &lt;logic:lessThan name="ch07_03" property="number"
value="8"&gt;</h2>
        <logic:lessThan name="ch07_03" property="number" value="8">
        Results: Less than
        </logic:lessThan>
        <BR>
```

You can see the results in Figure 7-3, where we discover that 6 is indeed less than 8.

Attribute Name	Description
cookie	The cookie whose value you want to compare.
header	The header whose value you want to compare (in this case, the comparison is case-insensitive).
name	If **property** is not used, this bean is the variable to be compared. If you use **property**, this is the bean whose property you're comparing.
parameter	The variable to be compared is the value of the request parameter specified by this attribute (or the first value if there are multiple values).
property	The property of a bean to compare.
scope	The bean scope (defaults to any scope).
value	The constant value to which the variable will be compared. This attribute is required.

Table 7-5 The Struts <logic:lessEqual> and <logic:lessThan> Tag Attributes

CRITICAL SKILL 7.5

Use the <logic:match> and <logic:notMatch> Tags

The **<logic:match>** and **<logic:notMatch>** tags let you search text for matches. Specifically, **<logic:match>** lets you search the text in a variable by providing a string; if your string is found inside the variable's text (matching either the entire text or a substring in that text), the body of the **<logic:match>** element is included in the result document; **<logic:notMatch>** works in the reverse way; the body of the element is included if the match is not found. You can see the significant attributes for these tags in Table 7-6.

In the **<logic>** sample project for this module, where the user enters the text "6", we'll check that text with **<logic:Match>** and **<logic:notMatch>**, first checking for the text "6" and then for the text "9":

```
<h2>Using &lt;logic:match&gt;</h2>
<logic:match name="ch07_03" property="text" value="6">
Results: Match
</logic:match>
<BR>

<h2>Using &lt;logic:notMatch name="ch07_03" property="number"
value="9"&gt;</h2>
<logic:notMatch name="ch07_03" property="number" value="9">
Results: No Match
</logic:notMatch>
<BR>
```

Attribute Name	Description
cookie	The cookie whose value you want to match.
header	The header whose value you want to match (in this case, the match is case-insensitive).
location	If not used, a match between the variable and the value can be at any position in the variable. If used, the match must occur at the specified location (start or end) of the variable.
name	If **property** is not used, this bean is the variable to be matched. If you use **property**, this is the bean whose property you're matching.
parameter	The variable to be matched is the value of the request parameter specified by this attribute (or the first value if there are multiple values).
property	The property of a bean to match.
scope	The bean scope (defaults to any scope).
value	The constant value which is to be matched as a substring of the specified variable. This attribute is required.

Table 7-6 The Struts <logic:match> and <logic:notMatch> Tag Attributes

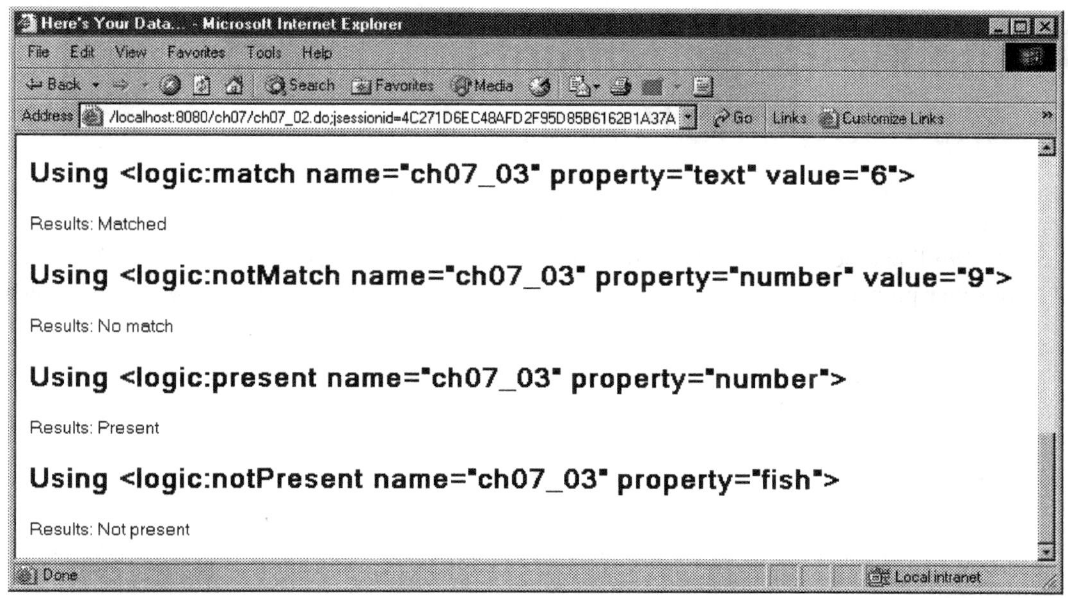

Figure 7-4 The Results page, part 3

You can see the results in Figure 7-4, where we have matched the text the user entered with **<logic:Match>** and also matched the case where the text was missing, using **<logic:notMatch>**.

Progress Check

1. If the **text** property of the bean named **bean** holds "abc", would this tag match: **<logic:match name="bean" property="text" value="a">**?
2. If the **text** property of the bean named **bean** holds "a", would this tag match: **<logic:match name="bean" property="text" value="abc">**?

---

1. Yes
2. No

CRITICAL SKILL 7.6

Use the <logic:present> and <logic:notPresent> Tags

These tags let you check for the presence or absence of variables, and you can see the attributes for these tags in Table 7-7.

We'll put these elements to work in the sample project for this module, checking for the **number** property, which does exist in our application, and for a fictitious property, **fish**, which doesn't:

```
<h2>Using &lt;logic:present name="ch07_03" property="number"&gt;</h2>
<logic:present name="ch07_03" property="number">
Results: Present
</logic:present>
<BR>

<h2>Using &lt;logic:notPresent name="ch07_03" property="fish"&gt;</h2>
<logic:notPresent name="ch07_03" property="fish">
Results: Not present
</logic:notPresent>
<BR>
```

You can see the results in Figure 7-4, where these tags have successfully identified the **number** property and also detected that the **fish** property doesn't exist.

Attribute Name	Description
cookie	The cookie whose value you want to check.
header	The header whose value you want to check (in this case, the check is case-insensitive).
name	If **property** is not used, this bean is the variable to be checked. If you use **property**, this is the bean whose property you're checking to make sure it's not **null**.
parameter	The variable to be checked is the value of the request parameter specified by this attribute (or the first value if there are multiple values).
property	The property of a bean to check to make sure it's not **null**.
role	Checks whether the currently authenticated user has been associated with any of the specified security roles. Set to a comma-delimited list to check for multiple roles.
scope	The bean scope (defaults to any scope).
user	Checks whether the currently authenticated user has the specified name.

Table 7-7 The Struts <logic:present> and <logic:notPresent> Tag Attributes

CRITICAL SKILL 7.7

Use the <logic:iterate> Tag

The **<logic:iterate>** element repeats the body content of this tag for every element of a collection, which must be an **Iterator** (including **ArrayList** and **Vector**) a **Collection**, a **Map** (including **HashMap**, **Hashtable**, and **TreeMap**), or an **array**. You can see the significant attributes for these tags in Table 7-8.

We've already seen this tag in Modules 3 and 6. In Module 6, we used it to iterate over properties like **multipleSelect**, which held an array of strings corresponding to the choices the user made in a **<select>** control:

```
<h2>The select control selections:</h2>
<logic:iterate id="select1" name="ch06_03" property="multipleSelect">
<%= select1 %>
<BR>
</logic:iterate>
<BR>
```

Attribute Name	Description
collection	The collection to be iterated over.
id	The name of a page scope bean containing the current element of the collection on each iteration. This attribute is required.
indexId	The name of a page scope bean that will contain the current index of the collection on each iteration.
length	The maximum number of entries to be iterated through on this page.
name	The name of the bean containing the collection to be iterated (if **property** is not specified), or the bean whose property getter method returns the collection to be iterated (if **property** is specified).
offset	The zero-relative index of the starting point at which entries the collection will be iterated.
property	Name of the bean property whose getter method returns the collection you want to use.
scope	The bean scope (defaults to any scope).
type	Java class name of the element to be exposed through the JSP bean named from the id attribute.

Table 7-8 The Struts <logic:iterate> Tag Attributes

In Module 3, we used **<logic:iterate>** with an array of strings returned by a custom JSP tag. We set a loop up to iterate over the items in the array of toppings selected by the user in The Struts Café project. That array was stored in the **toppings** attribute, which we referred to as **toppings1**:

```
<BODY>
    <H1>The Struts Cafe</H1>
    <html:errors/>
    <ch03:items/>
    <ch03:toppings/>
    <html:form action="ch03_04.do">
        <TABLE>
            <TR>
                <TD ALIGN="LEFT" VALIGN="TOP">
                    <bean:message key="toppings"/>
                    <BR>
                    <logic:iterate id="toppings1" name="toppings">
                        <html:multibox property="toppings">
                            <%= toppings1 %>
                        </html:multibox>
                        <%= toppings1 %>
                        <BR>
                    </logic:iterate>
                </TD>
                .
                .
                .
```

CRITICAL SKILL 7.8

Use the <logic:forward> and <logic:redirect> Tags

The **<logic:forward>** tag lets you forward to an action forward, and the **<logic:redirect>** tag lets you redirect the browser to a new URL. You can see the significant attributes for **<logic:forward>** in Table 7-9 and for **<logic:redirect>** in Table 7-10. Note that for the **<logic:redirect>** tag, you must specify exactly one of the **forward** attribute, the **href** attribute, or the **page** attribute.

Attribute Name	Description
name	The global **ActionForward** for the target. This attribute is required.

Table 7-9 The Struts <logic:forward> Tag Attributes

Attribute Name	Description
anchor	Anchor tag (such as **#item**) to be added to the generated hyperlink (don't use the # character in this attribute's value).
forward	Name of a global **ActionForward** that contains the URI of the redirect destination. You must specify exactly one of the **forward** attribute, the **href** attribute, or the **page** attribute.
href	The URL to which this redirect will go. You must specify exactly one of the **forward** attribute, the **href** attribute, or the **page** attribute.
name	The name of a JSP bean that contains a **Map** representing the query parameters (if **property** is not used), or a JSP bean whose property getter method is called to return a **Map** (if **property** is used).
page	The context-relative path beginning with a forward slash [/[). You must specify exactly one of the **forward** attribute, the **href** attribute, or the **page** attribute.
property	The name of a property of the bean specified by the `name` attribute, whose return value must be a **java.util.Map** containing the query parameters to be added to the hyperlink. You must specify the **name** attribute if you specify this attribute.
scope	The bean's scope.
transaction	Set to **true** to include the transaction control token included in the generated redirect URL.

Table 7-10 The Struts <logic:redirect> Tag Attributes

Using **<logic:forward>** is easy; you just supply the name of a global action forward you want to forward to.

The **<logic:redirect>** tag lets you redirect the browser to a new URL. The base URL for the redirect is based on of the following attributes, and you must specify one of them:

- **forward** Name of a global **ActionForward** that contains the URI of the redirect destination.
- **href** The URL to which this redirect will go.
- **page** The context-relative path (beginning with a forward slash [/]).

We've seen how to work with **<logic:redirect>** in the struts-blank application in Module 2. As you may recall, in that application, the Welcome page, index.jsp, was designed to forward the user on immediately to the application's actual Welcome page, welcome.jsp. The index.jsp file did that with a forward named **welcome** and **<logic:redirect>**:

```
<%@ taglib uri="/tags/struts-logic" prefix="logic" %>
<logic:redirect forward="welcome"/>
```

In struts-config.xml, the **welcome** global forward was connected to an action named **Welcome.do**:

```
<global-forwards>
    <!-- Default forward to "Welcome" action -->
    <!-- Demonstrates using index.jsp to forward -->
    <forward
        name="welcome"
        path="/Welcome.do"/>
</global-forwards>
```

The **Welcome.do** action used a **ForwardAction** to the real Welcome page, Welcome.jsp:

```
<action-mappings>
        <!-- Default "Welcome" action -->
        <!-- Forwards to Welcome.jsp -->
    <action
        path="/Welcome"
        type="org.apache.struts.actions.ForwardAction"
        parameter="/pages/Welcome.jsp"/>
</action-mappings>
```

Progress Check

1. What's the only attribute of the **<logic:forward>** tag?
2. Which three attributes must you include exactly one of in **<logic:redirect>**?

The <bean> Tags

The Struts **<bean>** tags are all about working with data, and you can see them all in Table 7-11. We'll take a look at a number of these tags in this module.

To demonstrate how the **<bean>** tags work, we'll create another project in this module, which you can see at work in Figure 7-5. The user enters some text, "No worries", here and clicks the Submit button.

1. **name**, the name of the global **ActionForward** for the target
2. **forward**, **href**, or **page**

Tag Name	Description
cookie	Create a scripting variable based on the value of the specified cookie.
define	Create a scripting variable based on the value of a bean property.
header	Create a scripting variable based on the value of a header.
include	Get the response from a dynamic application request and make it available as a bean.
message	Send an internationalized message string to the response.
page	Get a specified item from the page context and make it available as a bean.
parameter	Create a scripting variable based on the value of a request parameter.
resource	Load a web application resource and make it available as a bean.
size	Create a bean containing the number of elements in a Collection or Map.
struts	Expose a named Struts internal configuration object as a bean.
write	Send the value of the specified bean property to the current page.

Table 7-11 The Struts <bean> Tags

The Results page in this project, which you can see in Figure 7-6, puts a number of **<bean>** tags to work. We'll go over these tags in this module.

Figure 7-5 The <bean> tags project

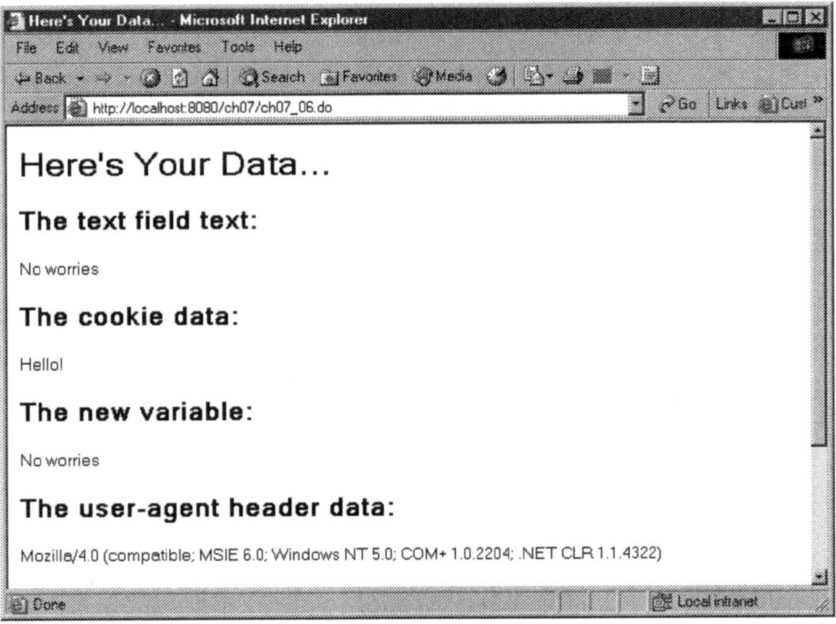

Figure 7-6 The <bean> tags project Results page, part 1

Here are the files for this project:

- **ch07_05.jsp** The Welcome page
- **ch07_06.java** The action
- **ch07_07.java** The action form
- **ch07_08.jsp** The Results page

Here's the Welcome page for this project, ch07_05.jsp:

```
<%@ taglib uri="/tags/struts-html" prefix="html" %>
<html:html>
    <head>
        <title>Using &lt;bean&gt; Tags</title>
    </head>

    <body>
        <h1>Using &lt;bean&gt; Tags</h1>

        <%
        Cookie cookie1 = new Cookie("message", "Hello!");
```

```
        cookie1.setMaxAge(24 * 60 * 60);
        response.addCookie(cookie1);
        %>

        <html:form action="ch07_06.do">

            <h2>Enter your data:</h2>
            <html:text property="text"/>

            <br>
            <br>

            <html:submit value="Submit"/>
            <html:cancel/>
        </html:form>
    </body>
</html:html>
```

The action just passes on the form bean to the Results page in this project. Here's the form bean, ch07_07.jsp, which just sets up a **text** property corresponding to what the user typed into the text field in the Welcome page:

```
package ch07;

import org.apache.struts.action.*;
import javax.servlet.http.HttpServletRequest;
import javax.servlet.http.HttpServletResponse;

public class ch07_07 extends ActionForm
{
    private String text = "";

    public String getText()
    {
        return text;
    }

    public void setText(String text)
    {
        this.text = text;
    }
}
```

We'll use various **<bean>** elements in the Results page, ch07_08.jsp, to demonstrate how to work with those elements. For example, the **<bean:cookie>** element lets you read the value of a cookie, and we'll start with that.

CRITICAL SKILL 7.9

Use the <bean:cookie> Tag

You can use the **<bean:cookie>** tag to recover (not set) the value of a cookie. The value will be a single value or multiple values, depending on the **multiple** attribute. The return value will be stored in a page scope attribute of type **Cookie** (if **multiple** is not used) or **Cookie[]** (if **multiple** is used). You can see the attributes for this tag in Table 7-12.

To see how this tag works, we'll create a cookie named **message** in the Welcome page in the JSP code. This cookie will last for a day and will hold the text "Hello!":

```
<%
Cookie cookie1 = new Cookie("message", "Hello!");
cookie1.setMaxAge(24 * 60 * 60);
response.addCookie(cookie1);
%>
```

Now that we've installed the cookie, we can use a **<bean:cookie>** element to read it. This creates a **Cookie** object named **messageCookie** holding our cookie in the response page:

```
<h2>The cookie data:</h2>
<bean:cookie id="messageCookie" name="message"/>
.
.
.
<BR>
```

Attribute Name	Description
id	The name of the scripting variable that will be made available with the value of the specified request cookie. This attribute is required.
multiple	Causes all matching cookies to be accumulated and stored into a bean of type **Cookie[]**. If not used, the first value for the specified cookie will be stored as a value of type **Cookie**.
name	Specifies the name of the cookie whose value, or values, is to be retrieved. This attribute is required.
value	The default cookie value to return if no cookie with the specified name was found.

Table 7-12 The Struts <bean:cookie> Tag Attributes

Ask the Expert

Q: **I want to set a cookie in my action's code, not in a JSP page. How can I do that?**

A: You can use the **response** object, passed to you in the action's **execute** method like this: **Cookie cookie1 = new Cookie("*name*", "*text*"); response.addCookie(cookie1);**.

Now that the **messageCookie** object is available, we can use the **Cookie** class's **getValue** method to read the value of the cookie (i.e., the text "Hello!") and display that in the Results page, like this:

```
<h2>The cookie data:</h2>
<bean:cookie id="messageCookie" name="message"/>
<%= messageCookie.getValue() %>
<BR>
```

You can see this at work in the Results page in Figure 7-6, where the cookie's text has been retrieved.

CRITICAL SKILL 7.10

Use the <bean:define> Tag

This tag creates a new scripting variable, named by the value of this tag's **id** attribute. You can create a new variable directly, or create it using a value from a bean. Here are the options:

- Use the **name** attribute. The created scripting variable will be of the type of the retrieved bean property.
- Use the **value** attribute. The created scripting variable will be of type **java.lang.String**, set to the value of this attribute.
- Use body content. The created scripting variable will be of type **java.lang.String**, set to the value of the nested body content.

You can see the attributes for this tag in Table 7-13.

We'll use **<bean:define>** in the **<bean>** example project to create a variable named **variable** that holds the value of the **text** property (which holds the text the user entered in the Welcome page):

```
<h2>The new variable:</h2>
<bean:define id="variable" name="ch07_07" property="text"/>
<%= variable %>
<BR>
```

Attribute Name	Description
id	The name of the scripting variable that will be created. This attribute is required.
name	If **property** is specified, the attribute name of the bean whose property you want to use to define a new variable. Or, if **property** is not specified, the attribute name of the bean that is duplicated with the new reference created by this tag. This attribute is required unless you specify a **value** attribute or nested body content.
property	The name of the bean property to use creating this variable.
scope	The variable scope searched to retrieve the bean specified by **name**.
toScope	The variable scope where the newly defined bean will be placed. The default is page scope.
type	The class name of the value used in the **id** attribute.
value	The string value to which the variable should be set. This attribute is required unless you specify the **name** attribute or nested body content.

Table 7-13 The Struts <bean:define> Tag Attributes

You can see this at work in Figure 7-6, where the value in the **text** property, "No worries", has been stored in a variable, which we've then inserted into the Results page using a JSP expression.

Progress Check

1. What three ways can you use to create a variable with this tag?
2. What attribute do you use to name the new scripting variable?

CRITICAL SKILL 7.11

Use the <bean:header> Tag

The **<bean:header>** tag retrieves the value of the specified request header as a single value or multiple values (depending on the **multiple** attribute). The results are stored as a page scope **String** attribute (if **multiple** is not used) or **String[]** (if **multiple** is used). You can see the attributes for this tag in Table 7-14.

1. Use the **name** attribute, the **value** attribute, or body content.
2. The **name** attribute

Attribute Name	Description
id	The name of the scripting variable that will be created. This attribute is required.
multiple	If any value is assigned to this attribute, creates a call to **HttpServletRequest.getHeaders** and returns headers as type **String[]**. By default, **HttpServletRequest.getHeader** is called, and the header is returned as type **String**.
name	The name of the request header whose value, or values, is to be retrieved. This attribute is required.
value	The default header value to return if no header with the given name was found.

Table 7-14 The Struts <bean:header> Tag Attributes

For example, in the **<bean>** example project in this module, we'll take a look at the request object's **user-agent** header, which indicates the type of browser the user has. Here's how we access that information:

```
<h2>The user-agent header data:</h2>
<bean:header id="headerObject" name="user-agent"/>
<%= headerObject %>
<BR>
```

You can see the results in Figure 7-6, which indicates that the browser is the Microsoft Internet Explorer.

CRITICAL SKILL 7.12

Use the <bean:message> Tag

The **<bean:message>** tag is already an old favorite of ours; you can use it to display a message in a page by retrieving data from a resource bundle like application.properties or from form beans. You can see the significant attributes for this tag in Table 7-15.

Attribute Name	Description
bundle	The name of the bean containing messages is stored.
key	The message key of the requested message. If not specified, the key is obtained from the **name** and **property** attributes.
name	The name of the bean whose property is accessed to retrieve the value specified by **property**. If **property** is not given, the value of this bean itself will be used as the message resource key.

Table 7-15 The Struts <bean:message> Tag Attributes

Attribute Name	Description
property	The name of the bean property to be accessed. If not specified, the value of the bean identified by **name** will itself be used as the message resource key.
scope	The scope searched to retrieve the bean.

Table 7-15 The Struts bean:message> Tag Attributes *(continued)*

For example, we saw how to use **<bean:message>** in Module 3, where we displayed messages from application.properties like this in The Struts Café project:

```
<%@ taglib uri="/tags/struts-bean" prefix="bean" %>
<%@ taglib uri="/tags/struts-logic" prefix="logic" %>

<HTML>
    <HEAD>
        <TITLE>Here's Your Order!</TITLE>
    </HEAD>

    <BODY>
        <H1>Here's Your Order!</H1>
        <bean:message key="items"/>
        <bean:write name="ch03_06" property="items"/>
        <BR>
        <BR>
        <bean:message key="toppings"/>
        <BR>
        <logic:iterate id="toppings1" name="ch03_06" property="toppings">
            <%= toppings1 %>
            <BR>
        </logic:iterate>
        <BR>
        <bean:message key="email"/>
        <bean:write name="ch03_06" property="email"/>
        <BR>
    </BODY>
</HTML>
```

These elements recovered these keys from application.properties:

```
email=<b>Email address:</b>
items=<b>Item:</b>
toppings=<b>Toppings:</b>
```

CRITICAL SKILL
7.13 Use the <bean:parameter> Tag

The **<bean:parameter>** tag gives you access to request object parameters. These are the parameters that hold data from the HTML controls that you can access with the **getParameter** method in Java code. You can see the attributes for this tag in Table 7-16.

For example, the text field in the **<bean>** sample project is named **text** in the Welcome page:

```
<html:form action="ch07_06.do">

<h2>Enter your data:</h2>
<html:text property="text"/>
        .
        .
        .
```

We'll recover the text in the text field with a **<bean:parameter>** element, storing that data in a variable named **text**. We'll display the value in that variable in the Results page this way:

```
<h2>The parameter data:</h2>
<bean:parameter id="text" name="text"/>
<%= text %>
<BR>
```

You can see the results in Figure 7-7, where as you see, the data from the **text** parameter, "No worries", was recovered from the **request** object and displayed.

Attribute Name	Description
id	The name of the scripting variable that will be created with the value of the specified request parameter. This attribute is required.
multiple	If any value is assigned to this attribute, creates a call to **ServletRequest.getParameterValues** and returns parameters as type **String[]**. By default, **ServletRequest.getParameter** is called, and the parameter is returned as type **String**.
name	The name of the request parameter whose value, or values, is to be retrieved. This attribute is required.
value	The default value to return if no parameter with the specified name was found.

Table 7-16 The Struts <bean:parameter> Tag Attributes

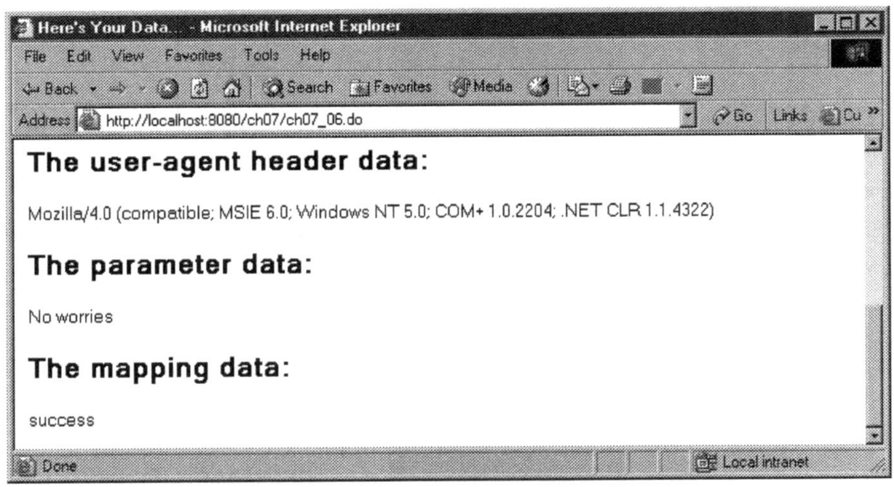

Figure 7-7 The <bean> tags project Results page, part 2

CRITICAL SKILL 7.14

Use the <bean:struts> Tag

You can use the **<bean:struts>** tag to read the value of Struts configuration objects, such as an action mapping. You can see the significant attributes for this tag in Table 7-17. You must specify exactly one of the **formBean**, **forward**, or **mapping** attributes to select the configuration object.

Attribute Name	Description
formBean	The name of the Struts **ActionFormBean** definition object to be exposed.
forward	The name of the global Struts **ActionForward** object to be exposed.
id	The name of the scripting variable that will be created. This attribute is required.
mapping	The path of the Struts **ActionMapping** definition object to be exposed.

Table 7-17 The Struts <bean:struts> Tag Attributes

For example, say you wanted to recover the name of the first **<forward>** in the action mapping for the action, **ch07_06**, for the **<bean>** project. That name is "success", as you see in the action mapping:

```
<action path="/ch07_06"
  type="ch07.ch07_06"
  name="ch07_07"
  scope="request"
  input="/ch07_05.jsp">
  <forward name="success" path="/ch07_08.jsp"/>
</action>
```

Here's how you can use the **<bean:struts>** tag to recover that forward's name; first, you get a Struts **ActionMapping** object:

```
<h2>The mapping data:</h2>
<bean:struts id="mapping" mapping="/ch07_06"/>
.
.
.
```

Then you can use the **ActionMapping** object's **findForwards** method in a JSP scriptlet to get all the forwards in the mapping. The first one will correspond to the "success" mapping, which we display in the Results page:

```
<h2>The mapping data:</h2>
<bean:struts id="mapping" mapping="/ch07_06"/>
<% String[] mappings = mapping.findForwards();
out.println(mappings[0]); %>
<BR>
```

You can see how this works in Figure 7-7, where we've recovered and displayed the name of the action mapping's forward for the **<bean>** project's action.

Progress Check

1. What attribute gives the name of the scripting variable that will be created?
2. Which three attributes must you include one of to use this tag?

---

1. **id**
2. You must specify exactly one of the **formBean**, **forward**, or **mapping** attributes.

CRITICAL SKILL 7.15

Use the <bean:write> Tag

The **<bean:write>** tag is another old favorite. This tag allows you to write the value of a bean property to a web page. You can see the attributes for this tag in Table 7-18.

We've used **<bean:write>** to write the value of various properties to web pages throughout the book. For example, here's how we use **<bean:write>** to write the value of the **text** property, which holds the text the user entered into the Welcome page's text field to the **<bean>** sample project's Results page:

```
<HTML>
    <HEAD>
        <TITLE>Here's Your Data...</TITLE>
    </HEAD>

    <BODY>
        <H1>Here's Your Data...</H1>

        <h2>The text field text:</h2>
        <bean:write name="ch07_03" property="text"/>
        <BR>
        .
        .
        .
```

Attribute Name	Description
bundle	The name of the bean under which the **MessageResources** object containing messages is stored.
filter	If this attribute is **true** (the default), the property value will be filtered for characters that are sensitive in HTML, and any such characters will be replaced by their entity equivalents.
format	A format string to use to convert bean or property value to the String.
name	The attribute name of the bean whose property is accessed to retrieve the value specified by **property**, if **property** is specified. If **property** is not specified, the value of this bean itself will be used. This attribute is required.
property	The name of the bean property you want to use.
scope	The variable scope searched to retrieve the bean specified by name.

Table 7-18 The Struts <bean:write> Tag Attributes

Use Struts 1.2

Everything in this module checks out okay with the early release version of Struts 1.2, including the new .tld files for the **<logic>** and **<bean>** tags. As usual, of course, if you use the **ActionError** and **ActionErrors** classes in your code, you'll have to switch to the **ActionMessage** and **ActionMessages** classes.

✓ Module 7 Mastery Check

1. Which **<logic>** tag would you use to redirect the browser?

   A. **<forward>**

   B. **<logic:forward>**

   C. **<logic:redirect>**

   D. **<redirect>**

2. Which **<logic>** tag searches for substrings in the text value of a variable?

   A. **<logic:search>**

   B. **<logic:find>**

   C. **<logic:substring>**

   D. **<logic:match>**

3. Which **<logic:empty>** element attribute do you use to specify the bean whose property you're checking?

   A. **bean**

   B. **form**

   C. **name**

   D. **actionForm**

4. When using the **<logic:equal>** tag, which attributes would you use if you wanted to test a bean property against a constant?

   A. **name, property, value**

   B. **name, value**

   C. **name, parameter**

   D. **name, property, value, parameter**

5. Which tag would you use to check if a cookie named **message** exists?
   - A. **<logic:present cookie="message">**
   - B. **<logic:match cookie="message">**
   - C. **<logic:header cookie="message">**
   - D. **<logic:search cookie="message">**
6. Which three attributes must you specify exactly one of to use **<logic:redirect>**?
   - A. **forward**, **href**, **page**
   - B. **forward**, **name**, **page**
   - C. **forward**, **name**, **property**
   - D. **forward**, **href**, **property**
7. Which **<bean>** tag would you use to create a scripting variable?
   - A. **<bean:include>**
   - B. **<bean:define>**
   - C. **<bean:write>**
   - D. **<bean:struts>**
8. Which Struts **<bean>** tag do you use to set the value of a cookie?
   - A. **<bean:define>**
   - B. **<bean:include>**
   - C. **<bean:cookie>**
   - D. You can't use a **<bean>** tag to do that.
9. Which Struts tag can you use to determine which browser the user has?
   - A. **<logic:browser>**
   - B. **<logic:define>**
   - C. **<bean:header>**
   - D. **<bean:scope>**
10. Which **<bean>** tag can you use to read the data from a text field?
   - A. **<bean:header>**
   - B. **<bean:parameter>**
   - C. **<bean:define>**
   - D. **<bean:message>**

Module 8

Creating Custom Tags

CRITICAL SKILLS

8.1 Use a Text-Inserting Tag

8.2 Create Iterating Tags

8.3 Create Cooperating Tags

8.4 Use Custom Tags that Create Variables

As you know, much of working with Struts revolves around working with custom JSP tags. In addition to the tags that come built into Struts, that also often means creating your own custom tags to augment what Struts provides.

For example, in The Struts Café project in Module 3 we saw how custom JSP tags can feed data to the Struts custom tags by setting attributes that the Struts custom tags can use. Here's what it looked like in code, where we used two of our own custom tags, **<ch03:items/>** and **<ch03:toppings/>**, to pass data to the **<logic:iterate>** and **<html:select>** Struts tags:

```
<%@ taglib uri="/tags/struts-bean" prefix="bean" %>
<%@ taglib uri="/tags/struts-html" prefix="html" %>
<%@ taglib uri="/tags/struts-logic" prefix="logic" %>
<%@ taglib uri="/ch03" prefix="ch03" %>

<HTML>
    <HEAD>
        <TITLE>The Struts Cafe</TITLE>
    </HEAD>

    <BODY>
        <H1>The Struts Cafe</H1>
        <html:errors/>
        <ch03:items/>
        <ch03:toppings/>
        <html:form action="ch03_04.do">
            <TABLE>
                <TR>
                    <TD ALIGN="LEFT" VALIGN="TOP">
                        <bean:message key="toppings"/>
                        <BR>
                        <logic:iterate id="toppings1" name="toppings">
                            <html:multibox property="toppings">
                                <%= toppings1 %>
                            </html:multibox>
                            <%= toppings1 %>
                            <BR>
                        </logic:iterate>
                    </TD>
                    <TD ALIGN="LEFT" VALIGN="TOP">
                        <bean:message key="items"/>
                        <BR>
                        <html:select property="items">
                            <html:options name="items"/>
                        </html:select>
                    </TD>
                </TR>
                <TR>
                    <TD ALIGN="LEFT">
```

```
                                        <BR>
                              <bean:message key="email"/>
                              <html:text property="email"/>
                          </TD>
                      <TR>
                  </TABLE>
                        <BR>
                  <html:submit value="Place Your Order!"/>
              </html:form>
          </BODY>
      </HTML>
```

In this module, we're going to discuss how to create custom JSP tags. In the real world, Struts applications are often mixes of your own custom tags and those built into Struts. For that reason, creating your own JSP tags that can work with Struts tags is a fundamental skill for Struts programmers, and we're going to develop that skill in this module. It's a skill that even many experienced JSP/servlet programmers lack, but as you start working with Struts, it's an important one to pick up.

CRITICAL SKILL 8.1

Use a Text-Inserting Tag

Our first example is going to be a simple project where we just create a tag that will insert some text ("This text is from the custom tag.") into a results web page. Here's how we'll use this tag, which we'll call **<ch08:message/>**, in the Welcome page, ch08_01.jsp:

```
<%@ taglib prefix="ch08" uri="WEB-INF/ch08_02.tld" %>
<HTML>
    <HEAD>
        <TITLE>Inserting Text With Custom Tags</TITLE>
    </HEAD>
    <BODY>
        <H1>Inserting Text With Custom Tags</H1>
        <ch08:message />
    </BODY>
</HTML>
```

Note the **<%@ taglib %>** JSP directive here, which connects the prefix for our custom tags, **ch08** in this module, with the tag library definition file, ch08_02.tld. There are various ways to make this connection, including using a **<taglib>** element in web.xml like this (as we did in Module 3, and as the Struts tag libraries do it):

```
<taglib>
  <taglib-uri>/ch08</taglib-uri>
  <taglib-location>/WEB-INF/ch08.tld</taglib-location>
</taglib>
```

But there's an easier way to do this that doesn't involve specially editing web.xml: you can simply give the URL of the .tld file directly in the **<%@ taglib %>** directive. Because this way is easier, it's more commonly used than the technique that requires you to edit web.xml, and that's the way we'll do it in this module:

```
<%@ taglib prefix="ch08" uri="WEB-INF/ch08_02.tld" %>
```

This lets the server find the .tld file for the custom tag **<ch08:message>**, which is ch08_02.tld. On the other hand, you still have to create the .tld file.

Creating TLD Files

We've tied the prefix used by our custom JSP tag in the Welcome page, ch08_01.jsp, to the .tld file ch08_02.tld. In ch08_02.tld, you start with a standard header, like this:

```
<?xml version="1.0" encoding="ISO-8859-1"?>
<!DOCTYPE taglib PUBLIC
    "-//Sun Microsystems, Inc.//DTD JSP Tag Library 1.2//EN"
    "http://java.sun.com/dtd/web-jsptaglibrary_1_2.dtd">
<taglib>
        .
        .
        .
</taglib>
```

To set up the tag library we'll be using, we'll use child elements of the **<taglib>** element here. You can see the allowed child elements of the **<taglib>** element in Table 8-1.

Element	Contains
<description>	Description of the library
<display-name>	Name that can be displayed by authoring tools
<jsp-version>	The JSP version the tag library needs
<large-icon>	Large icon that can be used by authoring tools
<listener>	Event listener classes that can handle events
<short-name>	Name that can be used by authoring tools
<small-icon>	Small icon that can be used by authoring tools
<tag>	A custom tag
<tlib-version>	The tag library's version
<uri>	URI that uniquely identifies the tag library

Table 8-1 Child Elements of the <taglib> Element

Here's how we'll add the child elements of the **<taglib>** element in the .tld file for the **<ch08:message>** element:

```
<?xml version="1.0" encoding="ISO-8859-1"?>
<!DOCTYPE taglib PUBLIC
    "-//Sun Microsystems, Inc.//DTD JSP Tag Library 1.2//EN"
    "http://java.sun.com/dtd/web-jsptaglibrary_1_2.dtd">
<taglib>
  <tlib-version>1.0</tlib-version>
  <jsp-version>1.2</jsp-version>
  <short-name>CustomTags</short-name>
  <description>Example tags.</description>
  <tag>
        .
        .
        .
  </tag>
</taglib>
```

Each custom tag is configured with a **<tag>** element. This element can contain the child elements you see in Table 8-2. The **<name>** and a **<tag-class>** child elements are required.

Element	Contains
<attribute>	Tag attribute definition
<body-content>	The type of body content
<description>	Tag-specific description
<display-name>	Name that can be displayed by authoring tools
<large-icon>	Large icon that can be used by authoring tools
<name>	The tag name
<small-icon>	Small icon that can be used by authoring tools
<tag-class>	The name of the tag's Java class
<tei-class>	Tag extra info data based on javax.servlet.jsp.tagext.TagExtraInfo
<variable>	Scripting variable definition

Table 8-2 Child Elements of the <tag> element

Here's the final .tld file, which connects the **<ch08:message>** tag to the Java class **ch08.ch08_03**:

```
<?xml version="1.0" encoding="ISO-8859-1"?>
<!DOCTYPE taglib PUBLIC
    "-//Sun Microsystems, Inc.//DTD JSP Tag Library 1.2//EN"
    "http://java.sun.com/dtd/web-jsptaglibrary_1_2.dtd">
<taglib>
  <tlib-version>1.0</tlib-version>
  <jsp-version>1.2</jsp-version>
  <short-name>CustomTags</short-name>
  <description>Example tags.</description>
  <tag>
    <name>message</name>
    <tag-class>ch08.ch08_03</tag-class>
</tag>
</taglib>
```

Now we've connected the **<ch08:message>** tag to the Java class **ch08.ch08_03**, so the next order of business is to create that class.

Progress Check

1. What element do you use to create a custom tag?
2. What element do you use to connect a tag to its Java support?

Supporting Custom Tags in Java

The Java class **ch08.ch08_03** starts off this way, where we're putting it in the **ch08** package:

```
package ch08;
        .
        .
        .
```

1. The **<tag>** element
2. The **<tag-class>** element

This class will support a custom JSP tag, so it's based on the Java **TagSupport** class:

```
package ch08;

import javax.servlet.jsp.tagext.*;
import javax.servlet.jsp.*;

public class ch08_03 extends TagSupport
{
        .
        .
        .
}
```

The methods of the **TagSupport** class appear in Table 8-3 for reference; we'll put a number of them to work here.

To support the **<ch08:message>** tag, you can insert text into the web page when the end tag, **</ch08:message>**, is encountered by the server's JSP processor. When the end tag is about

Method	Does This
int doAfterBody()	Is called after a custom element's body is processed
int doEndTag()	Is called after a custom element's end tag is encountered
int doStartTag()	Is called when a custom element's body is processed
java.lang.String getId()	Returns the value of the **id** attribute of this tag
Tag getParent()	Returns the parent enclosing this tag
java.lang.Object getValue(java.lang.String k)	Returns the value associated with a key
java.util.Enumeration getValues()	Enumerates the values kept by this tag handler
void removeValue(java.lang.String k)	Removes a value associated with a key
void setId(java.lang.String id)	Sets the **id** attribute for this tag
void setPageContext(PageContext pageContext)	Sets the page context to a particular **PageContext** object
void setParent(Tag t)	Sets the nesting tag of this tag
void setValue(java.lang.String k, java.lang.Object o)	Associates a value with a key

Table 8-3 Methods of the TagSupport Class

to be handled, the **TagSupport** class's **doEndTag** method is called, and you can support that method in the code for this tag:

```
package ch08;

import javax.servlet.jsp.tagext.*;
import javax.servlet.jsp.*;

public class ch08_03 extends TagSupport
{

  public int doEndTag()
  {
        .
        .
        .
  }
```

The code in this method is going to be called when the end of our custom tag is encountered, and we want to display the message "This text is from the custom tag." in the web page. How do you do that? You use the **TagSupport** class's **pageContext** field.

Using the Page Context

The page context gives you access to many resources in custom tag code, and you can see the methods of the **PageContext** class in Table 8-4.

Method	Does This
java.lang.Object findAttribute(java.lang.String name)	Searches for an attribute in page, request, session, and application scope(s). Returns the attribute's value or null.
void forward(java.lang.String relativeUrlPath)	Forwards the current **ServletRequest** and **ServletResponse** objects.
java.lang.Object getAttribute(java.lang.String name)	Returns the object associated with the attribute in the page scope, or **null** if not found.
java.lang.Object getAttribute(java.lang.String name, int scope)	Returns the object associated with the attribute in the specified scope, or **null** if not found.
java.util.Enumeration getAttributeNamesInScope(int scope)	Returns all the attributes in a given scope.
int getAttributesScope(java.lang.String name)	Returns the scope where a given attribute is defined.
java.lang.Exception getException()	Returns the value of the exception object.
JspWriter getOut()	Returns the out object (a **JspWriter** object).

Table 8-4 Methods of the pageContext Class

Method	Does This
java.lang.Object getPage()	Returns the page object (a **Servlet** object).
ServletRequest getRequest()	Returns the request object (a **ServletRequest** object).
ServletResponse getResponse()	Returns the response object (a **ServletResponse** object).
ServletConfig getServletConfig()	Returns the **ServletConfig** object.
ServletContext getServletContext()	Returns the **ServletContext** object.
HttpSession getSession()	Returns the session object (an **HttpSession** object).
void handlePageException(java.lang.Exception e)	Handles page exceptions.
void handlePageException(java.lang.Throwable t)	Same as **handlePageException(Exception)** except that it accepts a **Throwable** object.
void include(java.lang.String relativeUrlPath)	Includes the resource specified as part of the current **ServletRequest** and **ServletResponse** objects.
void initialize(Servlet servlet, ServletRequest request, ServletResponse response, java.lang.String errorPageURL, boolean needsSession, int bufferSize, boolean autoFlush)	Initializes a **PageContext** object.
void release()	Resets the internal state of a **PageContext** object.
void removeAttribute(java.lang.String name)	Removes the attribute associated with the given name in page scope.
void removeAttribute(java.lang.String name, int scope)	Removes the attribute associated with the given name in the given scope.
void setAttribute(java.lang.String name, java.lang.Object attribute)	Sets the name and value specified in page scope.
void setAttribute(java.lang.String name, java.lang.Object o, int scope)	Sets the name and value specified in the given scope.

Table 8-4 Methods of the pageContext Class *(continued)*

In this case, we're going to use the built-in JSP object **pageContext**, which holds the page context. As you can see in Table 8-3, this object supports a **getOut** method, which returns a **JSPWriter** object we'll call out. We'll use this object to print to the Results page:

```
package ch08;

import javax.servlet.jsp.tagext.*;
import javax.servlet.jsp.*;

public class ch08_03 extends TagSupport
{

  public int doEndTag() throws JspException
{
```

```
    try {
      pageContext.getOut().print("This text is from the custom tag.");
        .
        .
        .
    }
    return EVAL_PAGE;
  }
}
```

We're also returning a constant here, **EVAL_PAGE**, to indicate that the rest of the page should be evaluated normally. The final step is to add some exception-handling code, which Java will insist on. In this case, we'll just throw any possible exceptions back to the default JSP exception handler:

```
package ch08;

import javax.servlet.jsp.tagext.*;
import javax.servlet.jsp.*;

public class ch08_03 extends TagSupport
{

  public int doEndTag() throws JspException
{
    try {
      pageContext.getOut().print("This text is from the custom tag.");

    } catch (Exception e) {
      throw new JspException(e.toString());
    }
    return EVAL_PAGE;
  }
}
```

That's it; you can see the results in Figure 8-1 when you navigate to http://localhost:8080/ch08/ch08_01.jsp. As you can see, the **<ch08:message/>** element did indeed insert text into the Results page.

That gives you the basic framework of creating custom tags. However, what if you wanted to pass data to your tag? One way to do that is to add support for attributes to your custom tags.

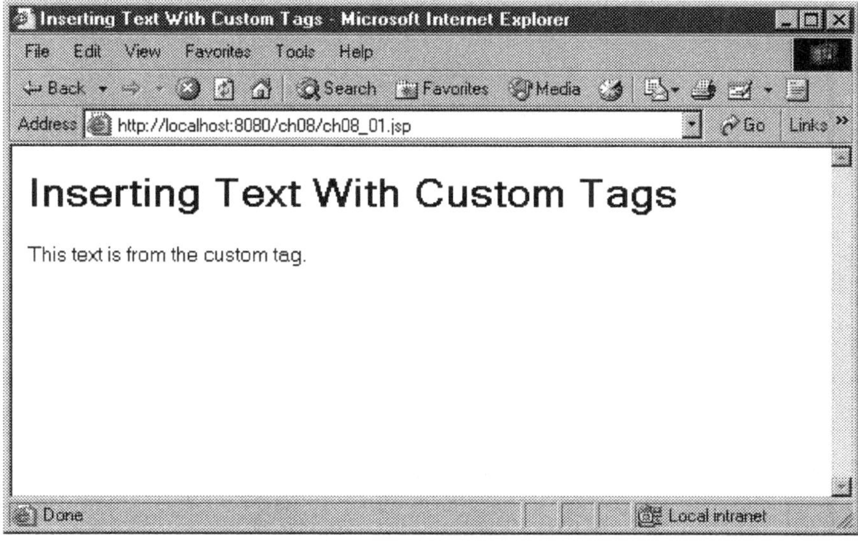

Figure 8-1 Inserting text into a web page

Progress Check

1. What import should you make to pick up Java support for custom tags?
2. What constant can you return from **doEndTag** to ensure the test of the page is evaluated?

Support Tag Attributes

Using attributes is a good way to pass data to your custom tag's code. As an example, we'll pass the text to the **<ch08:message>** tag to display using an attribute named **text**. In this case, we're passing the tag the text "This text was set using an attribute." to insert in the page:

```
<ch08:message text="This text was set using an attribute."/>
```

1. **import javax.servlet.jsp.tagext.*;**
2. **EVAL_PAGE**

Element	Contains
<description>	A description of the attribute.
<name>	The attribute name.
<required>	Specifies if an attribute is required to be present. Can contain **true**, **false**, **yes**, or **no**.
<rtexprvalue>	Specifies if the attribute can be assigned an expression's value at runtime. Can contain **true**, **false**, **yes**, or **no**.
<type>	Contains the Java type of the attribute.

Table 8-5 Child Elements of the <attribute> Element

So how do you create an attribute like this? You add support for the attribute in a .tld file and your Java code. In the .tld file, you use an **<attribute>** element, which supports the child elements you see in Table 8-5. Only the **<name>** child element is required.

Here's how you might put this new version of the **<ch08:message>** tag to work in a new JSP, ch08_04.jsp:

```
<%@ taglib prefix="ch08" uri="WEB-INF/ch08_05.tld" %>
<HTML>
  <HEAD>
        <TITLE>Handling Custom Tag Attributes</TITLE>
    </HEAD>
    <BODY>
        <H1>Handling Custom Tag Attributes</H1>
        <ch08:message text="This text was set using an attribute."/>
    </BODY>
</HTML>
```

We'll create this attribute now, starting with the new .tld file, ch08_05.tld. In this file, we'll add a new **<attribute>** element to support the **text** attribute, giving both the attribute's name and type (the default type if you don't specify one is **java.lang.String**):

```
<?xml version="1.0" encoding="ISO-8859-1"?>
<!DOCTYPE taglib PUBLIC
    "-//Sun Microsystems, Inc.//DTD JSP Tag Library 1.2//EN"
    "http://java.sun.com/dtd/web-jsptaglibrary_1_2.dtd">
<taglib>
  <tlib-version>1.0</tlib-version>
  <jsp-version>1.2</jsp-version>
  <short-name>CustomTags</short-name>
  <description>Example tags.</description>
  <tag>
    <name>message</name>
    <tag-class>ch08.ch08_06</tag-class>
    <attribute>
      <name>text</name>
```

```
      <type>java.lang.String</type>
    </attribute>
  </tag>
</taglib>
```

That declares the new attribute as far as the server is concerned. The next step is to add the Java support, which we'll do in ch08_06.java (as indicated in the preceding .tld file). The process of creating attributes is handled well in Java; all you need to do is to create a property corresponding to the attribute using the same name, and the JSP framework will call the property's **set** method automatically to pass the attribute's value to you.

In this new project, we'll create a write-only property named **text** to hold the text data passed to us. That property revolves around a **setText** method and a **String** variable named **text**:

```
public class ch08_06 extends TagSupport
{
  String text;

  public void setText(String s)
  {
    text = s;
  }

  public int doEndTag() throws JspException
{
    try {
        .
        .
        .
    }
    return EVAL_PAGE;
  }
}
```

The JSP framework will call the **setText** method when this code is loaded, assigning the **text** property the value of the **text** attribute. That means you can recover that text simply by using the **text String** variable in your code and display that text using **pageContext.getOut().print**, like this:

```
package ch08;

import javax.servlet.jsp.tagext.*;
import javax.servlet.jsp.*;

public class ch08_06 extends TagSupport
{
```

```
  String text;

  public void setText(String s) {
    text = s;
  }

  public int doEndTag() throws JspException
{
    try {
      pageContext.getOut().print(text);
    } catch (Exception e) {
      throw new JspException(e.toString());
    }
    return EVAL_PAGE;
  }
}
```

After compiling this code and (re)starting Tomcat, navigate to http://localhost:8080/ch08/ch08_04.jsp. You can see the results in Figure 8-2, where the text from the **<ch08:message>** tag's attribute was passed to the Java code, which displays that code in the results. In this way, you can pass data to custom tags at runtime.

So far, we've only created simple custom tags, but there are other options. For example, you can create your own iterating tags using the **IterationTag** interface (already implemented in the **TagSupport** class we've been using). This is the same interface that's implemented by the Struts **<logic:iterate>** tag. We'll take a look at creating iterating tags next, giving you a great deal more control than you'd get just by using the **<logic:iterate>** tag alone.

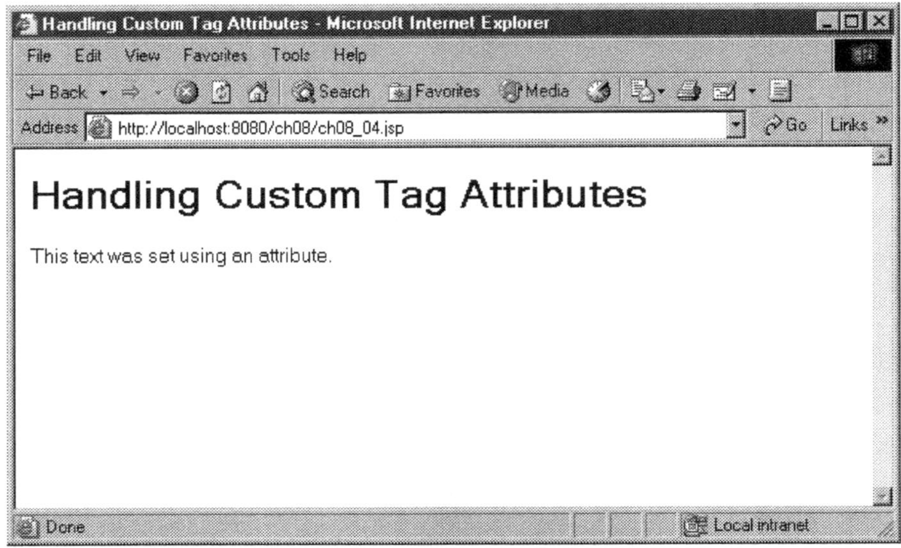

Figure 8-2 Using a custom tag attribute

CRITICAL SKILL 8.2

Create Iterating Tags

As an example, say that you want to display a list of pizza toppings in a web page as a list, like this:

```
Topping: Pepperoni
Topping: Sausage
Topping: Ed
Topping: Olives
```

We'll create an iterating tag, **<ch08:iterator>**, to display this list; by getting to the Java roots of iterating tags, you'll have more control than just using the Struts **<logic:iterate>** tag. The Welcome page for this new project, ch08_07.jsp, looks like the following—note that you place the text that will be iterated in each repetition ("Topping:" here) in the body of the **<ch08:iterator>** element:

```
<ch08:iterator>
    Topping:
</ch08:iterator>
```

You can hardcode the names of the toppings you want to display in your Java code, but it's usually better to store them in the page that'll display them directly where the Java code can get access to them, allowing you to use the same Java code across hundreds of different pages. For example, you might store the toppings in a page context attribute using the JSP **pageContext** built-in object, letting you communicate those toppings to your Java code.

Here's how you can add the toppings as a **String** array to the page context under the name **toppings** in a new Welcome page, ch08_07.jsp:

```
<%@ taglib prefix="ch08" uri="WEB-INF/ch08_08.tld" %>
<HTML>
    <HEAD>
        <TITLE>Creating Iterating Tags</TITLE>
    </HEAD>

    <BODY>
        <H1>Creating Iterating Tags</H1>
        <%
            String[] toppings = new String[]{ "Pepperoni", "Sausage", "Ham",
                "Olives" };
            pageContext.setAttribute("toppings", toppings);
        %>

        <ch08:iterator>
            Topping:
        </ch08:iterator>
    </BODY>
</HTML>
```

That sets up the Welcome page and stores the toppings we're going to display in a page context attribute. To connect that page to the Java code, we'll need a .tld file, ch08_08.tld:

```
<?xml version="1.0" encoding="ISO-8859-1"?>
<!DOCTYPE taglib PUBLIC
    "-//Sun Microsystems, Inc.//DTD JSP Tag Library 1.2//EN"
    "http://java.sun.com/dtd/web-jsptaglibrary_1_2.dtd">
<taglib>
  <tlib-version>1.0</tlib-version>
  <jsp-version>1.2</jsp-version>
  <short-name>CustomTags</short-name>
  <description>Example tags.</description>
  <tag>
    <name>iterator</name>
    <tag-class>ch08.ch08_09</tag-class>
  </tag>
</taglib>
```

How do you get access to the toppings in the Java code? You can use the **pageContext** object's **getAttribute** method to get the array of toppings set in this project's Welcome page. We'll do that as soon as JSP starts evaluating the **<ch08:iterator>** tag in the **doStartTag** method (note that this class is based on the **TagSupport** class, not the **IterationTag** interface, because **TagSupport** already implements **IterationTag**):

```
package ch08;

import javax.servlet.jsp.*;
import javax.servlet.jsp.tagext.*;

public class ch08_09 extends TagSupport
{
  private String[] toppings = null;

  public int doStartTag()
  {
    toppings = (String[]) pageContext.getAttribute("toppings");
    return EVAL_BODY_INCLUDE;
  }
        .
        .
        .
```

Passing data using page context attributes like this is a lot easier than using attributes if you've got a number of values to pass. How do you actually display these multiple values in the Results web page? You can use the **IterationTag** interface's **doAfterBody** method, which is called after the body has been evaluated (recall that the body of this element displays the text "Topping:" in the web page each iteration).

In the **doAfterBody** method, you can return the constant **EVAL_BODY_AGAIN** to make the body of the element be evaluated again. On the other hand, if you return the constant **SKIP_BODY**, the JSP framework will no longer iterate over the body.

To iterate the correct number of times, we'll create a counter named **iterationCounter** that will keep track of iterations. Here's how that looks in **doAfterBody**:

```
package ch08;

import javax.servlet.jsp.*;
import javax.servlet.jsp.tagext.*;

public class ch08_09 extends TagSupport
{
  private int iterationCounter = 0;
  private String[] toppings = null;

  public int doStartTag()
  {
    toppings = (String[]) pageContext.getAttribute("toppings");
    return EVAL_BODY_INCLUDE;
  }

  public int doAfterBody() throws JspException
  {
    try{
      pageContext.getOut().print(" " + toppings[iterationCounter] + "<BR>");
    } catch(Exception e){
      throw new JspException(e.toString());
    }
    iterationCounter++;
    if(iterationCounter >= toppings.length) {
      return SKIP_BODY;
    }
    return EVAL_BODY_AGAIN;
  }
}
```

The results appear in Figure 8-3, where, as you can see, the **<ch08:iterator>** tag is a success—not only was it able to recover the strings we passed it using a page context attribute, but it also iterated over those strings and inserted them in the Results page. Not bad.

In this project, we used the page context to store data we passed to Java code. Getting familiar with this way of passing data is important to Struts programming, as we've already seen. We'll develop this technique in the next project by creating cooperating tags that use the page context to pass data back and forth.

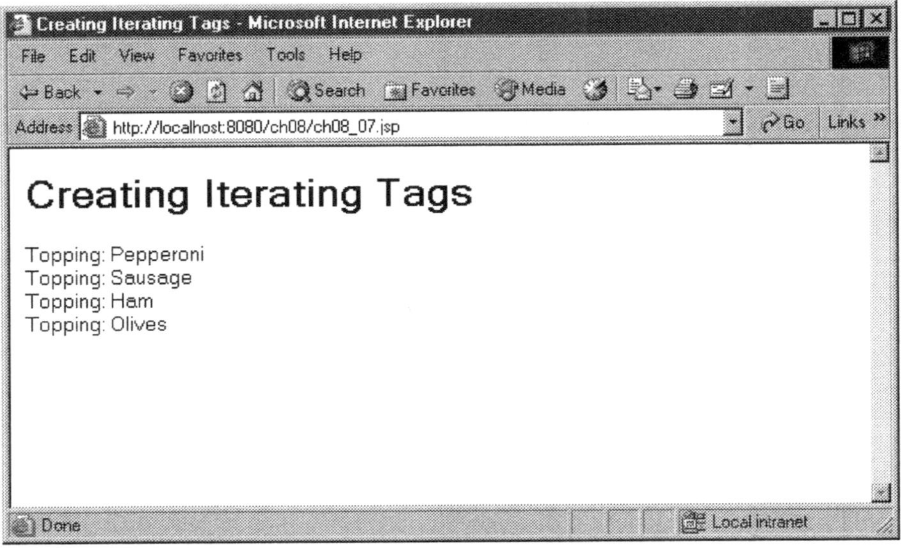

Figure 8-3 Creating an iterating tag

Progress Check

1. What method is executed after the body in an iterating tag is inserted into a web page?
2. What constant do you return if you want to iterate again?

CRITICAL SKILL 8.3

Create Cooperating Tags

In the previous project, we passed data to custom tags by setting **pageContext** object attributes. Here's how that worked with an attribute named **toppings**:

```
<%
    String[] toppings = new String[]{ "Pepperoni", "Sausage", "Ham",
        "Olives" };
    pageContext.setAttribute("toppings", toppings);
%>
```

---

1. **doAfterBody**
2. **EVAL_BODY_AGAIN**

In this project, we'll create a cooperating tag to go with our **<ch08:iterator>** tag, which will create the **toppings** page context attribute. This cooperating tag will be called **<ch08:createToppings>**. We saw in Module 3 that you can use custom tags like **<ch08:createToppings>** to store data in attributes that Struts tags like **<logic:iterate>** use, but we haven't seen how to create custom tags to do that until now.

Here's how we'll use this new tag, **<ch08:createToppings>**, in a new JSP page, ch08_10.jsp: all you have to do is to use **<ch08:createToppings/>** in a web page to store data in the **toppings** attribute, and then the **<ch08:iterator>** tag can recover the data from that attribute:

```
<%@ taglib prefix="ch08" uri="WEB-INF/ch08_11.tld" %>
<HTML>
    <HEAD>
        <TITLE>Creating Cooperating Tags</TITLE>
    </HEAD>

    <BODY>
        <H1>Creating Cooperating Tags</H1>
        <ch08:createToppings/>
        <ch08:iterator>
            Topping:
        </ch08:iterator>
    </BODY>
</HTML>
```

You also have to add this new tag to the .tld file:

```
<?xml version="1.0" encoding="ISO-8859-1"?>
<!DOCTYPE taglib PUBLIC
    "-//Sun Microsystems, Inc.//DTD JSP Tag Library 1.2//EN"
    "http://java.sun.com/dtd/web-jsptaglibrary_1_2.dtd">
<taglib>
  <tlib-version>1.0</tlib-version>
  <jsp-version>1.2</jsp-version>
  <short-name>CustomTags</short-name>
  <description>Example tags.</description>
  <tag>
    <name>iterator</name>
    <tag-class>ch08.ch08_09</tag-class>
  </tag>
  <tag>
    <name>createToppings</name>
    <tag-class>ch08.ch08_12</tag-class>
  </tag>
</taglib>
```

This new tag, **<ch08:createToppings>**, creates the **toppings** array that the **<ch08:iterator>** tag will use and stores that array in the **toppings** attribute this way:

```
package ch08;

import javax.servlet.jsp.tagext.*;

public class ch08_12 extends TagSupport
{

  public int doStartTag()
  {
    String[] toppings = new String[] {"Pepperoni", "Sausage", "Ham",
        "Olives"};
    pageContext.setAttribute("toppings", toppings);

    return SKIP_BODY;
  }
}
```

The results appear in Figure 8-4—the same as the previous version of this project, except that this time, the data the iterating tag displays comes from a cooperating tag, **<ch08:createToppings>**.

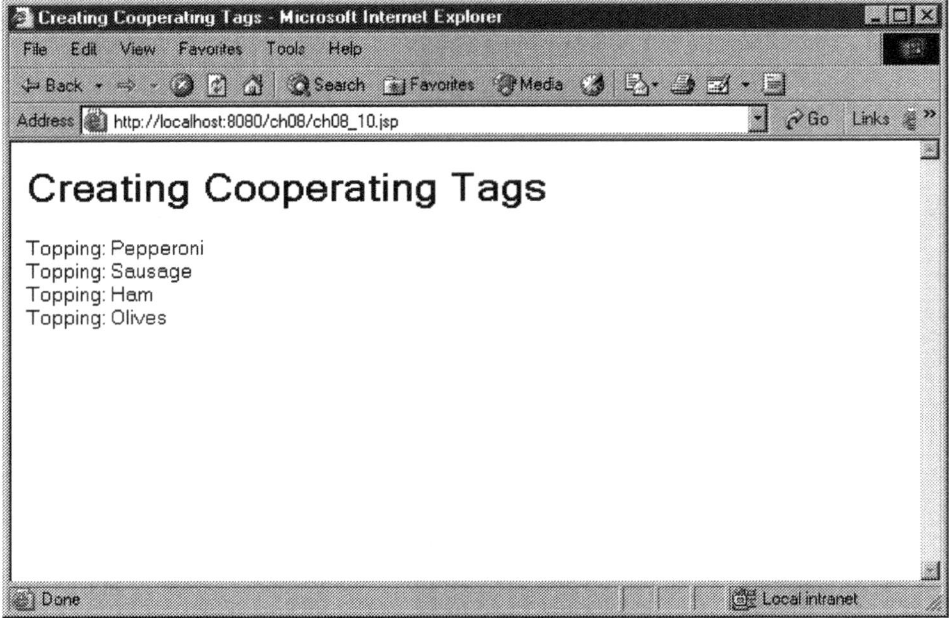

Figure 8-4 Using cooperating tags

The **<ch08:createToppings>** tag supplies its data using an attribute named **toppings**. Struts stores form beans using attributes that have the same names as the beans, so you can get the same results using our **<ch08:createToppings>** tag and the Struts **<logic:iterate>** tag, like this:

```
<%@ taglib uri="/tags/struts-logic" prefix="logic" %>
<%@ taglib prefix="ch08" uri="WEB-INF/ch08_11.tld" %>
<HTML>
    <HEAD>
        <TITLE>Creating Cooperating Tags</TITLE>
    </HEAD>

    <BODY>
        <H1>Creating Cooperating Tags</H1>
        <ch08:createToppings/>
        <logic:iterate id="toppings1" name="toppings">
            Topping: <%= toppings1 %>
            <BR>
        </logic:iterate>
    </BODY>
</HTML>
```

For that matter, if you wanted to display the toppings in a **<select>** control that stores user selections in a request parameter named **userToppings**, you could use our **<ch08:createToppings>** tag and the Struts **<html:select>** and **<html:options>**, like this:

```
<%@ taglib uri="/tags/struts-logic" prefix="logic" %>
<%@ taglib uri="/tags/struts-html" prefix="html" %>
<%@ taglib prefix="ch08" uri="WEB-INF/ch08_11.tld" %>
<HTML>
    <HEAD>
        <TITLE>Creating Cooperating Tags</TITLE>
    </HEAD>

    <BODY>
        <H1>Creating Cooperating Tags</H1>
        <ch08:createToppings/>
        <html:select property="userToppings">
            <html:options name="toppings"/>
        </html:select>
    </BODY>
</HTML>
```

We've used custom tags to feed data to Struts tags in The Struts Café project, and now you know how to create custom tags like those.

Ask the Expert

Q: Is there any other way to pass data from a web page to Struts tags?

A: You can, if you prefer, set the page context attribute that holds the data a Struts tag will use in a web page's JSP code. Here's an example:

```
  <%@ taglib uri="/tags/struts-logic" prefix="logic" %>
  <%@ taglib uri="/tags/struts-html" prefix="html" %>
<HTML>
  <HEAD>
    <TITLE>Select a Topping</TITLE>
  </HEAD>

  <BODY>
    <H1>Select a Topping</H1>
<%
  String[] toppings = new String[]{ "Pepperoni", "Sausage", "Ham",
    "Olives" };
  pageContext.setAttribute("toppings", toppings);%
>
    <logic:iterate id="toppings1" name="toppings">
      Topping: <%= toppings1 %>
      <BR>
    </logic:iterate>
  </BODY>
</HTML>
```

If you prefer, you can even use Struts tags like **<logic:notPresent>** with your own tags, as in this case where we're checking if the **toppings** attribute needs to be created before creating it ourselves:

```
<%@ taglib uri="/tags/struts-logic" prefix="logic" %>
<%@ taglib prefix="ch08" uri="WEB-INF/ch08_11.tld" %>
<HTML>
    <HEAD>
        <TITLE>Creating Cooperating Tags</TITLE>
    </HEAD>

    <BODY>
```

```
            <H1>Creating Cooperating Tags</H1>
            <logic:notPresent name="toppings">
                <ch08:createToppings/>
            </logic:notPresent>
            <ch08:iterator>
                Topping:
            </ch08:iterator>
        </BODY>
</HTML>
```

We'll take a look at one more custom tag project in this module: creating scripting variables using custom tags.

CRITICAL SKILL 8.4

Use Custom Tags That Create Variables

The **<ch08:createToppings/>** element creates a page context attribute named **toppings** that holds the **toppings** array. You can access that array in JSP code like this, using the **getAttribute** method:

```
<%@ taglib prefix="ch08" uri="WEB-INF/ch08_11.tld" %>
<HTML>
    <HEAD>
        <TITLE>Getting the Toppings</TITLE>
    </HEAD>

    <BODY>
        <H1>Getting the Toppings</H1>
        <ch10:createToppings/>
        <%
          String[] toppings = (String [])
                pageContext.getAttribute("toppings");

          for(int loopIndex = 0; loopIndex < toppings.length; loopIndex++) {
              out.println("Topping: " + toppings[loopIndex] + "<BR>");
          }
        %>
    </BODY>
</HTML>
```

However, there's an easier way to do this. You can modify the **<ch08:createToppings>** tag so that it'll create the **toppings** array as a scripting variable available in JSP code directly, which means you can use that array like this in ch08_13.jsp (note that no **getAttribute** call is needed):

```
<%@ taglib prefix="ch08" uri="WEB-INF/ch08_15.tld" %>
<HTML>
```

```
    <HEAD>
        <TITLE>Custom Tags and Variables</TITLE>
    </HEAD>

    <BODY>
        <H1>Custom Tags and Variables</H1>
        <ch08:createToppings/>
        <%
            for(int loopIndex = 0; loopIndex < toppings.length; loopIndex++)
            {
                out.println("Topping: " + toppings[loopIndex] + "<BR>");
            }
        %>
    </BODY>
</HTML>
```

Scripting variables make it easy to send data from custom tags to JSP code and back without the use of **pageContext** attributes. To support a scripting variable, you use the **<variable>** element in a .tld file. The **<variable>** element supports the child elements you see in Table 8-6. Note that you need to use at least the **<name-given>** element or the **<name-from-attribute>** element.

Element	Does This
<declare>	Specifies if the variable refers to a new object. Set to **true** (the default) or **false**.
<name-from-attribute>	Sets the name of an attribute whose value will give the name of the variable.
<name-given>	Gives the variable a name.
<scope>	Specifies the scope of the scripting variable: AT_BEGIN means from start tag to end of page, AT_END means after end tag to end of page, NESTED means between start tag and end tag. NESTED is the default.
<variable-class>	Specifies the name of the class of the variable. The default is java.lang.String.

Table 8-6 Child Elements of the <variable> Element

As an example, we'll implement the **toppings** array as a scripting variable using the **<ch08:createToppings>** tag. When you do, that array will become available in your JSP code automatically. To create this new scripting variable, you declare it in the .tld file:

```
<?xml version="1.0" encoding="ISO-8859-1"?>
<!DOCTYPE taglib PUBLIC
    "-//Sun Microsystems, Inc.//DTD JSP Tag Library 1.2//EN"
    "http://java.sun.com/dtd/web-jsptaglibrary_1_2.dtd">
<taglib>
  <tlib-version>1.0</tlib-version>
  <jsp-version>1.2</jsp-version>
  <short-name>CustomTags</short-name>
  <description>Example tags.</description>
  <tag>
    <name>iterator</name>
    <tag-class>ch08.ch08_09</tag-class>
  </tag>
  <tag>
    <name>createToppings</name>
    <tag-class>ch08.ch08_12</tag-class>
    <variable>
      <name-given>toppings</name-given>
      <variable-class>java.lang.String []</variable-class>
      <declare>true</declare>
      <scope>AT_END</scope>
    </variable>
  </tag>
</taglib>
```

Now the **toppings** variable will be filled automatically with the **toppings** array by the **<ch08:createToppings>** tag, and you can access it directly in your JSP code. The results appear in Figure 8-5, where you can see how easy it is to pass data from custom tags to JSP code.

That completes our discussion of creating custom tags for use in Struts applications. Struts applications often use custom tags to make life easier for the developer and to allow for easy code reuse. With custom tags, you can augment the resources Struts gives you in its own custom tags.

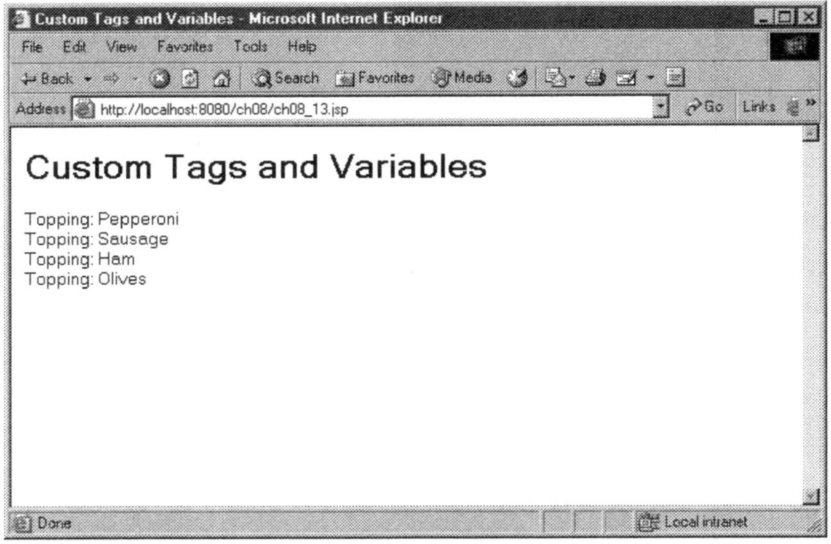

Figure 8-5 Creating scripting variables using custom tags

Module 8 Mastery Check

1. What JSP directive do you use to connect a tag library prefix with the tag library's .tld file?

   A. **<% taglibrary %>**

   B. **<%@ taglibrary %>**

   C. **<%@ taglib %>**

   D. **<% taglib %>**

2. Which element do you use to set up a tag library in a .tld file?

   A. **<name>**

   B. **<taglib>**

   C. **<%taglib%>**

   D. **<%@taglib>**

3. What elements are required inside a **<tag>** element in a .tld file?

   A. The **<taglib>** and **<class>** child elements are required.

   B. The **<tagname>** and **<class>** child elements are required.

   C. The **<name>** and **<class-name>** child elements are required.

   D. The **<name>** and **<tag-class>** child elements are required.

4. What class do you base the Java code for a custom tag on?

   A. **TagSupport**

   B. **Tag**

   C. **TagLib**

   D. **TagLibrary**

5. What method do you use to handle the case where the end of an element is encountered?

   A. **endElement**

   B. **doEndElement**

   C. **doEndTag**

   D. **doEnd**

6. How can you access a **JSPWriter** object in your tag's code that will enable you to write to the result web page?

   A. You can call **pageContext.getOut()**.

   B. You can call **page.getWriter()**.

   C. You can call **servletContext.getWriter()**.

   D. You can call **pageContext.getWriter()**.

7. What child element is required inside the .tld file **<attribute>** element?

   A. **<class>**

   B. **<type>**

   C. **<length>**

   D. **<name>**

8. What method do you use in the Java code for a tag to pass data to a web page?

   A. **pageContext.setValue**

   B. **pageContext.setParameter**

   C. **pageContext.setAttribute**

   D. You can't use a method to do that.

9. Which interface must you implement to create an iterating tag?

   A. **Iterate**

   B. **IIterate**

   C. **Iteration**

   D. **IterationTag**

10. When you don't want to iterate any more in an iterating tag, what constant should you return from the **doAfterBody** method?

    A. **STOP_ITERATION**

    B. **CANCEL**

    C. **SKIP_BODY**

    D. **EVAL_PAGE**

Module 9

The Struts Validator Framework

CRITICAL SKILLS

Up to this point, we've been handling user-data validation ourselves by writing customized code in either the action or form bean code. That means we've been responsible for reading form properties and validating data ourselves.

However, there's another mechanism that Struts offers to perform validation: the Validator framework. This module is about seeing that framework at work. There are all kinds of built-in validation rules in this framework, and once you connect your data up to it, it'll handle your data validation automatically.

We'll start with the application shown in Figure 9-1. This application lets us enter various values of various data types, as shown in the figure.

When you click the Submit button, the data the user entered is displayed in the application's Results page, as shown in Figure 9-2. We're going to implement data validation using this project and all the data types shown in the figure.

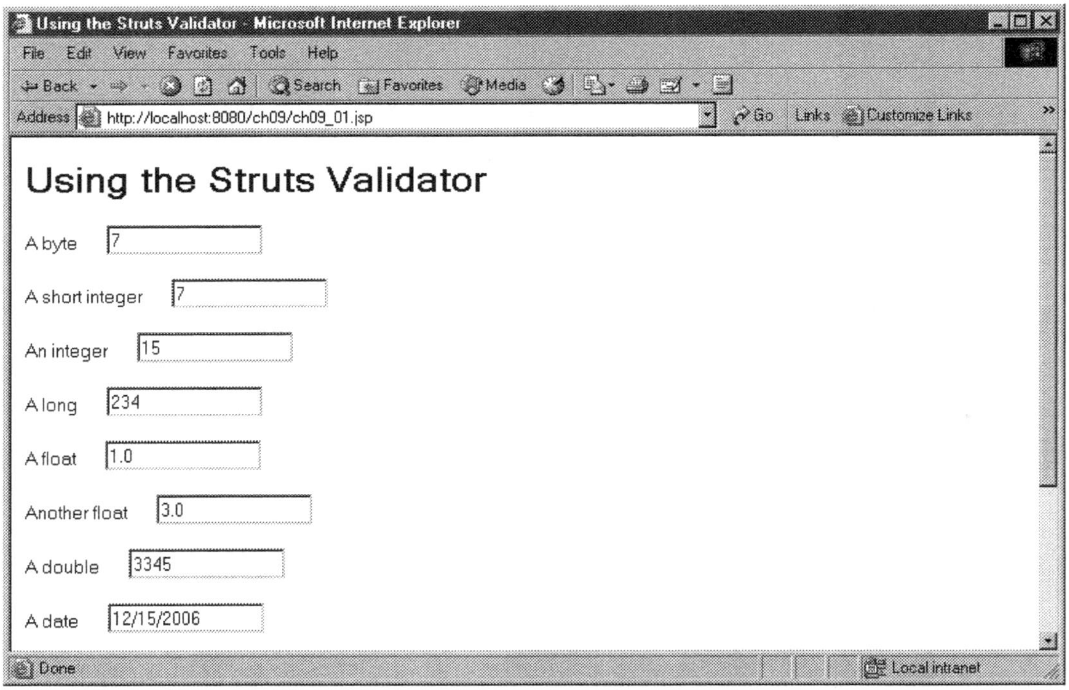

Figure 9-1 Entering data into a web page

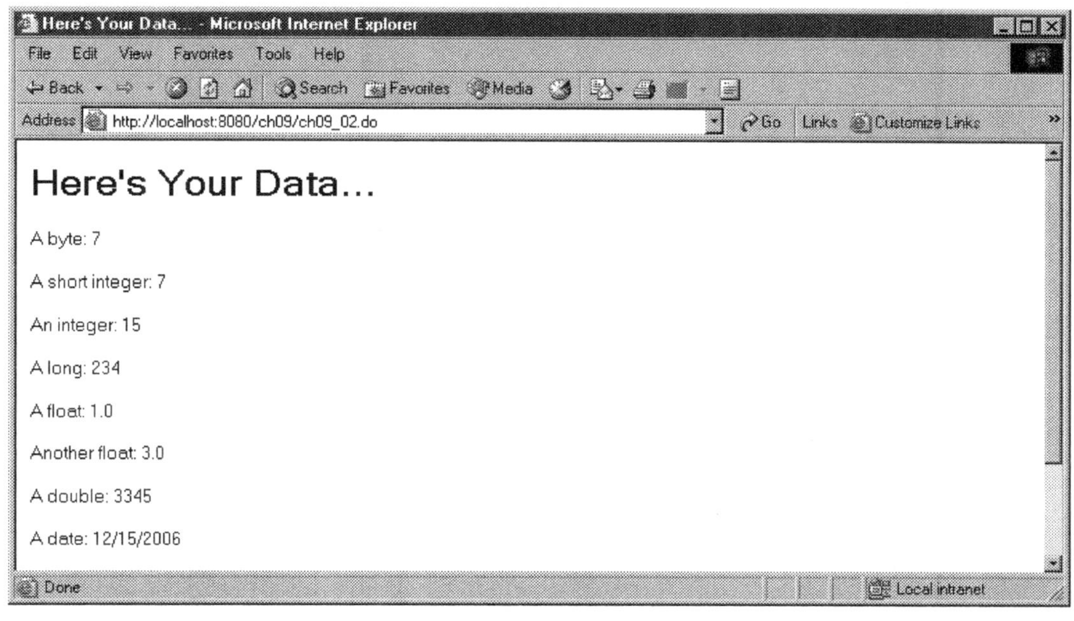

Figure 9-2 The Results page

Here's what the Welcome page shown in Figure 9-1 looks like—the plan is to change this page to handle automatic validation in this module:

```
<%@ taglib uri="/WEB-INF/struts-bean.tld" prefix="bean" %>
<%@ taglib uri="/WEB-INF/struts-html.tld" prefix="html" %>
<%@ taglib uri="/WEB-INF/struts-logic.tld" prefix="logic" %>

<html:html>
    <head>
    <title>Using the Struts Validator</title>
    <html:base/>
</head>

<body>
    <h1>Using the Struts Validator</h1>

    <html:form action="ch09_02">
```

```
        <bean:message key="ch09_03.byte.text"/>
         
         
         
        <html:text property="byte" size="15" maxlength="15"/>
        <br>
        <br>
        <bean:message key="ch09_03.short.text"/>
         
         
         
        <html:text property="short" size="15" maxlength="15"/>
        <br>
        <br>
        <bean:message key="ch09_03.integer.text"/>
         
         
         
        <html:text property="integer" size="15" maxlength="15"/>
        <br>
        <br>
          .
          .
          .
        <bean:message key="ch09_03.zip.text"/>
         
         
         
        <html:text property="zip" size="5" maxlength="5"/>
        <br>
        <br>
        <html:submit property="submit">
           Submit
        </html:submit>
         
        <html:reset>
           Reset
        </html:reset>
  </html:form>
  </body>
  </html:html>
```

The prompts shown in Figure 9-1 that label the various text fields are stored in application.properties:

```
ch09_03.byte.text=A byte
ch09_03.short.text=A short integer
ch09_03.integer.text=An integer
ch09_03.long.text=A long
ch09_03.float.text=A float
ch09_03.floatRange.text=Another float
ch09_03.double.text=A double
ch09_03.date.text=A date
ch09_03.creditCard.text=A credit card
ch09_03.city.text=Your city
ch09_03.zip.text=Your zip
```

The action is very simple in this project; all it does is forward control to the Results page:

```
package ch09;

import javax.servlet.http.HttpServletRequest;
import javax.servlet.http.HttpServletResponse;
import org.apache.struts.action.*;

public final class ch09_02 extends Action {

    public ActionForward execute(ActionMapping mapping,
        ActionForm form,
        HttpServletRequest request,
        HttpServletResponse response)
        throws Exception
    {
        return mapping.findForward("success");
    }
}
```

The form bean has one property for each of the text fields shown in the Welcome page shown in Figure 9-1:

```
package ch09;

import javax.servlet.http.HttpServletRequest;
import org.apache.struts.action.ActionMapping;
import org.apache.struts.validator.ValidatorForm;

public final class ch09_03 extends ActionForm {

    private String byteData = null;
    private String shortData = null;
```

```
private String integerData = null;
private String longData = null;
private String floatData = null;
private String floatDataRange = null;
private String doubleData = null;
private String dateData = null;
private String creditData = null;
private String cityData = null;
private String zipData = null;

public String getByte()
{
   return byteData;
}

public void setByte(String byteData)
{
        this.byteData = byteData;
}

public String getShort()
{
   return shortData;
}

public void setShort(String shortData)
{
         this.shortData = shortData;
}
    .
    .
    .
public String getZip()
{
   return zipData;
}

public void setZip(String zipData)
{
        this.zipData = zipData;
}

public void reset(ActionMapping mapping, HttpServletRequest request)
{
   byteData = null;
   shortData = null;
```

```
        integerData = null;
        longData = null;
        floatData = null;
        floatDataRange = null;
        doubleData = null;
        dateData = null;
        creditData = null;
        cityData = null;
        zipData = null;
    }
}
```

Finally, the Results page displays the data the user entered, using **<bean:write>** to recover the data in each of the bean properties:

```
<%@ taglib uri="/WEB-INF/struts-bean.tld" prefix="bean" %>

<HTML>
    <HEAD>
        <TITLE>Here's Your Data...</TITLE>
    </HEAD>

    <BODY>
        <H1>Here's Your Data...</H1>

        <bean:message key="ch09_03.byte.text"/>:
        <bean:write name="ch09_03" property="byte"/>
        <BR>
        <BR>
        <bean:message key="ch09_03.short.text"/>:
        <bean:write name="ch09_03" property="short"/>
        <BR>
        <BR>
        <bean:message key="ch09_03.integer.text"/>:
        <bean:write name="ch09_03" property="integer"/>
        .
        .
        .
        <bean:message key="ch09_03.city.text"/>:
        <bean:write name="ch09_03" property="city"/>
        <BR>
        <BR>
        <bean:message key="ch09_03.zip.text"/>:
        <bean:write name="ch09_03" property="zip"/>
        <BR>
    </BODY>
</HTML>
```

That's our project for this module; the next step is to implement the Validator framework and add validation support to this project.

CRITICAL SKILL 9.1

Use the Validator Framework

Earlier in the book, we would have added validation code to the form bean or the action to check our data. That would have looked something like this, where we check the data ourselves, as in this case, where we check for required text:

```
String byte = form.getByte();

if(byte.trim().equals("")) {
    actionerrors.add("ActionErrors.GLOBAL_ERROR", new
     ActionError("error.required"));
}
        .
        .
        .
if(actionerrors.size() != 0) {
    saveErrors(request, actionerrors);
    return new ActionForward(mapping.getInput());
}
```

In this module, we're going to let the Struts Validator framework handle the validation. That starts by deriving our form bean from the **ValidatorForm** class, not **ActionForm**, so make this change to ch09_03.java:

```
package ch09;

import javax.servlet.http.HttpServletRequest;
import org.apache.struts.action.ActionMapping;
import org.apache.struts.validator.ValidatorForm;

public final class ch09_03 extends ValidatorForm {
        .
        .
        .
```

Why the **ValidatorForm** class? This class overrides the **validate** method and implements that method to use the validation rules you specify (in two files, validation.xml and validator-rules.xml) to validate the data instead of asking you to do your own validation. The idea is

Field	Means
private **static org.apache.commons.logging.Log log**	Logging instance variable
protected **int page**	Indicates the current page of a multipage form
protected **org.apache.commons.validator.ValidatorResults validatorResults**	Results returned from the validation

Table 9-1 Fields of the ValidatorForm Class

simple—the Validator framework handles the **validate** method for you; no code is needed. You can see the fields of the **ValidatorForm** class in Table 9-1 and its methods in Table 9-2.

Now that we're using the **ValidatorForm** class, we have to add the Validator as a Struts *plug-in*. To do that, we make this change to struts-config.xml, where we're creating a new plug-in using a **<plug-in>** element, the **org.apache.struts.validator.ValidatorPlugIn** class,

Method	Means
int getPage()	Gets a page.
java.util.Map getResultValueMap()	Returns the values from any validation that are not other null or Boolean.
org.apache.commons.validator.ValidatorResults getValidatorResults()	Returns results of the validation performed by the Validator.
protected **void log(java.lang.String message)**	Deprecated. Use common logging to log debug messages.
protected **void log(java.lang.String message, java.lang.Throwable throwable)**	Deprecated. Use common logging to log debug messages.
void reset(ActionMapping mapping, javax.servlet.http.HttpServletRequest request)	Resets all properties to default values.
void setPage(int page)	Sets a page.
void setValidatorResults(org.apache.commons .validator.ValidatorResults validatorResults)	Sets the results of the validation.
ActionErrors validate(ActionMapping mapping, javax.servlet.http.HttpServletRequest request)	Validates the properties that have been set from this HTTP request.

Table 9-2 Methods of the ValidatorForm Class

and associating the files validation.xml and validator-rules.xml (which set the validation rules we want to use and which we'll store in **ch09/WEB-INF**) with the plug-in:

```
<?xml version="1.0" encoding="ISO-8859-1" ?>

<!DOCTYPE struts-config PUBLIC
          "-//Apache Software Foundation//DTD Struts Configuration 1.1//EN"
          "http://jakarta.apache.org/struts/dtds/struts-config_1_1.dtd">

<struts-config>

  <form-beans>
    <form-bean name="ch09_03"
        type="ch09.ch09_03"/>
  </form-beans>

  <action-mappings>
    <action path="/ch09_02"
            type="ch09.ch09_02"
            name="ch09_03"
            scope="request"
            validate="true"
            input="/ch09_01.jsp">
       <forward name="success"  path="/ch09_04.jsp"/>
    </action>
  </action-mappings>

  <message-resources
    parameter="resources.application"/>

<plug-in className="org.apache.struts.validator.ValidatorPlugIn">
  <set-property property="pathnames" value="/WEB-INF/validator-rules.xml,
        /WEB-INF/validation.xml"/>
  </plug-in>

</struts-config>
```

The validator-rules.xml file contains the definition of the *standard rules* that come built into the Validator framework, and validation.xml holds your own validation rules, built on the standard rules. We'll take a look at the standard, built-in rules first.

CRITICAL SKILL 9.2

Use the Standard Rules

You can see the standard Validator rules in Table 9-3; for example, the **required** rule says that a field is required. When you set up your own rules, you can refer to the standard rules by name.

Rule	Means
byte	Must be a byte
creditcard	Must be a valid credit card number
date	Must be a date
double	Must be a double
email	Must be is a valid e-mail address
float	Must be a float
floatRange	Sets the allowed float range
integer	Must be an integer
intRange	Sets the allowed integer range
invalid	Data is considered invalid
long	Must be a long
maxlength	Sets maximum length
minlength	Sets minimum length
required	Required field
short	Must be a short

Table 9-3 The Standard Validator Rules

The standard rules are set up in validator-rules.xml, including the JavaScript that can be used to enforce them in the browser. For example, here's how the **required** standard rule is defined in validator-rules.xml:

```
<validator name="required"
            classname="org.apache.struts.validator.FieldChecks"
               method="validateRequired"
         methodParams="java.lang.Object,
                       org.apache.commons.validator.ValidatorAction,
                       org.apache.commons.validator.Field,
                       org.apache.struts.action.ActionErrors,
                       javax.servlet.http.HttpServletRequest"
                  msg="errors.required">

         <javascript><![CDATA[
            function validateRequired(form) {
                var isValid = true;
                var focusField = null;
                var i = 0;
```

```
            var fields = new Array();
            oRequired = new required();
            for (x in oRequired) {
               var field = form[oRequired[x][0]];

                if (field.type == 'text' ||
                    field.type == 'textarea' ||
                    field.type == 'file' ||
                    field.type == 'select-one' ||
                    field.type == 'radio' ||
                    field.type == 'password') {
                    .
                    .
                    .
        // Trim whitespace from left and right sides of s.
        function trim(s) {
            return s.replace( /^\s*/, "" ).replace( /\s*$/, "" );
        }

        ]]>
     </javascript>

  </validator>
```

The beginning of validator-rules.xml lists the default error messages you should add to your application.properties file. Here they are; add them to application.properties now: These are the default error messages associated with each validator defined in this file. They should be added to your project's ApplicationResources.properties file or you can associate new ones by modifying the pluggable validators msg attributes in this file.

```
# Struts Validator Error Messages
errors.required={0} is required.
errors.minlength={0} can not be less than {1} characters.
errors.maxlength={0} can not be greater than {1} characters.
errors.invalid={0} is invalid.

errors.byte={0} must be a byte.
errors.short={0} must be a short.
errors.integer={0} must be an integer.
errors.long={0} must be a long.
errors.float={0} must be a float.
errors.double={0} must be a double.

errors.date={0} is not a date.
errors.range={0} is not in the range {1} through {2}.
errors.creditcard={0} is an invalid credit card number.
errors.email={0} is an invalid e-mail address.
```

Here, parameters like **{0}** and **{1}** will be replaced with text we supply to make these error messages make sense to the user. We can edit these error messages as we like in application.properties, of course. In addition to these error messages, we'll also add this text to application.properties for the header of the errors list that will be displayed:

```
errors.header=<h2><font color="red">Errors</font></h2>Please correct
the following error(s):
```

Note that the validator-rules.xml file will be different in different versions of Struts; validator-rules.xml is quite different in Struts 1.1 versus Struts 1.2, so be sure to use the version that matches your version of Struts.

To put these standard rules to work, you create your own rules that build on them.

CRITICAL SKILL 9.3

Create Your Own Rules

You create your own validation rules in validation.xml. This file starts with the usual XML declaration and an XML **<!DOCTYPE>** element to tell XML software where to find the DTD (Document Type Definition) for this kind of file:

```
<?xml version="1.0" encoding="ISO-8859-1" ?>

<!DOCTYPE form-validation PUBLIC
    "-//Apache Software Foundation//DTD Commons Validator Rules
Configuration 1.0//EN"
    "http://jakarta.apache.org/commons/dtds/validator_1_0.dtd">
        .
        .
        .
```

The document element here is **<form-validation>**. To set up the rules for our form bean, **ch09_03**, you use a **<form>** element and the **name** attribute inside a **<formset>** element, like this:

```
<?xml version="1.0" encoding="ISO-8859-1" ?>

<!DOCTYPE form-validation PUBLIC
    "-//Apache Software Foundation//DTD Commons Validator Rules
Configuration 1.0//EN"
    "http://jakarta.apache.org/commons/dtds/validator_1_0.dtd">

<form-validation>
```

```
    <formset>

        <form name="ch09_03">
          .
          .
          .
        </form>

    </formset>
</form-validation>
```

You set up your validation rules inside the **<form>** element. You'll do that now, starting with the **byte** field that's at the top of the Welcome page shown in Figure 9-1.

CRITICAL SKILL 9.4 Handle Bytes

To demand that the value entered into a field be a valid byte, we can use the standard **byte** rule. To make this field required, we can use the **required** rule. In our Welcome page, we give the name **byte** to the field that should contain a byte value:

```
<html:form action="ch09_02">

  <bean:message key="ch09_03.byte.text"/>
   
   
   
  <html:text property="byte" size="15" maxlength="15"/>
  <br>
  <br>
```

To constrain the legal values for this field, you create a rule for the **byte** field in the **ch09_03** bean with the **<field>** element, setting the property attribute to the name of the property you want to constrain:

```
<form name="ch09_03">
   <field property="byte"
     .
     .
     .
   </field>
```

To use a standard rule or rules, we assign a comma-delimited list of rules to the **depends** attribute of the **<field>** element like this, where we're using the standard **byte** and **required** rules:

```
<form name="ch09_03">
   <field property="byte"
       depends="required,byte">?
       .
       .
       .
   </field>
```

If the value the user entered is not a value that can be stored as a byte, the error message **errors.byte** will be displayed; that message looks like this in application.properties:

```
errors.byte={0} must be a byte.
```

To fill in a value for the **{0}** parameter, we can use an element named **<arg0>** inside the **<field>** element. In this case, we'll use the label text for the byte field that's displayed in the Welcome page. That label text is **ch09_03.byte.text**, as we've defined it earlier in this module in application.properties:

```
ch09_03.byte.text=A byte
```

Here's how we set the **{0}** parameter to **ch09_03.byte.text** in the rule we're creating using the **<arg0>** element's **key** attribute (to set a second parameter's value, you'd use an **<arg1>** element, a third, **<arg2>**, and so on):

```
<form name="ch09_03">
   <field property="byte"
       depends="required,byte">
       <arg0 key="ch09_03.byte.text"/>
   </field>
```

That's it; if the user omits this required field, this application will display an error in the Welcome page, as shown in Figure 9-3. (We're going to add the tags necessary to do this to the Welcome page later in this module.)

If the user enters a value that won't fit into a byte, the error message reflects that, as shown in Figure 9-4.

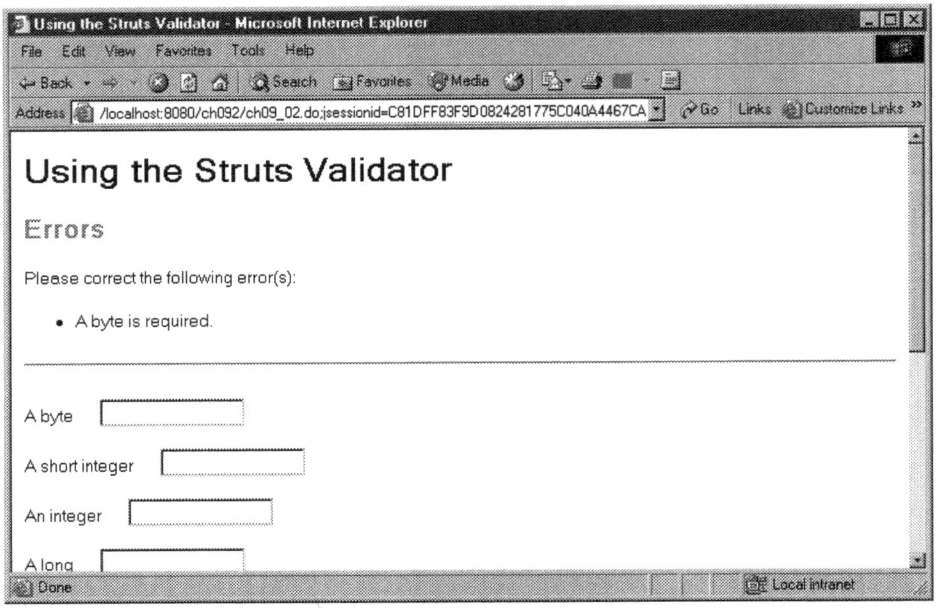

Figure 9-3 Catching an error: required field is missing

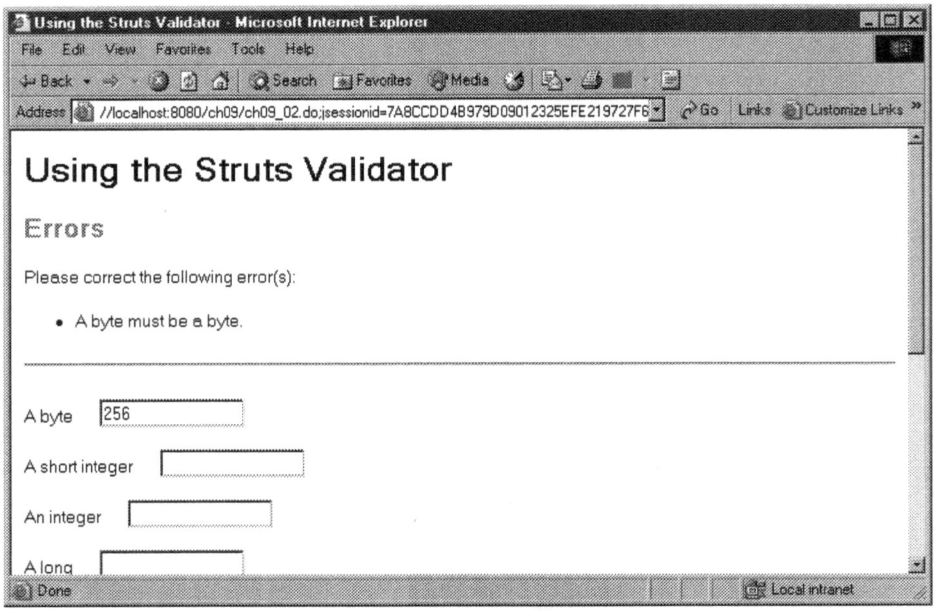

Figure 9-4 Catching an error: not a byte

CRITICAL SKILL 9.5 Handle Shorts

The **short** rule lets us make sure that the value the user enters fits into a short integer. We can handle that easily in validation.xml; for example, here's how we specify that the value entered into the Welcome page's short field must be a valid short integer:

```
<field property="short"
       depends="short">
        <arg0 key="ch09_03.short.text"/>
 </field>
```

CRITICAL SKILL 9.6 Handle Integers

The **integer** rule makes sure that the entered value will fit into an integer. Here's how we enforce that rule for the Welcome page's **integer** field:

```
<field property="integer"
      depends="integer">
        <arg0 key="ch09_03.integer.text"/>
.
.
.
</field>
```

What if you want to restrict the value of the integer to a certain range? That's coming up next.

CRITICAL SKILL 9.7 Handle Integer Ranges

To restrict the value of an integer to a certain range, we can use the **intRange** rule, which we add to the rules checking our **integer** field:

```
<field property="integer"
      depends="integer,intRange">
.
.
.
```

How do you restrict allowed integers to a certain range, say 15 to 25? Rules like **intRange** have variables associated with them, and in this case those variables are named **max** and **min**. You can set the values of the **min** and **max** variables with **<var>** elements, which contain the name of the variable in **<var-name>** elements and the value you're assigning the variable in **<var-value>** elements. To set **min** to 15 and **max** to 25, you'd do this:

```
<field property="integer"
      depends="integer,intRange">
        <arg0 key="ch09_03.integer.text"/>
        <arg1 name="intRange" key="${var:min}" resource="false"/>
        <arg2 name="intRange" key="${var:max}" resource="false"/>
        <var>
           <var-name>min</var-name>
           <var-value>15</var-value>
        </var>
        <var>
            <var-name>max</var-name>
            <var-value>25</var-value>
        </var>
</field>
```

The error message for range errors takes two parameters, corresponding to **min** and **max**, like this:

```
errors.range={0} is not in the range {1} through {2}.
```

To set the **{1}** and **{2}** parameters using the values of **min** and **max**, we can use **<arg1>** and **<arg2>** elements, setting the **name** attribute to **intRange** to indicate what error we're creating parameters for, the **key** value to the value of **min** or **max**, and the **resource** attribute to **false** to indicate that Struts shouldn't search application.properties for these values:

```
<field property="integer"
      depends="integer,intRange">
        <arg0 key="ch09_03.integer.text"/>
        <arg1 name="intRange" key="${var:min}" resource="false"/>
        <arg2 name="intRange" key="${var:max}" resource="false"/>
        <var>
            <var-name>min</var-name>
            <var-value>15</var-value>
        </var>
        <var>
            <var-name>max</var-name>
            <var-value>25</var-value>
        </var>
</field>
```

Now when the user enters a value outside allowed range, they'll see an error like the one that appears in Figure 9-5.

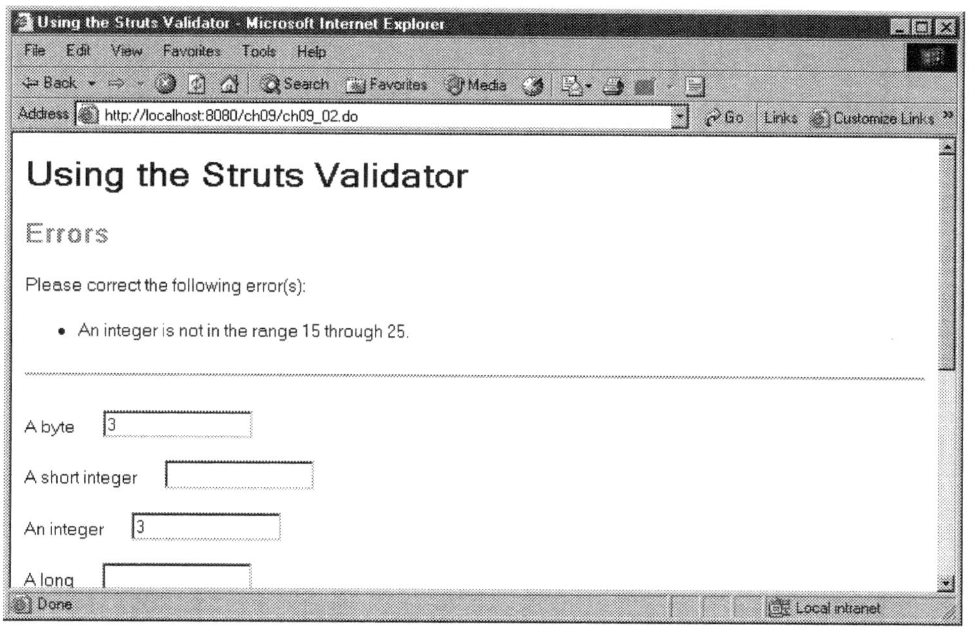

Figure 9-5 Catching an error: out of range

CRITICAL SKILL 9.8

Handle Longs

To ensure a value can fit into a long integer, we can use the **long** standard rule, as here in validation.xml, where we're checking the **long** field from the Welcome page:

```
<field property="long"
       depends="long">
         <arg0 key="ch09_03.long.text"/>
</field>
```

CRITICAL SKILL 9.9

Handle Floats

To make sure that a value will fit into a float value, we can use the standard **float** rule:

```
<field property="float"
       depends="float">
         <arg0 key="ch09_03.float.text"/>
</field>
```

CRITICAL SKILL

9.10 Handle Float Ranges

What if we wanted to confine float values to a certain range? We can do that with **floatRange**, which works much as **intRange** does for integers. Here's how we use **floatRange** in validation.xml to limit floating point values to the range –1.0 to 10.5:

```
<field property="floatRange"
      depends="float,floatRange">
        <arg0 key="ch09_03.floatRange.text"/>
        <arg1 name="floatRange" key="${var:min}" resource="false"/>
        <arg2 name="floatRange" key="${var:max}" resource="false"/>
            <var>
              <var-name>min</var-name>
              <var-value>-1.0</var-value>
            </var>
            <var>
              <var-name>max</var-name>
              <var-value>10.5</var-value>
            </var>
</field>
```

CRITICAL SKILL

9.11 Handle Doubles

We can handle validation for doubles using the **double** standard rule. Here's how we make sure that the **double** field in the Welcome page holds a value that can be held in a double, if one is entered:

```
<field property="double"
      depends="double">
        <arg0 key="ch09_03.double.text"/>
</field>
```

CRITICAL SKILL

9.12 Handle Dates

What about dates? We can handle dates using the **date** standard rule, which allows dates in many different formats to be entered. In this project, however, we'll set a variable named **datePatternStrict** to restrict allowed dates to the pattern **MM/dd/yyyy**:

```
<field property="date"
      depends="date">
        <arg0 key="ch09_03.date.text"/>
        <var>
```

```
                <var-name>datePatternStrict</var-name>
                <var-value>MM/dd/yyyy</var-value>
            </var>
    </field>
```

CRITICAL SKILL 9.13

Handle Credit Cards

There's even a **creditCard** rule to check if the value entered is a legal credit card number. Here's how we use that rule in this module's project:

```
<field property="creditCard"
      depends="creditCard">
        <arg0 key="ch09_03.creditCard.text"/>
</field>
```

This rule simply checks credit card numbers by checking whether the number satisfies the algorithm for valid credit card numbers.

CRITICAL SKILL 9.14

Handle Masks

One very powerful validation rule is **mask**, which lets you use regular expressions to validate text. Although their syntax is outside the scope of this book, regular expressions let you specify exactly how text strings should read—whether they should be all text, contain punctuation, letters, digits, and so on. In the project for this module, we ask the user to enter their city in a field named **city** in the Welcome page. To make sure that this field contains only lowercase and/or uppercase letters, we can use the simple regular expression **^[a-zA-Z]*$** (^ corresponds to the beginning of a line of text, **$** to the end, and the character set **[a-zA-Z]*** stands for multiple lowercase and/or uppercase letters). Here's what that looks like in validation.xml, using the **mask** variable with the **mask** standard rule:

```
<field property="city"
      depends="mask">
        <arg0 key="ch09_03.city.text"/>
        <var>
            <var-name>mask</var-name>
            <var-value>^[a-zA-Z]*$</var-value>
        </var>
</field>
```

CRITICAL SKILL 9.15

Validate Using Constants

It's also possible to create named constants in validation.xml. For example, to check zip codes, you might create a constant named **zip** corresponding to a regular expression that can check for five-digit zip code. You can create a global constant in an element named **<global>** under the **<form-validation>** document element, like this:

```
<form-validation>
   <global>
      <constant>
        <constant-name>zip</constant-name>
        <constant-value>^\d{5}\d*$</constant-value>
      </constant>
   </global>
        .
        .
        .
```

Or, you can create a local constant in a **<formset>** element:

```
<formset>
   <constant>
     <constant-name>zip</constant-name>
     <constant-value>^\d{5}\d*$</constant-value>
   </constant>
   <form name="ch09_03">
     .
     .
     .
   </form>
```

Now you can refer to that constant in your rules like this, where you're using the zip constant in a rule to ensure the zip field from the Welcome page contains valid five-digit zips:

```
<field property="zip"
      depends="mask">
        <arg0 key="ch09_03.zip.text"/>
        <var>
            <var-name>mask</var-name>
            <var-value>${zip}</var-value>
        </var>
</field>
```

CRITICAL SKILL

9.16 Display Errors

At this point, we've seen how to connect validation rules to the contents of various Welcome page fields. So how do we display a list of errors in the Welcome page if there's been a problem?

Error text is handled as messages with the Validator framework. That means we can use the Struts **<logic:messagesPresent>** tag in the Welcome page to see if any messages are present. If so, we'll display the header text for the list of errors, setting up the error list with a **<ul>** unordered list tag:

```
<logic:messagesPresent>
    <bean:message key="errors.header"/>
    <ul>
    .
    .
    .
```

You recover the various possible errors one by one. For example, to recover and display the error for the **byte** field, if there is such an error, use these elements:

```
<html:messages id="error" property="byte">
    <li><bean:write name="error"/></li>
</html:messages>
```

Here's what you should add to the Welcome page to display the list of errors returned by the Validator framework. The **<html:form>** element that holds the controls that appear in the Welcome page follows this list.

```
<%@ taglib uri="/WEB-INF/struts-bean.tld" prefix="bean" %>
<%@ taglib uri="/WEB-INF/struts-html.tld" prefix="html" %>
<%@ taglib uri="/WEB-INF/struts-logic.tld" prefix="logic" %>

<html:html>
    <head>
    <title>Using the Struts Validator</title>
    <html:base/>
</head>

<body>
    <h1>Using the Struts Validator</h1>

    <logic:messagesPresent>
        <bean:message key="errors.header"/>
```

```
        <ul>
            <html:messages id="error" property="byte">
                <li><bean:write name="error"/></li>
            </html:messages>
            <html:messages id="error" property="short">
                <li><bean:write name="error"/></li>
            </html:messages>
            <html:messages id="error" property="integer">
                <li><bean:write name="error"/></li>
            </html:messages>
            <html:messages id="error" property="long">
                <li><bean:write name="error"/></li>
            </html:messages>
            <html:messages id="error" property="float">
                <li><bean:write name="error"/></li>
            </html:messages>
            <html:messages id="error" property="floatRange">
                <li><bean:write name="error"/></li>
            </html:messages>
            <html:messages id="error" property="double">
                <li><bean:write name="error"/></li>
            </html:messages>
            <html:messages id="error" property="date">
                <li><bean:write name="error"/></li>
            </html:messages>
            <html:messages id="error" property="creditCard">
                <li><bean:write name="error"/></li>
            </html:messages>
            <html:messages id="error" property="city">
                <li><bean:write name="error"/></li>
            </html:messages>
            <html:messages id="error" property="zip">
                <li><bean:write name="error"/></li>
            </html:messages>
        </ul>
        <hr>
    </logic:messagesPresent>

    <html:form action="ch09_02">
        .
        .
        .
```

That completes all the files in our project for this module. This project works as we want it to; we've been able to support full validation in this example using the Struts Validator framework. But there's more to consider, such as using that framework with **DynaActionForm** objects.

CRITICAL SKILL 9.17

Use DynaActionForm Objects and Validation

What if you wanted to perform validation when using a **DynaActionForm** instead of a standard form bean? As you saw, you can convert a form bean's code to use the Validator framework if you use the **ValidatorForm** class instead of the **ActionForm** class. But what about **DynaActionForm** objects?

It turns out that this is easier than you might think: all you have to do is to use the **DynaValidatorForm** class instead of the **DynaActionForm** class. Here's how that might look in struts-config.xml:

```
<form-bean
    name="logonForm"
    type="org.apache.struts.action.DynaValidatorForm">
    <form-property
        name="username"
        type="java.lang.String"/>
    <form-property
        name="password"
        type="java.lang.String"/>
```

As before, you connect the Validator framework to Struts by creating a new plug-in using the **org.apache.struts.validator.ValidatorPlugIn** class and associating the files validation.xml and validator-rules.xml with the plug-in. You can find the fields of the **DynaActionForm** class in Table 9-4 and its methods in Table 9-5.

Field	Means
private **static org.apache.commons.logging.Log log**	Logging instance variable
protected **int page**	Indicates the current page of a multipage form
protected **org.apache.commons.validator.ValidatorResults validatorResults**	Results returned from the validation

Table 9-4 The Fields of the DynaActionForm Class

Method	Means
int getPage()	Gets a page.
java.util.Map getResultValueMap()	Returns the values from any validation that are not other null or Boolean.
org.apache.commons.validator.ValidatorResults getValidatorResults()	Returns results of the validation performed by the Validator.
protected **void log(java.lang.String message)**	Deprecated. Use common logging to log debug messages.
protected **void log(java.lang.String message, java.lang.Throwable throwable)**	Deprecated. Use common logging to log debug messages.
void reset(ActionMapping mapping, javax.servlet.http.HttpServletRequest request)	Resets all properties to default values.
void setPage(int page)	Sets a page.
void setValidatorResults(org.apache.commons .validator.ValidatorResults validatorResults)	Sets the results of the validation.
ActionErrors validate(ActionMapping mapping, javax.servlet.http.HttpServletRequest request)	Validates the properties that have been set from this HTTP request.

Table 9-5 The Methods of the DynaActionForm Class

Use JavaScript for Validation

It's worth noting that we can also use JavaScript for validation in the client browser. Here's an example where we're checking to make sure that the user entered a value when asked for their name:

```
<HTML>
    <HEAD>
        <TITLE>Validation Example</TITLE>
        <SCRIPT LANGUAGE="JavaScript">
            <!--
            function checkData()
            {
                if(document.form1.text1.value == ""){
                    window.alert("Please enter your name.")
                    return false
                } else {
                    return true
                }
```

```
            }
            // -->
        </SCRIPT>
    </HEAD>

    <BODY>
        <H1>Validation Example</H1>
        <FORM NAME="form1" METHOD="POST"
            ACTION="http://www.strutspower.com/data.jsp"
            ONSUBMIT="return checkData()">
            Please enter your name:
            <INPUT TYPE="TEXT" ID="text1" VALUE="">
            <BR>
            <INPUT TYPE="SUBMIT" NAME="Submit" VALUE="Submit">
            <INPUT TYPE="RESET">
        </FORM>
    </BODY>
</HTML>
```

If the user hasn't entered a name, they'll see a message box with the message "Please enter your name."

Use Struts 1.2

In the early release version of Struts 1.2 available as of this writing, there have been big internal changes in the Validator framework. Once you use the new classes in struts.jar and the new validation-rules.xml, this module's project will work without any other changes. However, the Validator framework is one of the big issues in Struts 1.2, so don't be surprised if other changes are coming.

✓ Module 9 Mastery Check

1. What class do you use in your form bean to support validation?

   A. **ActionForm**

   B. **ValidationForm**

   C. **ValidatorForm**

   D. **ValidatorActionForm**

2. What class do you use in the **<plug-in>** element to work with the Validator framework?

   A. **org.apache.struts.ValidatorPlugIn**

   B. **org.apache.struts.validation.ValidatorPlugIn**

   C. **org.apache.validator.ValidatorPlugIn**

   D. **org.apache.struts.validator.ValidatorPlugIn**

3. What file do you use to set up your own validation rules?

   A. validator.xml

   B. validation.xml

   C. validation-rules.xml

   D. validator-rules.xml

4. What element do you use inside a <plug-in> element to specify where to find the two XML files used to set validation rules?

   A. **<set-property>**

   B. **<property>**

   C. **<filename>**

   D. **<location>**

5. What standard rule lets you specify maximum length?

   A. **length**

   B. **maximumLen**

   C. **maxLen**

   D. **maxLength**

6. What standard rule(s) do you use to specify maximum and minimum integer values?

   A. **max** and **min**

   B. **maxInt** and **minInt**

   C. **integerRange**

   D. **intRange**

7. What standard rule do you use to make sure the user enters data in the corresponding field?

   A. **necessary**

   B. **standard**

C. **requirement**

D. **required**

8. What variable do you use to set the minimum value of an integer range?

A. **minimum**

B. **min**

C. **minInt**

D. **minInteger**

9. What element do you use to set the first argument passed to an error string?

A. **<arg0>**

B. **<arg>**

C. **<argument>**

D. **<arg1>**

10. What two elements do you use to set up a constant's name and contents?

A. **<name>** and **<contents>**

B. <**constant**> and <**contents**>

C. **<constant-name>** and **<constant-value>**

D. **<constant-name>** and **<constant-contents>**

Module 10

The Tiles Framework

CRITICAL SKILLS

10.1 Create a Basic Page

10.2 Use <tiles:putList>

10.3 Use the <definition> Tag

10.4 Use XML-Based Definitions

10.5 Overload Definitions

10.6 Extend Definitions

10.7 Use Definitions as Attributes

10.8 Use a Definition as an ActionForward

Another big aspect of Struts programming that you should know about is using the Tiles framework. Like the name Struts, Tiles is not an acronym—the idea is that you can construct the appearance of application pages using "tiles" that you construct yourself. All you need to do is to create a template that lays out the appearance of a page as you want it, and then tell the Tiles framework what tiles you want to include. Each tile is just a web page in its own right, and they'll all be inserted where you want them.

This connects well with Struts because the pages you arrange with Tiles can all be Struts-aware, containing forms that connect to various actions. Also, as we'll see at the end of this module, you can use a Tiles definition (corresponding to a Tiles layout) as a Struts action forward. Tiles interfaces so well with Struts that it's included in the Struts 1.1 struts.jar file, which means the Java support is already there for us to use.

There are other mechanisms to include pages in a template page like this, such as the **<jsp:include>** action. But Tiles has more to offer; while **<jsp:include>** just includes a page at a specific point, Tiles lets you specify the format of the final page by specifically including headers, footers, and other page elements. You can see an example page built with Tiles in Figure 10-1, with these elements showing.

So how does the Tiles framework work?

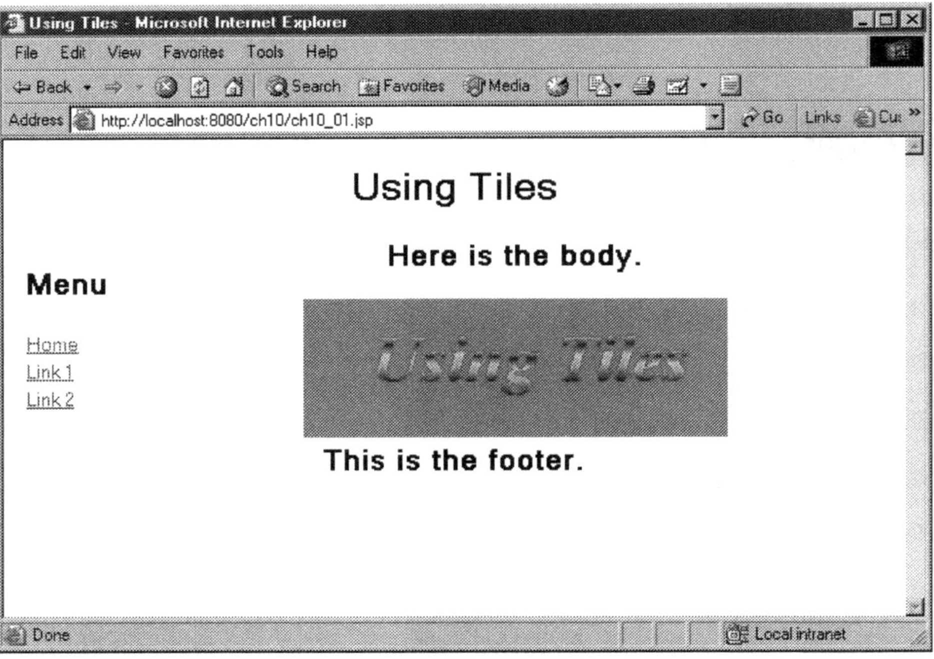

Figure 10-1 A page created using the Tiles framework

Working with Tiles

The Tiles framework depends on you first creating a layout template and then creating individual tiles that will be placed in various places in the template. The idea is that this model promotes reusability, as well as easy internationalization of your pages. If the only thing that changes between the 500 web pages on your site is the individual page's body and you want to keep the header, footer, and a navigation menu the same for each page, Tiles can help you out.

To use Tiles, you create a layout page, often using HTML tables or Cascading Style Sheet (CSS) styles to arrange elements where you want them. The tile pages you create will be inserted into that layout. Although you're free to lay out your pages as you want them using Tiles, you typically use Tiles to construct a page using these common four page elements (as we have done in Figure 10-2):

- **Header** Text and graphics that appear at the top of the Results page.
- **Footer** Text and graphics that appear at the bottom of the Results page.
- **Menu** A set of navigation hyperlinks, usually appearing to the left of the Results page's body, as you see in Figure 10-1.
- **Body** The page's content, sandwiched between the header and footer vertically and placed to the right of the menu.

For example, here's what ch10_01.jsp, which you see in Figure 10-1, looks like (we'll take this web page apart in a few pages):

```
<%@ taglib uri="/WEB-INF/struts-tiles.tld" prefix="tiles" %>

<tiles:insert page="Layout.jsp" flush="true">
  <tiles:put name="title"  value="Using Tiles" />
  <tiles:put name="header" value="header.jsp" />
  <tiles:put name="footer" value="footer.jsp" />
  <tiles:put name="menu"   value="menu.jsp" />
  <tiles:put name="body"   value="body.jsp" />
</tiles:insert>
```

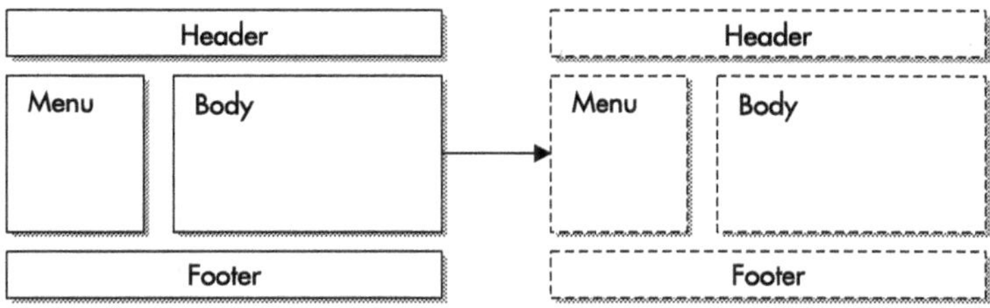

Figure 10-2 Tiles Page elements

You can see what's going on here—we specify the layout page we want to insert items into with the **<tiles:insert>** element, which contains **<tiles:put>** elements that set attributes we've given names to like **title**, **header**, **footer**, and so on to various values. In the layout page, we'll be able to recover those attributes and assemble our Results page (we'll use an HTML table to arrange the various items we want to display).

Installing Tiles

How do you actually get Struts working? The Tiles .class files you need come built into the Struts 1.1 struts.jar file, but like the Validator framework, you have to install Tiles as a plug-in in struts-config.xml. Here's what that looks like—in this case, we're connecting a file named tiles-definitions.xml to the Tiles plug-in to hold template definitions (these definitions can appear in .jsp pages or in XML documents, as we're going to see):

```
<struts-config>
         .
         .
         .
  <plug-in className="org.apache.struts.tiles.TilesPlugin" >
    <set-property property="definitions-config"
         value="/WEB-INF/tiles-definitions.xml" />
    <set-property property="moduleAware" value="true" />
  </plug-in>
         .
         .
         .
</struts-config>
```

As is apparent in ch10_01.jsp, which uses the **<tiles:insert>** element and **<tiles:put>** elements, Tiles is based on custom JSP tags. As you can see in the **<%@ taglib %>** directive at the top of ch10_01.jsp, the .tld file for these tags is struts-tiles.tld:

```
<%@ taglib uri="/WEB-INF/struts-tiles.tld" prefix="tiles" %>
```

To register struts-tiles.tld with the server, you add a **<taglib>** element to web.xml, just as you do for the Struts tag libraries (such as struts-html.tld and so on), like this:

```
<web-app>
.
         .
         .
<taglib>
    <taglib-uri>/WEB-INF/struts-tiles.tld</taglib-uri>
    <taglib-location>/WEB-INF/struts-tiles.tld</taglib-location>
```

```
  </taglib>
        .
        .
        .
</web-app>
```

Now the server will look for the Tiles tags definitions in struts-tiles.tld, which comes with Struts 1.1 and which we'll store in ch10/WEB-INF. This .tld file connects the Tiles tags to classes found in struts.jar. For example, this is how the Tiles **<tiles:insert>** element is tied to the class **org.apache.struts.taglib.tiles.InsertTag** and its various attributes in struts-tiles.tld:

```
<?xml version="1.0" encoding="UTF-8"?>

<!DOCTYPE taglib PUBLIC "-//Sun Microsystems, Inc.//DTD JSP Tag Library
1.1//EN" "http://java.sun.com/j2ee/dtds/web-jsptaglibrary_1_1.dtd">
<taglib>
<tlibversion>1.0</tlibversion>
<jspversion>1.1</jspversion>
<shortname>Tiles Tag Library</shortname>
<uri>http://jakarta.apache.org/struts/tags-tiles-1.1</uri>
<tag>
<name>insert</name>
<tagclass>org.apache.struts.taglib.tiles.InsertTag</tagclass>
<bodycontent>JSP</bodycontent>
<attribute>
<name>template</name>
<required>false</required>
<rtexprvalue>true</rtexprvalue>
</attribute>
<attribute>
<name>component</name>
<required>false</required>
<rtexprvalue>true</rtexprvalue>
</attribute>
<attribute>
<name>page</name>
<required>false</required>
<rtexprvalue>true</rtexprvalue>
</attribute>
<attribute>
<name>definition</name>
<required>false</required>
<rtexprvalue>true</rtexprvalue>
</attribute>
<attribute>
<name>attribute</name>
<required>false</required>
<rtexprvalue>false</rtexprvalue>
</attribute>
<attribute>
        .
        .
        .
```

Tag Name	Description
insert	Inserts a tile into a template.
definition	Creates a tile template definition.
put	Puts an attribute into the template context.
putList	Declares a list that will be passed as an attribute to the tile context.
add	Adds an element to the enclosing list. Just like "put," but for lists.
get	Gets the content from request scope that was stored by a put tag.
getAsString	Retrieves the value of the specified attribute.
useAttribute	Uses attribute value inside a page as a JSP-accessible variable.
importAttribute	Imports a Tiles attribute.
initComponentDefinitions	Initializes the Tiles definitions factory.

Table 10-1 The Tiles Tags

You can see the Tiles tags in Table 10-1.

That installs Tiles. How about putting it to work?

CRITICAL SKILL 10.1

Create a Basic Page

As our first example, we're going to create the page you see in Figure 10-1, ch10_01.jsp. We'll start with a **<tiles:insert>** element, which lets you insert tiles into a layout page. In this case, we're going to insert our tiles into a page named Layout.jsp using **<tiles:insert>** and the **page** attribute (setting the **flush** attribute to "true" means the current page's output stream will be flushed):

```
<%@ taglib uri="/WEB-INF/struts-tiles.tld" prefix="tiles" %>

<tiles:insert page="Layout.jsp" flush="true">
        .
        .
        .
</tiles:insert>
```

You can see the attributes of the **<tiles:insert>** element in Table 10-2.

Attribute Name	Means
attribute	Name of an attribute in current tile context.
beanName	Name of the bean used as the value.
beanProperty	The bean property name.
beanScope	Scope which is searched for the bean.
component	Same as **page**.
controllerUrl	URL of a controller called immediately before page is inserted (can denote a Struts action).
definition	Name of the definition to insert.
flush	If **true**, current page out stream is flushed before the insertion operation.
ignore	If **true** and the attribute specified by **name** does not exist, return without writing anything.
name	Name of the entity to insert.
page	Path of the page to insert.
role	If the user is not in the specified role, the tag is ignored.
template	Same as **page**.

Table 10-2 The <tiles:insert> Attributes

To insert the tiles in Layout.jsp, we'll use **<tiles:put>** elements inside the **<tiles:insert>** element. In each **<tiles:put>** element, we specify the name of the tile we want to insert and its value—for example, the body of the Results page will be inserted from the page body.jsp. In this way, we're creating what are called *attributes* in Tiles and assigning each a value:

```
<%@ taglib uri="/WEB-INF/struts-tiles.tld" prefix="tiles" %>

<tiles:insert page="Layout.jsp" flush="true">
  <tiles:put name="title"  value="Using Tiles" />
  <tiles:put name="header" value="header.jsp" />
  <tiles:put name="footer" value="footer.jsp" />
  <tiles:put name="menu"   value="menu.jsp" />
  <tiles:put name="body"   value="body.jsp" />
</tiles:insert>
```

You can see the **<tiles:put>** attributes in Table 10-3.

Attribute	Means
content	Same as **value**
direct	Same as setting type to "string"
name	The identifier for this Tiles attribute
type	The type of the value (set to "string", "page", "template" or "definition")
value	The value associated with this attribute

Table 10-3 The <tiles:put> Attributes

The next step is to create the layout we're going to use, Layout.jsp.

Creating the Layout

In ch10_01.jsp, we "put" the value of several attributes, such as setting the attribute we've named **header** to "header.jsp". We also set the attribute **title** to the text "Using Tiles". Layout.jsp acts like a template you can insert tiles into, and in this case, we're going to use an HTML table to arrange those tiles.

To start, we'll recover the value of the attribute we've named title in ch10_01.jsp, which holds the text we want in the Results page's title. You can do that with the **<tiles:getAsString>** element like this:

```
<%@ taglib uri="/WEB-INF/struts-tiles.tld" prefix="tiles" %>

<html>
    <head>
        <title><tiles:getAsString name="title"/></title>
    </head>
        .
        .
        .
    </body>
</html>
```

The **<tiles:getAsString>** element recovers the value of the attribute you specify and inserts it into the template as you direct—in this case, as the title text for the Results page. You can also use the **<tiles:insert>** element to insert the pages—that is, the tiles—we want to display. Here's how we insert the header, footer, menu, and body, using an HTML table:

```
<%@ taglib uri="/WEB-INF/struts-tiles.tld" prefix="tiles" %>

<html>
    <head>
        <title><tiles:getAsString name="title"/></title>
    </head>

    <body>
        <table width="100%">

            <tr>
                <td colspan="2">
                    <tiles:insert attribute="header" />
                </td>
            </tr>
            <tr>
                <td width="80">
                    <tiles:insert attribute="menu" />
                </td>
                <td>
                    <tiles:insert attribute="body" />
                </td>
            </tr>
            <tr>
                <td colspan="2">
                    <tiles:insert attribute="footer" />
                </td>
            </tr>
        </table>
    </body>
</html>
```

The various tiles like menu.jsp are easy to write. The menu.jsp file just holds the navigation menu you see on the left in Figure 10-1:

```
<table>
<tr>
  <td>
    <h2>Menu</h2>
  </td>
</tr>
<tr>
  <td width="80" valign="top">
    <a href="<%=request.getContextPath()%>/ch10_01.jsp">Home</a>
  </td>
</tr>
```

```
<tr>
  <td width="80" valign="top">
    <a href="">Link 1</a>
  </td>
</tr>
<tr>
  <td width="80" valign="top">
    <a href="">Link 2</a>
  </td>
</tr>
</table>
```

The header.jsp file holds the header text:

```
<center><h1>Using Tiles</h1></center>
```

The body.jsp file just holds the body's text, and in this case also inserts an image, image.jpg, which we'll store in the ch10 directory and refer to as **<%=request.getContextPath()%>/image.jpg** using a little JSP code:

```
<div align="center">
    <h2>Here is the body.</h2>
    <img src="<%=request.getContextPath()%>/image.jpg"
        align="center" border="0">
</div>
```

Finally, here's footer.jsp, which holds the footer's text:

```
<div align="center">
    <h2>This is the footer.</h2>
</div>
```

When you open ch10_01.jsp, the tiles we've created are inserted into the layout. Here's what the HTML sent to the browser ends up as:

```
<html>
<head>
    <title>Using Tiles</title>
</head>

<body>
<TABLE width="100%">

  <TR>
```

```
    <TD colspan="2"><center><h1>Using Tiles</h1></center>

</TD></TR>
  <TR>
    <TD width="80"><table>
<tr>
  <td>
    <h2>Menu</h2>
  </td>
</tr>
<tr>
  <td width="80" valign="top">
    <a href="/ch10/ch10_01.jsp">Home</a>
  </td>
</tr>
<tr>
  <td width="80" valign="top">
    <a href="">Link 1</a>
  </td>
</tr>
<tr>
  <td width="80" valign="top">
    <a href="">Link 2</a>
  </td>
</tr>
</table>
</TD>
    <TD><div align="center">
    <h2>Here is the body.</h2>
    <img src="/ch10/image.jpg" align="center" border="0">
</div></TD></TR>
  <TR>
    <TD colspan="2"><div align="center">
    <h2>This is the footer.</h2>
</div>
</TD>
  </TR>
</TABLE>

</body>
</html>
```

That's our first Tiles example at work; the Results page appears in Figure 10-1. As you can see, it's not too hard to put the Tiles framework to work.

Progress Check

1. What Tiles element do you use to recover the value of a text attribute?
2. What Tiles element do you use to place a tile in the Results page?

CRITICAL SKILL 10.2

Use <tiles:putList>

There's also a utility element, **<tiles:putList>**, that lets you handle lists of tiles all at once. This element is useful when you have many pages to display at once, as when you want to arrange news stories in columns. We'll put this element to work in a new example, ch10_02.jsp, which you can see at work in Figure 10-3. In this case, the body of the Results page is displaying two lists, each in their own column, of web pages (each web page just contains the text "Page 0", "Page 1", and so on in this example).

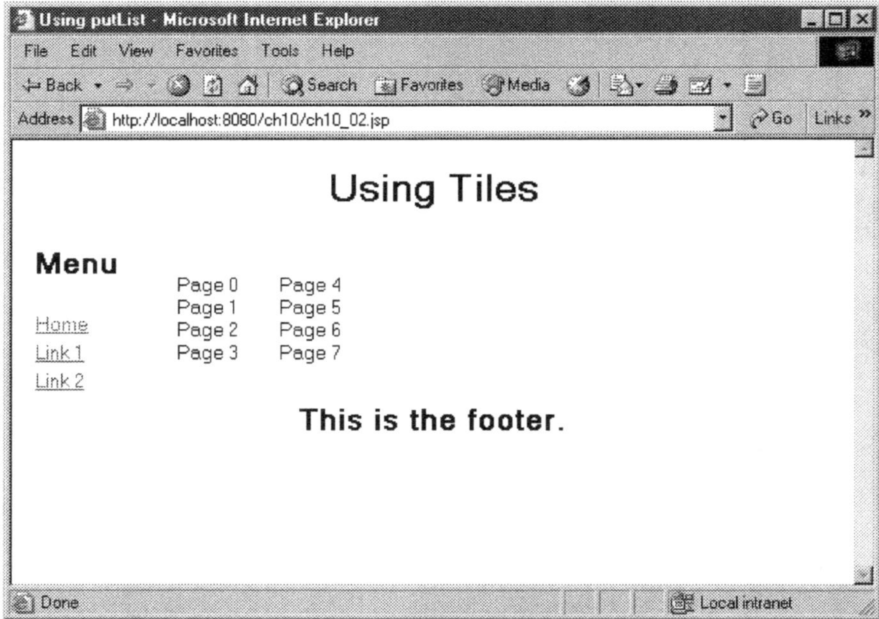

Figure 10-3 Using <tiles:putList>

---

1. **<tiles:getAsString>**
2. **<tiles:insert>**

Here's what ch10_02.jsp looks like—note that the new body of this page is now list.jsp, not body.jsp:

```
<%@ taglib uri="/WEB-INF/struts-tiles.tld" prefix="tiles" %>

<tiles:insert page="Layout.jsp" flush="true">
  <tiles:put name="title"  value="Using putList" />
  <tiles:put name="header" value="header.jsp" />
  <tiles:put name="footer" value="footer.jsp" />
  <tiles:put name="menu"   value="menu.jsp" />
  <tiles:put name="body"   value="list.jsp" />
</tiles:insert>
```

In list.jsp, we'll create two lists of tiles, **itemList0** and **itemList1**, using **<tiles:putList>**. In each **<tiles:putList>** element, we add each item in the list using **<tiles:add>**. Note that we also set an attribute named **numberColumns** to the number of columns we want, and that we're using a new layout here, columnsLayout.jsp (each of the tiles we're inserting, page0.jsp to page7.jsp, just contains text like "Page 0", "Page 1", and so on, as you see in Figure 10-3):

```
<%@ taglib uri="/WEB-INF/struts-tiles.tld" prefix="tiles" %>

<tiles:insert page="/columnsLayout.jsp" flush="true">
  <tiles:put name="numberColumns" value="2" />
  <tiles:putList name="itemList0" >
    <tiles:add value="/page0.jsp" />
    <tiles:add value="/page1.jsp" />
    <tiles:add value="/page2.jsp" />
    <tiles:add value="/page3.jsp" />
  </tiles:putList>
  <tiles:putList name="itemList1" >
    <tiles:add value="/page4.jsp" />
    <tiles:add value="/page5.jsp" />
    <tiles:add value="/page6.jsp" />
    <tiles:add value="/page7.jsp" />
  </tiles:putList>
</tiles:insert>
```

The **<tiles:putList>** element only has one attribute, **name**, which holds the name of the list you're creating. On the other hand, the **<tiles:add>** element has a number of attributes, as you see in Table 10-4.

In columnsLayout.jsp, we will recover the number of columns from the **numberColumns** attribute, storing that value in a JSP-accessible variable named **numberColumnsString** using the **<tiles:useAttribute>** element. This element's purpose is exactly that—to store the value of a Tiles attribute in a JSP-accessible variable.

Attribute Name	Description
beanName	Name of the bean used as the value.
beanProperty	Bean property name.
beanScope	Scope that searched for the bean.
content	The element value; can be a string or an object. Same as **value**.
direct	If **true**, content is printed directly; if **false** (the default), content is included.
role	If the user is in the specified role, the tag is taken into account; otherwise, the tag is ignored.
type	Content type (set to: **string**, **page**, **template**, or **instance**).
value	The element value; can be a string or an object.

Table 10-4 The <tiles:add> Attributes

When we know how many columns there are, we can loop over each column in JSP code, inserting each list in the Results page. When we loop over each column of tiles, we'll use a new layout, internalLayout.jsp, to lay out each column, like this in columnsLayout.jsp:

```
<%@ page import="org.apache.struts.tiles.ComponentContext"%>
<%@ taglib uri="/WEB-INF/struts-tiles.tld" prefix="tiles" %>

<tiles:useAttribute id="numberColumnsString" name="numberColumns"
classname="java.lang.String" />

<table>
    <tr>
    <%
        int number = Integer.parseInt(numberColumnsString);
        ComponentContext context = ComponentContext.getContext(request);
        for(int intLoopIndex = 0; intLoopIndex < number; intLoopIndex++)
        {
            java.util.List listObject =
                (java.util.List)context.getAttribute("itemList" +
                    intLoopIndex);
            pageContext.setAttribute("list", listObject);
    %>
        <td>
           <tiles:insert page="/internalLayout.jsp" flush="true" >
             <tiles:put name="itemsList" beanName="list" beanScope="page" />
           </tiles:insert>
        </td>
    <%
        }
    %>
    </tr>
</table>
```

Attribute Name	Description
classname	Class of the variable.
id	Name of the declared attribute and variable.
ignore	If **true** and the attribute specified by the name does not exist, return without error.
name	The tile's attribute name. This attribute is required.
scope	Scope of the declared attribute. The default is **page**.

Table 10-5 The <tiles:useAttribute> Attributes

You can find the attributes of the **<tiles:useAttribute>** element in Table 10-5.

In the layout for each column, internalLayout.jsp, we insert the items in a list into the Results page, separating them with **
** elements:

```
<%@ page import="java.util.Iterator"%>
<%@ taglib uri="/WEB-INF/struts-tiles.tld" prefix="tiles" %>

<tiles:useAttribute id="listObject" name="itemsList"
classname="java.util.List" />

<%
    Iterator iterator = listObject.iterator();
    while(iterator.hasNext())
    {
        String item = (String)iterator.next();
%>
    <tiles:insert name="<%=item%>" flush="true" />
    <br>
<%
    }
%>
```

You can see the results in Figure 10-3, where we've handled lists of tiles by displaying those lists in columns.

Progress Check

1. What attribute is required for the **<tiles:putList>** element?
2. What's the purpose of the **<tiles:useAttribute>** element?

---

1. **name**
2. This element creates a JSP-accessible variable from a Tiles attribute.

CRITICAL SKILL 10.3

Use the <definition> Tag

There's another way of working with Tiles besides using the **<tiles:insert>** element directly—you can use Tiles *definitions*. Definitions are useful because you can use them simply by referring to them by name, as well as extending them as we're going to see.

As an example, we'll create a new Tiles page, ch10_03.jsp, where we replace the **<tiles:insert>** element with **<tiles:definition>**, specifying the layout page with the **page** attribute:

```
<%@ taglib uri="/WEB-INF/struts-tiles.tld" prefix="tiles" %>

<tiles:definition id="theDefinition" page="/Layout.jsp" >
  <tiles:put name="title"  value="My first page" />
  <tiles:put name="header" value="/header.jsp" />
  <tiles:put name="footer" value="/footer.jsp" />
  <tiles:put name="menu"   value="/menu.jsp" />
  <tiles:put name="body"   value="/body.jsp" />
</tiles:definition>
        .
        .
        .
```

What we've done is to create a new Tiles definition named **theDefinition**. This definition corresponds exactly to what we created in our first example, ch10_01.jsp, with the same layout, header, footer, and so on.

After you've created a Tiles definition, you can use the **beanName** attribute of the **<tiles:insert>** element to put that definition to work. Here's what that looks like in ch10_03.jsp:

```
<%@ taglib uri="/WEB-INF/struts-tiles.tld" prefix="tiles" %>

<tiles:definition id="theDefinition" page="/Layout.jsp" >
  <tiles:put name="title"  value="My first page" />
  <tiles:put name="header" value="/header.jsp" />
  <tiles:put name="footer" value="/footer.jsp" />
  <tiles:put name="menu"   value="/menu.jsp" />
  <tiles:put name="body"   value="/body.jsp" />
</tiles:definition>

<tiles:insert beanName="theDefinition" flush="true" />
```

The Results page looks just the same as you see in Figure 10-1—all that's changed is that we've used a new named definition to achieve the same results. You can see the attributes of the **<tiles:definition>** element in Table 10-6.

Attribute Name	Description
id	The name of the newly created definition bean. This attribute is required.
scope	The scope of the newly defined bean. The default is page scope.
template	Same as **page**.
page	A string representing the URI of a template JSP page.
role	If the user is in the specified role, the tag is taken into account; otherwise, the tag is ignored.
extends	Name of a parent definition that is used as the base for this new definition.

Table 10-6 The <tiles:definition> Attributes

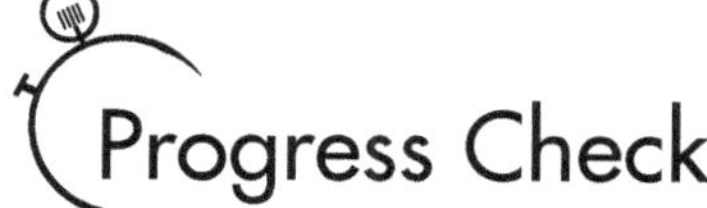

Progress Check

1. What attribute do you use to specify the layout page in **<tiles:definition>**?
2. What attribute do you use in **<tiles:definition>** to specify the definition you want to use?

Besides creating a definition in a JSP file, you can also store Tiles definitions in XML documents, and it's more usual to do that.

CRITICAL SKILL 10.4

Use XML-Based Definitions

As you recall, we connected a file named tiles-definitions.xml to the Tiles plug-in in struts-config.xml:

```
<plug-in className="org.apache.struts.tiles.TilesPlugin" >
    <set-property property="definitions-config"
        value="/WEB-INF/tiles-definitions.xml" />
    <set-property property="moduleAware" value="true" />
</plug-in>
```

This document, tiles-definitions.xml, contains an element named **<tiles-definitions>**. We can place our definition, which we'll name **tilesDefinition** here, inside that element. Doing

1. **template**
2. **beanName**

this is similar to the previous project, where we created a definition in a JSP page, but this time you can omit the **tiles:** prefix:

```
<?xml version="1.0" encoding="ISO-8859-1"?>

 <!DOCTYPE tiles-definitions PUBLIC
       "-//Apache Software Foundation//DTD Tiles Configuration 1.1//EN"
       "http://jakarta.apache.org/struts/dtds/tiles-config_1_1.dtd">

<tiles-definitions>

  <definition name="tilesDefinition" template="/Layout.jsp">
        <put name="title"  value="Using Definitions" />
        <put name="header" value="/header.jsp" />
        <put name="footer" value="/footer.jsp" />
        <put name="menu"   value="/menu.jsp" />
        <put name="body"   value="/body.jsp" />
  </definition>
        .
        .
        .
```

Now that we've created this new definition, **tilesDefinition**, we can refer to it in JSP files. Here's how that works in ch10_04.jsp, where we're putting this definition to work with the **<tiles:insert>** element:

```
<%@ taglib uri="/WEB-INF/struts-tiles.tld" prefix="tiles" %>

<tiles:insert definition="tilesDefinition" flush="true" />
```

The results in this project are just the same as you see in our first project in this module, which appears in Figure 10-1.

Progress Check

1. What property do you set in struts-config.xml to connect a Tiles XML definition document to the Tiles plug-in?
2. What XML element do you place **<definition>** elements in inside a Tiles XML definition document?

You can do more with definitions: you can overload them as well.

---

1. **definitions-config**
2. **<tiles-definitions>**

CRITICAL SKILL 10.5

Overload Definitions

Say that you wanted to change some aspect of a Tiles definition—for example, you might want to use a different header file than that specified in the definition. To see how that would work, take a look at ch10_05.jsp, where we're doing exactly that—replacing the header used in our definition **tilesDefinition**.

In ch10_05.jsp, we use the **tilesDefinition** definition:

```
<%@ taglib uri="/WEB-INF/struts-tiles.tld" prefix="tiles" %>

<tiles:insert definition="tilesDefinition" flush="true" >
        .
        .
        .
</tiles:insert>
```

But we also change some aspects of the definition by overloading them with new **<tiles:put>** elements. In particular, we'll change the titles text and the JSP page used as the header:

```
<%@ taglib uri="/WEB-INF/struts-tiles.tld" prefix="tiles" %>

<tiles:insert definition="tilesDefinition" flush="true" >
  <tiles:put name="title" value="Overloading Definitions" />
  <tiles:put name="header" value="/overloadedHeader.jsp" />
</tiles:insert>
```

Here's what the new header file, overloadedHeader.jsp looks like:

```
<center><h1>Overloading Definitions</h1></center>
```

You can see the results in Figure 10-4, in both the header text and title bar text, which display the text "Overloading Definitions".

Progress Check

1. What Tiles element do you use to overload a definition?
2. How do you indicate which attribute you're overloading in the Tiles element that's the answer to the previous question?

---

1. **<tiles:insert>**
2. You use the **name** attribute.

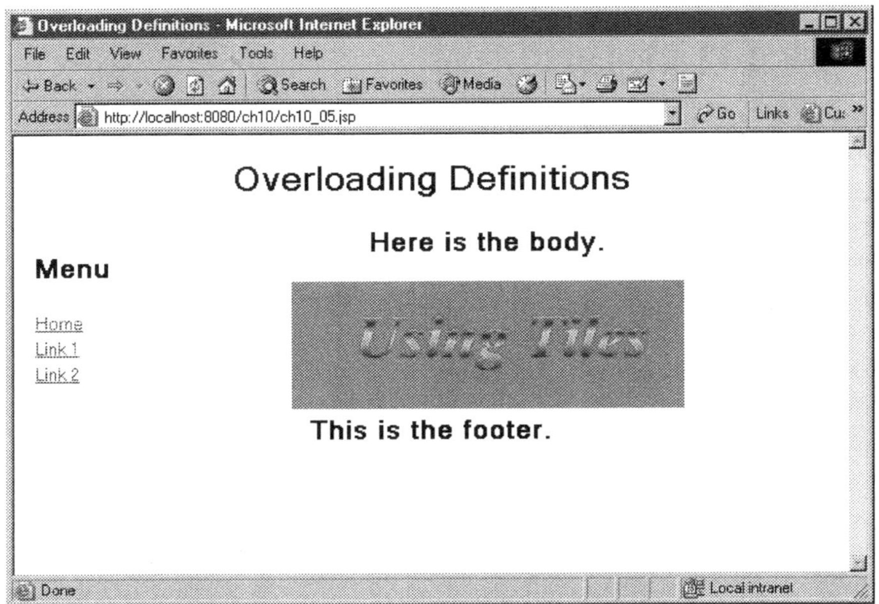

Figure 10-4 Overloading a definition

CRITICAL SKILL 10.6

Extend Definitions

You can also extend definitions, something like inheriting between Java classes. As an example, take a look at ch10_06.jsp. In this JSP, we're going to use an extended definition that we'll create, **tilesExtendedDefinition**:

```
<%@ taglib uri="/WEB-INF/struts-tiles.tld" prefix="tiles" %>

<tiles:insert definition="tilesExtendedDefinition" flush="true" />
```

This new definition, **tilesExtendedDefinition**, builds on our previous **tilesDefinition** definition. Here's how **tilesDefinition** looks in tiles-definitions.xml:

```
<definition name="tilesDefinition" path="/Layout.jsp">
      <put name="title"  value="Using Definitions" />
      <put name="header" value="/header.jsp" />
      <put name="footer" value="/footer.jsp" />
      <put name="menu"   value="/menu.jsp" />
      <put name="body"   value="/body.jsp" />
</definition>
      .
      .
      .
```

To extend this definition in **tilesExtendedDefinition**, you use the **extends** attribute when defining this new definition:

```
<definition name="tilesExtendedDefinition" extends="tilesDefinition" >
        .
        .
        .
</definition>
```

Now you can add new attribute definitions to the **tilesDefinition** definition like this, using **<put>** elements:

```
<definition name="tilesExtendedDefinition" extends="tilesDefinition" >
  <put name="title" value="Extending Definitions" />
  <put name="header" value="/extendedHeader.jsp" />
</definition>
```

In this case, we're changing the title text to "Extending Definitions" and using the same text in the header, using this file, extendedHeader.jsp:

```
<center><h1>Extending Definitions</h1></center>
```

You can, of course, also add entirely new attributes as well. You can see the results in Figure 10-5, where we're using the new definition, **tilesExtendedDefinition**.

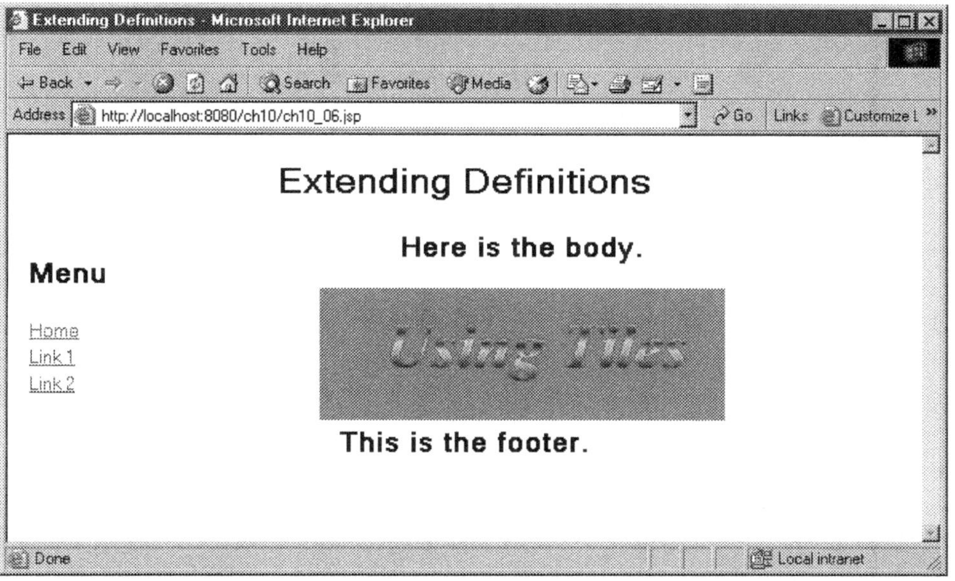

Figure 10-5 Using an extended definition

Progress Check

1. What element do you use to create an extended definition?
2. What attribute do you use to extend a definition from another one?

CRITICAL SKILL 10.7

Use Definitions as Attributes

You can also use a Tiles definition as a Tiles attribute. For example, say you had this definition in tiles-definitions.xml (note that the Tiles **body** attribute is set to a definition, **attribute.body**):

```
<definition name="attributeDefinition" extends="tilesDefinition" >
  <put name="title" value="An Attribute Definition" />
  <put name="body"  value="attribute.body" />
</definition>
```

This is the way we might define **attribute.body** in tiles-definitions.xml:

```
<definition name="attribute.body" path="/Layout.jsp" >
        <put name="title"  value="Dynamic Definitions" />
        <put name="header" value="/header.jsp" />
       <put name="footer" value="/footer.jsp" />
       <put name="menu"   value="/menu.jsp" />
       <put name="body"   value="/body.jsp" />
  </definition>
```

Now we can make use of our new definition, **attributeDefinition**, in a new JSP, ch10_07.jsp:

```
<%@ taglib uri="/WEB-INF/struts-tiles.tld" prefix="tiles" %>

<tiles:insert definition="attributeDefinition" flush="true" />
```

You can see the results in Figure 10-6, where we're using a definition as an attribute value—in this case, inserting our entire layout as the body of the Results page.

---

1. **<definition>**
2. **extends**

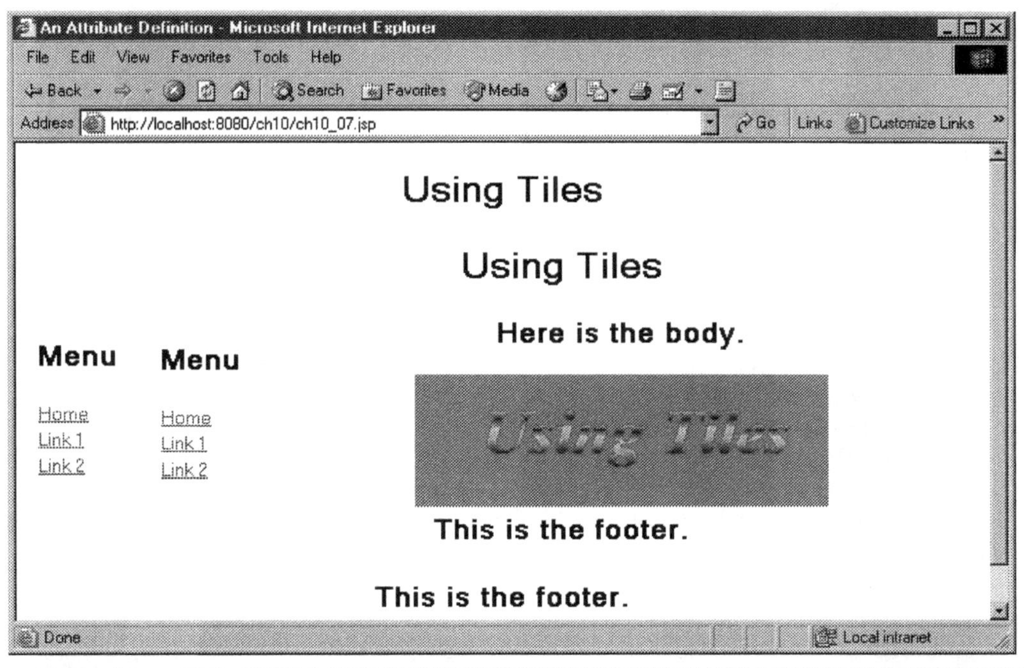

Figure 10-6 Using a definition as an attribute

CRITICAL SKILL 10.8

Use a Definition as an ActionForward

You can also use a definition as an **ActionForward** in a Struts application—that is, as the target of an action mapping's **<forward>** element, like this:

```
<forward name="success" path="tilesDefinition"/>
```

To make this work, we'll modify the ch07_01 project from Module 7. The Welcome page, ch07_01.jsp, which we'll rename ch10_08.jsp for this module, asks the user to enter some data:

```
<%@ taglib uri="/tags/struts-html" prefix="html" %>
<%@ taglib uri="/tags/struts-logic" prefix="logic" %>

<html:html>
    <head>
        <title>Using &lt;logic&gt; Tags</title>
    </head>
```

```
    <body>
        <h1>Using &lt;logic&gt; Tags</h1>

        <html:form action="ch10_08.do">

            <h2>Enter your data:</h2>
            <html:text property="text"/>

            <br>
            <br>

            <html:submit value="Submit"/>
            <html:cancel/>
        </html:form>
    </body>
</html:html>
```

The action and form bean just pass this data on to the Results page after some processing. You can see the Welcome page in Figure 10-7.

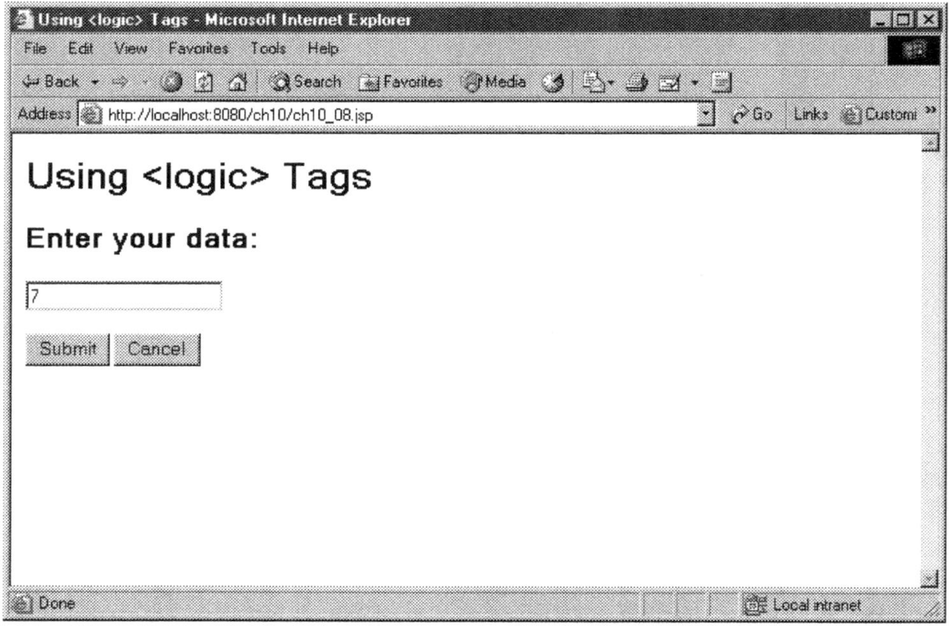

Figure 10-7 A Welcome page

In struts-config.xml, we'll change the path of the **success** forward to our Tiles definition, **tilesDefinition**, instead of the JSP page this application used in Module 7:

```
    <action path="/ch10_08"
      type="ch10.ch10_08"
      name="ch10_09"
      scope="request"
      input="/ch10_07.jsp">
      <forward name="success" path="tilesDefinition"/>
</action>
```

This means that when the user clicks the Submit button in Figure 10-7, we'll forward to **tilesDefinition** automatically, as you see in Figure 10-8 (note the URL in the address bar in the figure, which corresponds to the Struts action for this project).

Progress Check

1. What element can you use to forward to a Tiles definition?
2. To what attribute can you assign a Tiles definition?

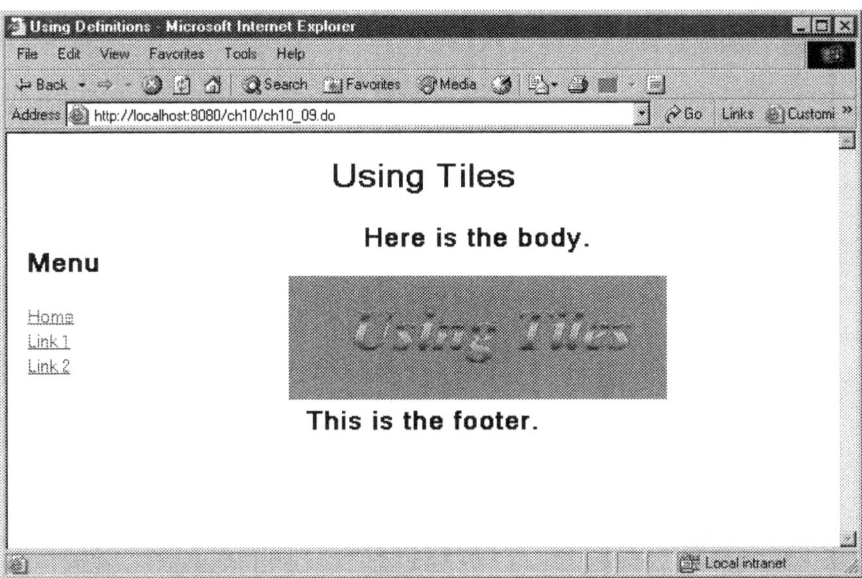

Figure 10-8 Forwarding to a Tiles definition

1. **<forward>**
2. **path**

Module 10 Mastery Check

1. What element do you use with struts-config.xml to install Tiles?

   A. **<struts-configuration>**

   B. **<tiles>**

   C. **<tiles-config>**

   D. **<plug-in>**

2. What element do you use to associate a definition file with Tiles in struts-config.xml?

   A. **<config-file>**

   B. **<set-property>**

   C. **<tiles-definition>**

   D. **<definition>**

3. What attributes do you use to associate a definition file with Tiles in struts-config.xml?

   A. **property** and **value**

   B. **config** and **item**

   C. **config-file** and **item**

   D. **configuration** and **item**

4. What .tld file comes with Struts 1.1 to support the Tiles custom tags?

   A. **tiles.tld**

   B. **struts-tiles.tld**

   C. **tiles-taglib.tld**

   D. **tiles-library.tld**

5. What is the effect of setting the **<tiles:insert>** element's flush attribute to **true**?

   A. The Struts input stream will be flushed.

   B. The Struts output stream will be flushed.

   C. The current page's input stream will be flushed.

   D. The current page's output stream will be flushed.

6. You use **<tiles:put>** elements inside which other element?

   A. **<tiles:insert>**

   B. **<tiles:list>**

   C. **<tiles:putList>**

   D. **<tiles:attribute>**

7. What Tiles element can you use to recover the value of a Tiles attribute as text?

   A. **<tiles:text>**

   B. **<tiles:getAsText>**

   C. **<tiles:getAsString>**

   D. **<tiles:astext>**

8. What elements do you use to create a list of tiles?

   A. **<tiles:list>** and **<tiles:put>**

   B. **<tiles:putList>** and **<tiles:add>**

   C. **<tiles:putList>** and **<tiles:put>**

   D. **<tiles:list>** and **<tiles:add>**

9. What attribute in the **<tiles:useAttribute>** element sets the name of the variable to be created?

   A. **id**

   B. **name**

   C. **variable-name**

   D. **ref**

10. What element do you use to invoke a Tiles definition?

    A. **<tiles:definition>**

    B. **<tiles:put>**

    C. **<tiles:def>**

    D. **<tiles:insert>**

Module 11

Using Eclipse with Struts

CRITICAL SKILLS

11.1 Download and Install Eclipse

11.2 Use Eclipse Views, Editors, and Perspectives

11.3 Create a Struts Application with Eclipse

11.4 Create a New Eclipse Project

11.5 Add a JSP to an Eclipse Project

11.6 Create a Java Class

11.7 Edit struts-config.xml

11.8 Add the Results Page to the Project

11.9 Connect Eclipse to Ant

As you progress with Struts and develop larger projects, working with the Java command-line compiler, javac, becomes more and more cumbersome. Even with small Java projects, Java can be very finicky—you might forget to add a semicolon at the end of a line or to declare a variable or something similar, and javac can suddenly reel off pages of errors. But when your Struts applications become large, managing many files in different locations and working on the code can become very difficult if you're doing it all by hand.

A Java Integrated Development Environment (IDE) is the answer, and in this module we'll discuss using the most popular (and free) one: Eclipse. Using Eclipse can make Struts development far easier, as we're going to see in this module, where we'll develop a Struts application using Eclipse. Eclipse lets you automate the entire build process, reducing the whole thing to a single menu item selection. And Eclipse can not only pinpoint problems before you try to compile your code, but can also suggest solutions. Struts applications involve many files, and one of the biggest advantages to using an IDE like Eclipse is that doing so centralizes access to all those files. They're all listed in a single window, and you don't have to worry anymore about specifying paths seven levels deep to access them; you can simply double-click a file to open it.

Eclipse is the premiere Java IDE these days; you can see it in Figure 11-1. Eclipse can act as an IDE for many languages (Eclipse calls itself a universal tool platform), from C to Cobol, but it's most widely used with Java. It comes with Java tools and the Java IDE built in, although you can load plug-ins for other languages as well.

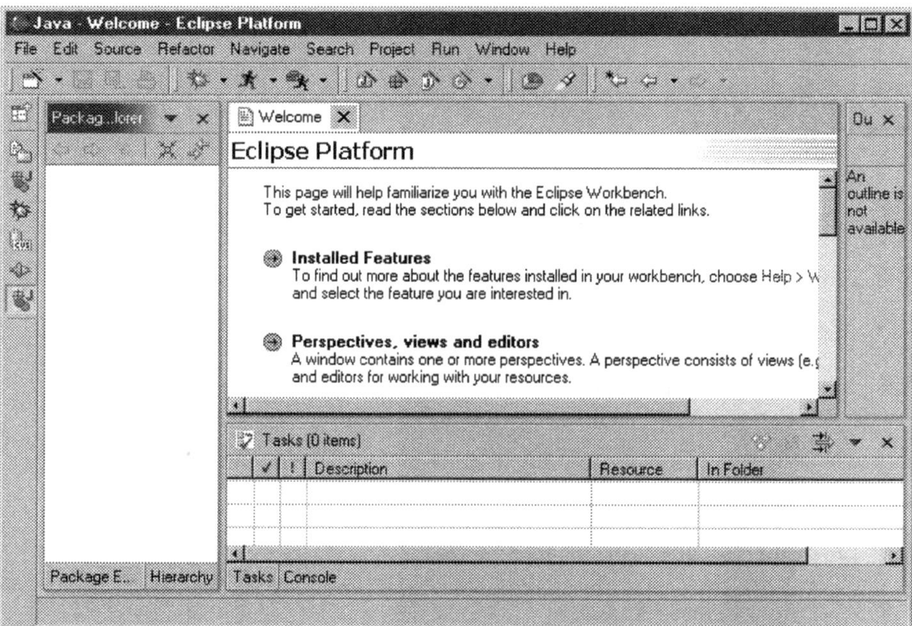

Figure 11-1 Eclipse

Eclipse is free. That doesn't make it cheap, however—at least, not cheap to create. A major player behind Eclipse is IBM, which has reportedly spent some $40 million to develop it. The first version, 1.0, came out in November 2001, and it's been undergoing changes ever since.

Eclipse is now an open source project. It's still largely under IBM's development, but it's part of a software consortium named eclipse.org. You can see the consortium's web page, www.eclipse.org, in Figure 11-2.

The Eclipse consortium now contains more than 45 members, including such corporations as Borland, IBM, MERANT, QNX Software Systems, Rational Software3, Red Hat, SuSE, Sybase, Hitachi, Oracle, Hewlett Packard, Intel, and others.

Eclipse is actually a project that has three subparts:

- The Eclipse platform itself, which forms the backbone of the whole application
- The Java Development Toolkit (JDT), led by Erich Gamma
- The Plug-in Development Environment (PDE), which lets you develop your own tools for Eclipse, called plug-ins.

You can learn more about these three subprojects at http://www.eclipse.org/eclipse/.

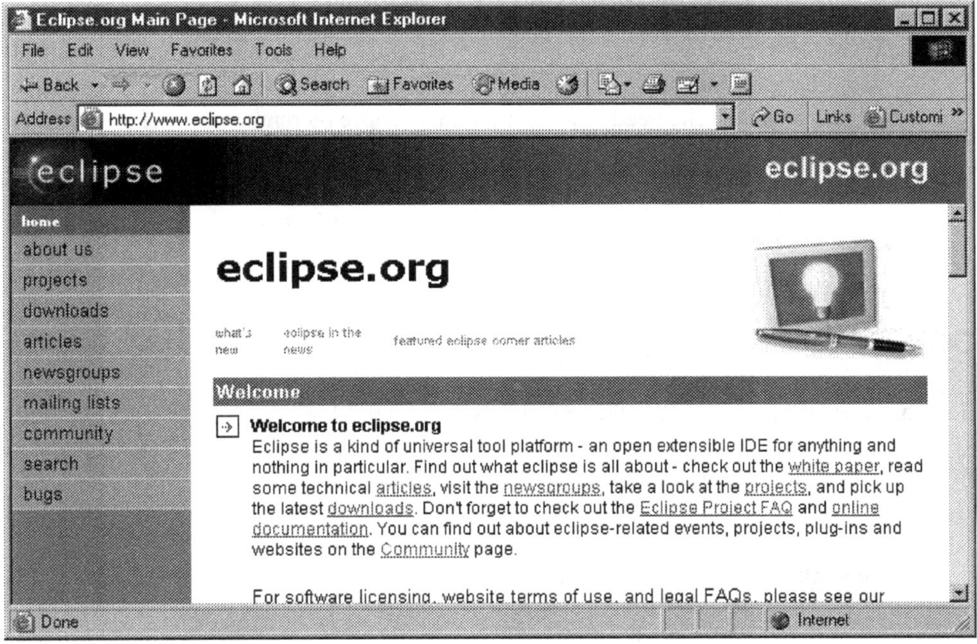

Figure 11-2 The Eclipse consortium web page

CRITICAL SKILL 11.1

Download and Install Eclipse

Getting your own copy of Eclipse is not hard. It's available for free—just go to www.eclipse.org/downloads and select one of the download mirrors available on that page. You'll be presented with a list of the available downloads of various types:

- **Release builds** These versions are for general use. Most often, when you download Eclipse, you'll use one of the release versions. These builds have been well tested, and the chance of coming across serious bugs is minimal.
- **Stable builds** These versions are like beta versions. A stable build is a step along the way towards a release version. It's considered to be relatively stable, but there may be problems. New features are often available here.
- **Integration builds** These versions consist of components that have been tested, but their operation together may still have some problems. If things work out, an integration build may be elevated to a stable version.
- **Nightly builds** These are the most experimental of all publicly available Eclipse versions. They're created nightly, without any guarantee that things will work as you expect. Experience with these builds indicates that they can have serious problems.

Select the most recent release version of Eclipse for your operating system and click the link to download it.

To install Eclipse, just unzip or untar it depending on what operating system you have, and you'll find an executable file, ready to run. You start Eclipse by running the Eclipse executable, such as eclipse.exe. When you start it the first time, it may ask you to wait while it completes the installation, which does not take long (Eclipse is creating the workspace directories it'll be using). Note that Eclipse is Java-based, so you have to have Java on your machine to run it.

Progress Check

1. What versions of Eclipse are the most ready for general use?
2. What versions of Eclipse are the most experimental?

Before working with Eclipse, you have to understand how it works and creates Java projects.

1. Release builds
2. Nightly builds

The Parts of Eclipse

Most developers think of Eclipse as a Java IDE, and when you download Eclipse, you get the Java IDE (this is the Java Development Toolkit, the JDT) and the Plug-in Development Environment (the PDE, which lets you develop Eclipse plug-ins) with it.

As already mentioned, however, Eclipse considers itself a universal tool platform. The JDT is itself an addition to Eclipse; in fact, it's an Eclipse plug-in. Eclipse is really the Eclipse platform, and the platform provides support for other tools. These tools are implemented as plug-ins, so the platform only needs be a small software package.

The Eclipse platform is made up of several components: the platform kernel, the workbench, the workspace, the team component, and the help component.

The Platform Kernel

The Eclipse kernel gets everything started and loads the plug-ins used by the platform. This is the component that runs first when you start Eclipse, and it loads the other plug-ins that perform such tasks as displaying the visual IDE, which is done by the Eclipse workbench.

The Eclipse Workbench

The workbench is what you see in Figure 11-1. This is the essential graphical interface you work with when you use Eclipse. It comes with toolbars and menus built in, and its job is to present those items and the internal windows you see in Figure 11-1. It's the workbench that displays the welcome message you see in that figure. On the other hand, when you start working with Java, the JDT takes over.

The Eclipse Workspace

The workspace component manages your resources, such as files, for you. When you work with Java code in Eclipse, you work with projects. Each project has its own folder in the Eclipse workspace. Eclipse projects can contain many folders, each with subfolders.

The workspace component manages all the resources in a project, and that includes maintaining a history of all the changes to those resources so you can undo changes as you want. The workspace will then inform the various Eclipse plug-ins of those changes.

The resources in the workspace are held in a directory named **workspace**. The fact that each Eclipse project has its own folder in that directory makes things easier when you install a new version of Eclipse because you can migrate old projects to the new version just by copying over their folders (you can also use the Eclipse File | Import menu item).

When we develop a Struts application, our Java code will be stored in the Eclipse workspace, but the generated .class files will automatically be stored in the appropriate Tomcat directory. You can also link to and open files that are not in the Eclipse workspace but are important to your project, such as web.xml, as we're going to see in this module.

The Team Component

The Eclipse team component lets you share code with others in a team environment. If you've ever been part of a corporate programming team, you know all about version control. Program code is checked into or out of a repository as needed so that the changes to that software can be tracked. The idea here is to avoid random changes being made by team members so that changes do not overlap or obliterate each other as various team members work on different versions of the code at the same time.

This component acts like a Concurrent Versions System (CVS) client that interacts with a CVS server. You'll need a CVS server to make this work; such servers are available for free on the Internet.

The Help Component

As its name implies, the help component built into Eclipse provides help. Actually, it's an extensible documentation system. Besides the help files that come with Eclipse, Eclipse plug-ins, which extend Eclipse, can provide HTML-based documentation that the help component makes available to the user.

That's it for the components that come built into the Eclipse platform. There's one more set of concepts to master before starting to work with Eclipse: views, editors, and perspectives.

CRITICAL SKILL 11.2

Use Eclipse Views, Editors, and Perspectives

As with any IDE, Eclipse presents you with many different windows. Some of these windows are called *views*, because they give you a view into your project's resources or your data. For example, one view, called the Package Explorer, displays the Java packages and classes in your project. Another view lets you navigate between projects.

Also, as in any IDE where screen space is at a premium, views are often stacked. You can access various views by clicking the tabs that will appear along the edges of the stack.

Besides views, there's a special kind of window that appears in the center of the Eclipse workbench, and that's the *editor* windows. Whenever you use Eclipse to open a document or other resources, they'll appear in an editor. Eclipse will use the correct kind of editor for the document you've opened—for example, a plain text editor for plain text files, or a source code editor from the JDT for a Java source code file.

The central space where editors, which can be stacked using tabs just as views can, appears in Figure 11-1, displaying the welcome message you see in that figure. You can close an editor by clicking the X button in its tab. If you have too many editors open to conveniently navigate between them using tabs, you can use the Window | Switch to Editor menu item (or CTRL-F6).

You don't usually select the views and editors that appear at a particular time. Instead, you use collections of editors and views called *perspectives*. For example, when you debug, you use the Debug perspective, which displays the code you're working on using special debug editors, various other views let you keep track of breakpoints, immediate values, and so on. When you develop Java code, you use the Java perspective, which displays stacked Java source code editors that support syntax checking and highlighting, and other views, such as the Console view, which displays what your application prints to the console, and the Package Explorer, which lets you navigate between the packages and classes in your project.

That is to say, perspectives are predefined collections of views and editors that appear automatically when you perform certain tasks. For example, when you create a Java project, Eclipse will open the Java perspective by default. When you run an application with the Run | Debug menu items, the Debug perspective opens by itself.

You can also customize perspectives, adding and removing views and editors, using the Window | Customize Perspective menu item.

The JDT supports a number of perspectives associated with Java development—for example, the Java perspective itself, which is used for Java development, and the Debug perspective, which is specially designed to debug Java applications.

At this point, we're up to speed on the concepts we'll need to use Eclipse, so that's what we're going to do now. Our purpose here will be to create a working Struts project using Eclipse.

CRITICAL SKILL

11.3 Create a Struts Application with Eclipse

In this module, we're going to pick the HTML controls project from Module 6 as our example project, with the files renamed for this module. The idea here will be to translate that project into an Eclipse project. Here are the files we'll be using:

- **ch11_01.jsp** HTML controls page
- **Ch11_02.java** The action
- **Ch11_03.java** The action form
- **ch11_04.jsp** The Results page

These are the files we'll develop and install using Eclipse. When you first start Eclipse, you'll see the Resource perspective, which is the default perspective that appears in Figure 11-1. To work with Struts, you'll need to create a new project.

CRITICAL SKILL 11.4

Create a New Eclipse Project

To create a new project in Eclipse, select the File | New | Project menu item, opening the New Project dialog you see in Figure 11-3. To create a Java project, select Java in the box at left and Java Project in the box at right, and click Next.

In the next dialog, give the new project a name—ch11, as shown in Figure 11-4—and click Next.

In the next dialog, we'll set the output folder for the compiled code in our project. That way, although the source for those files will be in the Eclipse workspace, the compiled code created from them will go into the Tomcat directories automatically, ready for use. To set the output folder, click the Browse button next to the Default output folder text box to open the Folder Selection dialog, click the Create New Folder button to open the New Folder dialog, click the Advanced button in this dialog, then click the Link to folder in the file system check box, followed by the Browse button in this dialog.

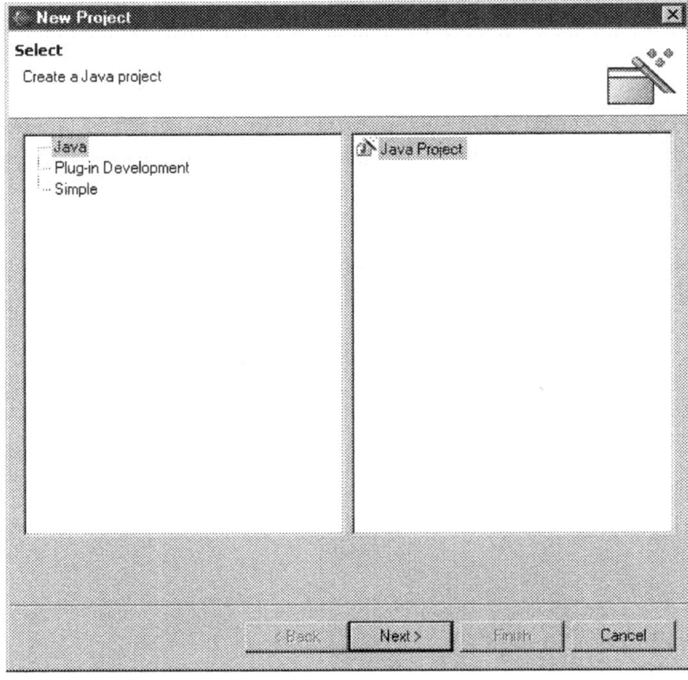

Figure 11-3 The New Project dialog

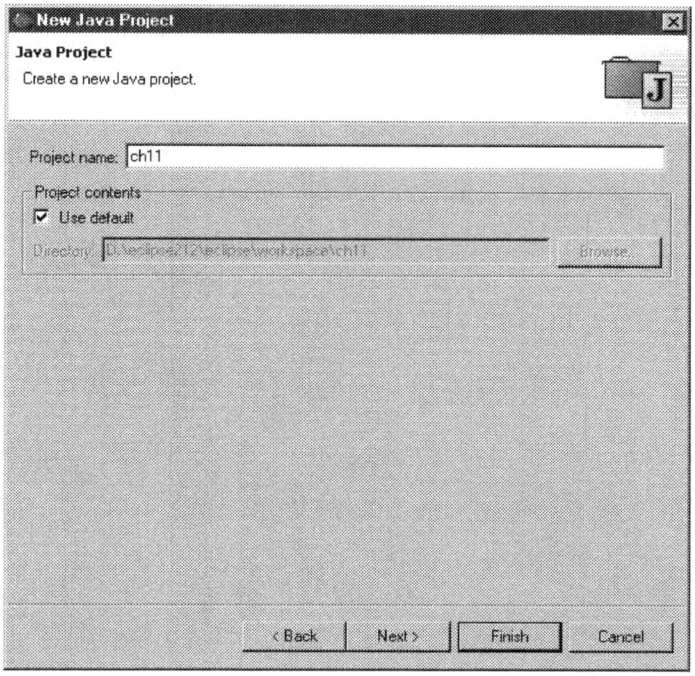

Figure 11-4 Naming a project

This opens the Browse for Folder dialog. Browse to the Tomcat webapps directory and, using the New Folder button repeatedly in this dialog, create this directory structure (i.e., ch11 will be webapps/ch11, WEB-INF will be webapps/ch11/WEB-INF, and so on):

```
ch11
|___WEB-INF
    |___classes
    |___lib
```

Then select the WEB-INF/classes directory and click OK, closing the Browse for Folder dialog and returning control to the New Folder dialog. Type "output" in the Folder Name box and click OK. Then click OK again to close the Folder Selection dialog. This sets the output folder to webapps/ch11/WEB-INF/classes. This folder is called output in Eclipse now, and you can see that it's the new default output folder, as indicated in the text box at the bottom of Figure 11-5. Now when we compile Java source code, the .class files will go to the webapps/ch11/WEB-INF/classes folder automatically.

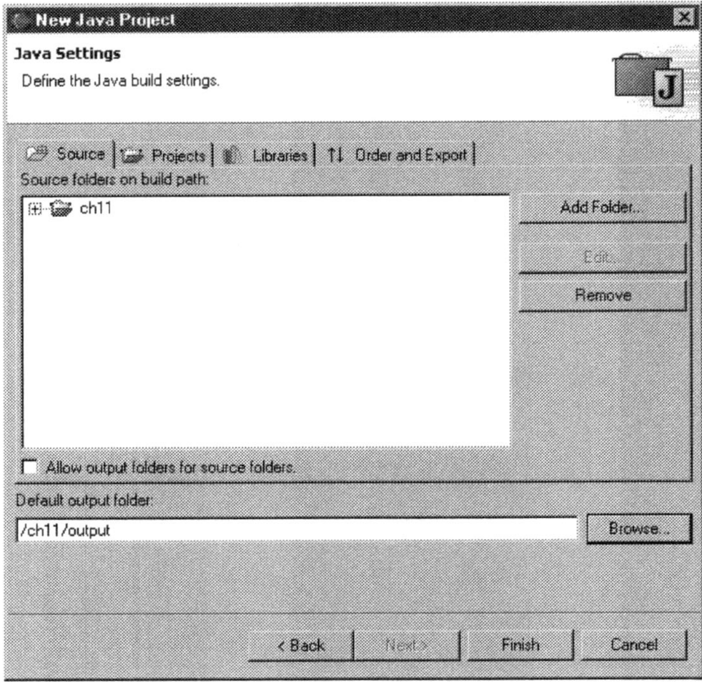

Figure 11-5 Setting the output folder

Click Finish in the New Project dialog to create the new Java project. Eclipse switches to the Java perspective, and you can see the new project, ch11, in the Package Explorer view at left in Figure 11-6.

The Eclipse project is ready for us to start working with source code files.

Progress Check

1. What menu item do you use to create a new project?
2. How do you set the output folder of an Eclipse project?

---

1. File | New | Project

2. Click the Browse button next to the Default output folder text box. That opens the Folder Selection dialog. Click the Create New Folder button to open the New Folder dialog, click the Advanced button in this dialog, and then click the Link to folder in the file system check box. Then you're free to navigate to the output folder you want to use by clicking the Browse button in this dialog.

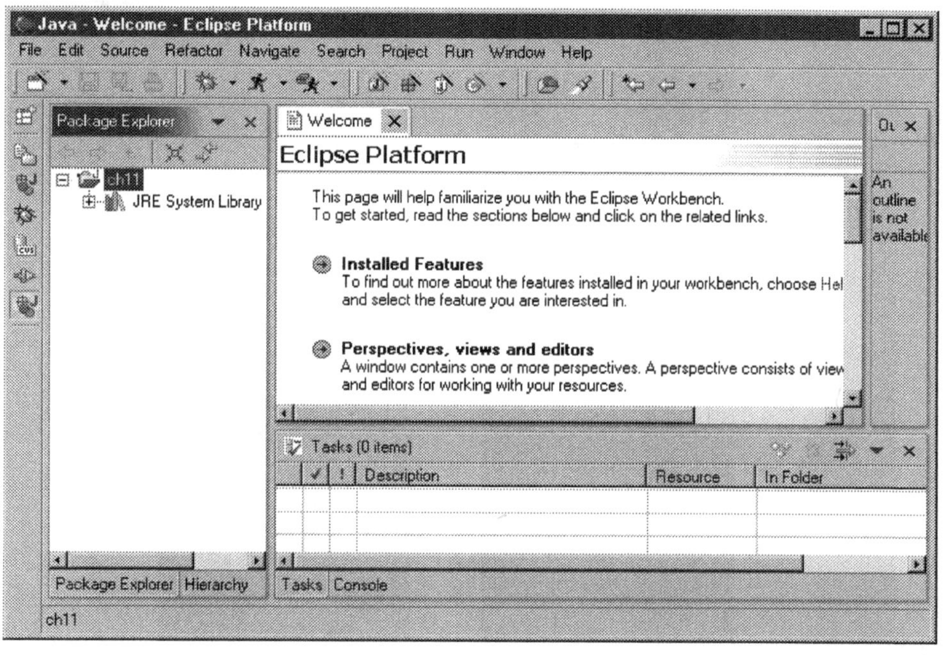

Figure 11-6 A new Java project

CRITICAL SKILL 11.5

Add a JSP to an Eclipse Project

The next step is to add the first JSP, ch11_01.jsp, to our Eclipse project. To do that, place this code in the new file ch11_01.jsp and store that file in the Tomcat directory webapps/ch11:

```
<%@ taglib uri="/tags/struts-html" prefix="html" %>
<%@ taglib uri="/tags/struts-logic" prefix="logic" %>

<html:html>
    <head>
        <title>Using &lt;html&gt; Tags</title>
        <script language="JavaScript">
            function clicker()
            {
                confirm("You clicked the button.");
            }
        </script>
    </head>

    <body>
```

```
<h1>Using &lt;html&gt; Tags</h1>

<html:errors/>

<html:form action="ch11_02.do" method="POST"
    enctype="multipart/form-data">

    <h2>Text Fields:</h2>
    <html:text property="text"/>
    <br>

    <h2>Text Areas:</h2>
    <html:textarea property="textarea" rows="10"/>
    <br>

    <h2>Checkboxes:</h2>
    <html:checkbox property="checkbox"/>Check Me
    <br>

    <h2>Radio Buttons:</h2>
    <html:radio property="radio" value="red"/>red
    <html:radio property="radio" value="green"/>green
    <html:radio property="radio" value="blue"/>blue
    <br>

    <h2>Buttons:</h2>
    <html:button onclick="clicker()" value="Click Me"
        property="text"/>
    <br>

    <h2>Links:</h2>
    <html:link action="ch11_02">Click Me</html:link>
    <br>

    <h2>Images:</h2>
    <html:img page="/image.jpg"/>
    <br>

    <h2>Image Controls:</h2>
    <html:image page="/imagecontrol.jpg" property=""/>
    <br>

    <h2>Select Controls:</h2>
    <html:select property="multipleSelect" size="9" multiple="true">
        <html:option value="Multi 0">Multi 0</html:option>
        <html:option value="Multi 1">Multi 1</html:option>
        <html:option value="Multi 2">Multi 2</html:option>
        <html:option value="Multi 3">Multi 3</html:option>
        <html:option value="Multi 4">Multi 4</html:option>
        <html:option value="Multi 5">Multi 5</html:option>
        <html:option value="Multi 6">Multi 6</html:option>
        <html:option value="Multi 7">Multi 7</html:option>
        <html:option value="Multi 8">Multi 8</html:option>
    </html:select>
```

```
            <h2>Multibox Controls:</h2>
                <html:multibox property="multiBox" value="a" />a
                <html:multibox property="multiBox" value="b" />b
                <html:multibox property="multiBox" value="c" />c
                <html:multibox property="multiBox" value="d" />d
                <html:multibox property="multiBox" value="e" />e
            <br>

            <h2>File Controls:</h2>
            <html:file property="file" />

            <br>
            <br>

            <html:submit value="Submit"/>
            <html:cancel/>
        </html:form>
    </body>
</html:html>
```

To add this file to our Eclipse project, right-click the ch11 project in the Package Explorer and select New | File to open the New File dialog. Enter "ch11_01.jsp" in the File Name text box, click the Advanced button, and select the Link to File in the file system check box. Then click the Browse button next to the text box and browse to ch11_01.jsp in the Tomcat webapps/ch11 directory. Select ch11_01.jsp and click Open. Then click Finish to close the New File dialog, adding ch11_01.jsp to the Eclipse project, as you see in Figure 11-7. Double-clicking ch11_01.jsp in the Package Explorer opens it in an Eclipse editor, as shown in the figure.

In addition, this page displays two images, image.jpg and imagecontrol.jpg, so copy them over from webapps/ch06.

Progress Check

1. How do you add a file to an Eclipse project?

CRITICAL SKILL 11.6

Create a Java Class

This project also relies on two Java classes, the action, **Ch11_02**, and the form bean, **Ch11_03**. We'll start by creating the action, **Ch11_02**. To do that, right-click the ch11 project in the Package Explorer and select New | Class to open the New Class dialog you see in Figure 11-8.

---

1. You select New | File to open the New File dialog, click the Advanced button, and select the Link to File in the file system check box. Then click the Browse button and browse to the file you want to add.

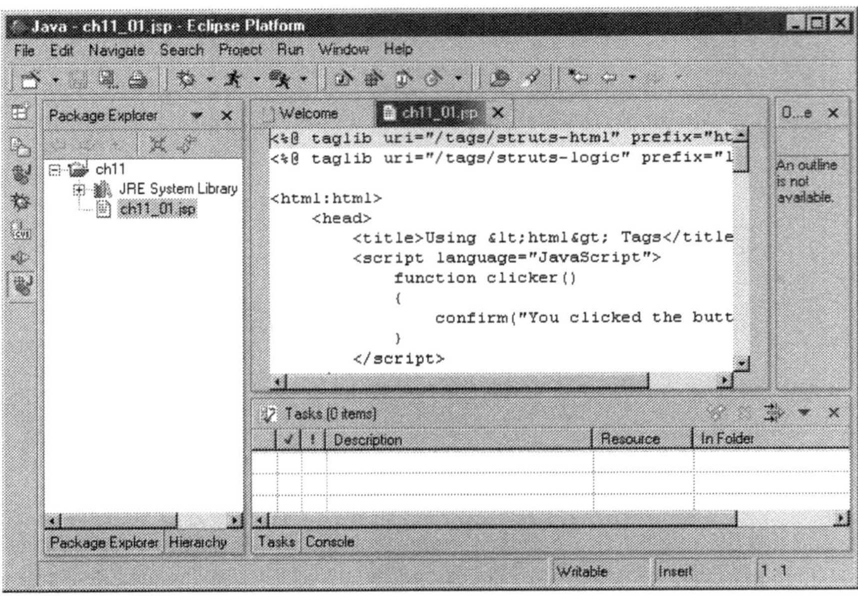

Figure 11-7 Linked to a new file

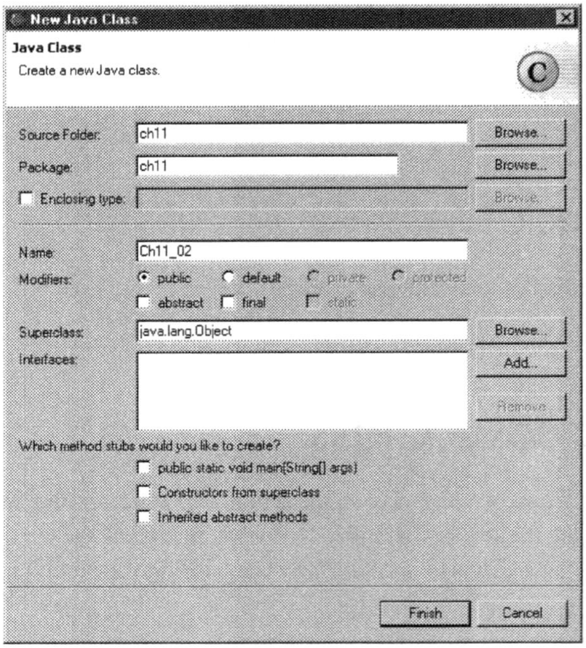

New Java Class
Java Class
Create a new Java class.
Source Folder: ch11 Browse...
Package: ch11 Browse...
Enclosing type: Browse...
Name: Ch11_02
Modifiers: public default private protected
abstract final static
Superclass: java.lang.Object Browse...
Interfaces: Add... Remove
Which method stubs would you like to create?
public static void main(String[] args)
Constructors from superclass
Inherited abstract methods
Finish Cancel

Figure 11-8 Creating a new Java class

Give the name of the new class as Ch11_02 in the Name text box and set the package to ch11 in the package text box. Make sure the bottom three check boxes, which provide stub methods, are not selected, and click Finish.

This creates a skeletal version of Ch11_02.java, which opens in the Eclipse editor:

```
/*
 * Created on May 20, 2004
 *
 * To change the template for this generated file go to
 * Window&gt;Preferences&gt;Java&gt;Code Generation&gt;Code and Comments
 */
package ch11;

/**
 *
 * To change the template for this generated type comment go to
 * Window&gt;Preferences&gt;Java&gt;Code Generation&gt;Code and Comments
 */
public class Ch11_02
{

}
```

Edit this file by adding the code we'll need for this action:

```
/*
 * Created on May 20, 2004
 *
 * To change the template for this generated file go to
 * Window&gt;Preferences&gt;Java&gt;Code Generation&gt;Code and Comments
 */
package ch11;

import java.io.*;
import javax.servlet.http.HttpServletRequest;
import javax.servlet.http.HttpServletResponse;
import javax.servlet.ServletException;
import org.apache.struts.action.*;
/**
 *
 * To change the template for this generated type comment go to
 * Window&gt;Preferences&gt;Java&gt;Code Generation&gt;Code and Comments
 */
public class Ch11_02 extends Action
{
      public ActionForward execute(ActionMapping mapping,
        ActionForm form,
```

```
            HttpServletRequest request,
            HttpServletResponse response)
            throws IOException, ServletException {

                  return mapping.findForward("success");
            }
}
```

When you insert this code in Eclipse, much of the code will be marked in red and underlined with wavy lines, as shown in Figure 11-9. That's Eclipse's way of indicating that there's an error. To determine what the problem is, let the mouse cursor rest over a marked line, as you see in Figure 11-9, and a tool tip will give you the details. In this case, Eclipse is indicating that it can't satisfy the imports we've used.

In this case, we'll need struts.jar and servlet-api.jar to satisfy the imports. We'll also need all the other standard Struts files, such as the Struts .tld files, so we'll copy over all those support files from our earlier version of this project, in webapps/ch06. That means copying over the contents of webapps/ch06/WEB-INF to webapps/ch11/WEB-INF and the contents of webapps/ch06/WEB-INF/lib to webapps/ch11/WEB-INF/lib. (Make sure the new lib directory contains servlet-api.jar, since we'll use it from that location.)

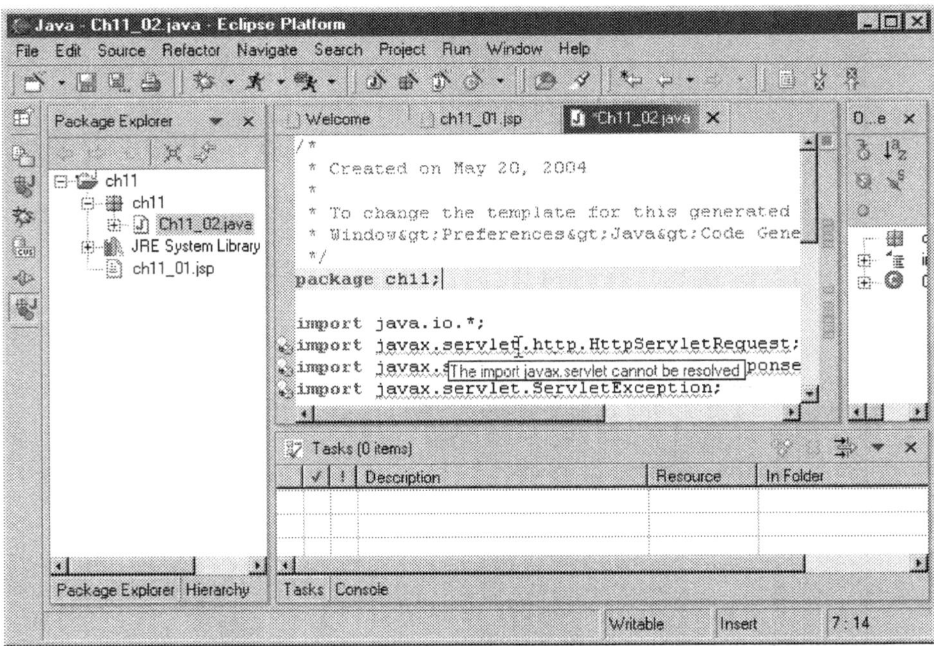

Figure 11-9 A new Java file

Now you can add struts.jar and servlet-api.jar to the ch11 project's build path by selecting the Project | Properties menu item and clicking the Libraries tab in the Properties for ch11 dialog. Now click the Add External Jars button, navigate to webapps/ch11/WEB-INF/lib in the JAR Selection dialog, select struts.jar and servlet-api.jar, and click Open. This adds these .jar files to the build path, as shown in Figure 11-10. Click OK to close the Properties for ch11 dialog, then save the Ch11_02.java file with the File | Save menu item or by clicking the diskette icon in the toolbar.

This lets Eclipse find the imports it needs and removes the red markings in Ch11_02.jar, as shown in Figure 11-11. (If the markings don't disappear, save the file; if that doesn't work, close Ch11_02.jar by clicking the X button in its editor tab and then reopen this file by double-clicking it in the Package Explorer.)

Note the syntax highlighting in Eclipse at this point; Eclipse checks your syntax as it's entered and highlights Java keywords in bold red by default. If there are errors, you'll see them marked in bright red with wavy underlines. Warnings will be underlined and marked in yellow (as an example, you'll get a warning when you have an import statement that's not needed).

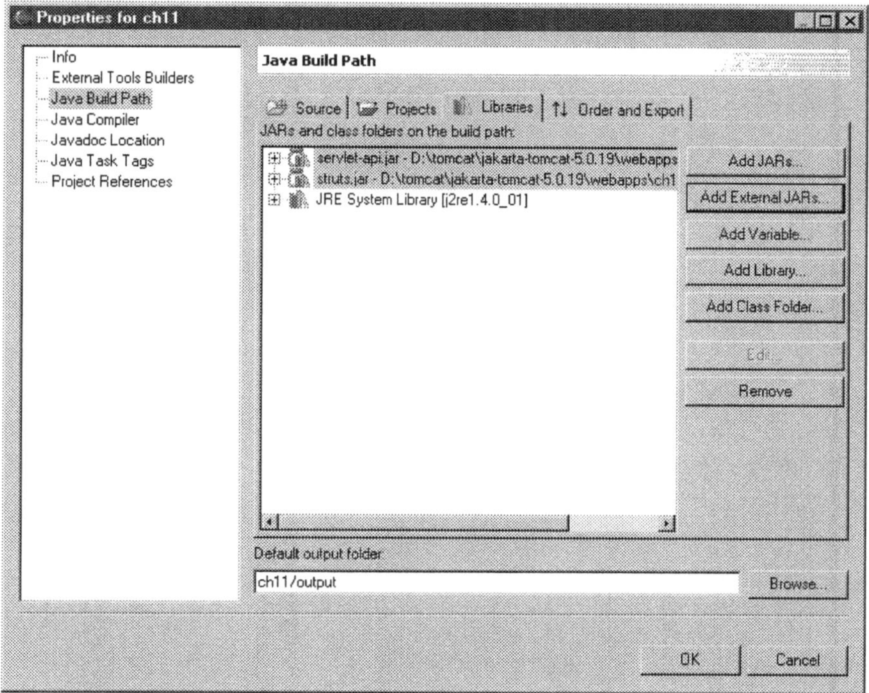

Figure 11-10 Adding .jar files to the build path

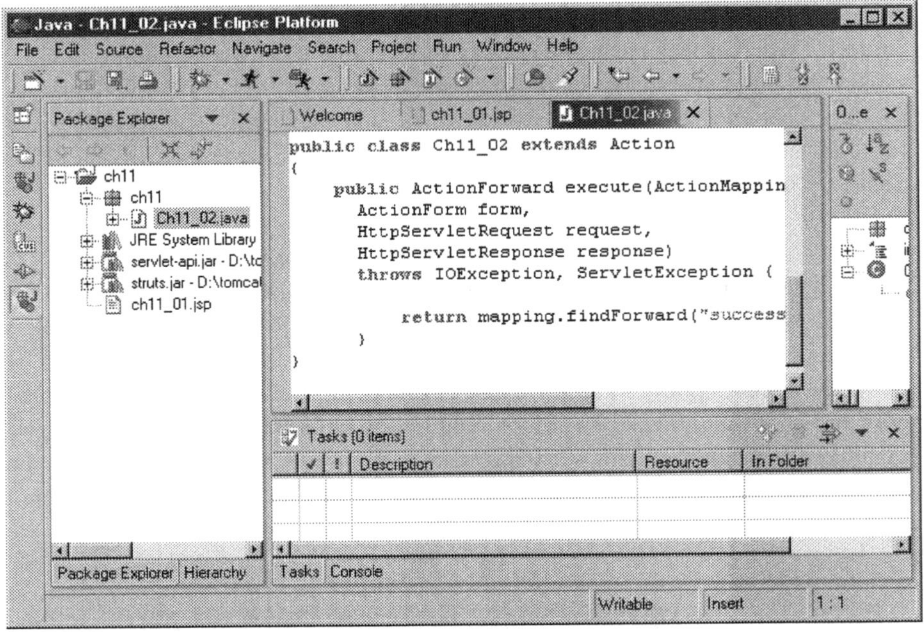

Figure 11-11 The Ch11_02.java code

Progress Check

1. How do you create a new Java class in an Eclipse project?
2. How do you add .jar files to an Eclipse build path?

Eclipse will do more than tell you what's wrong; it can also offer suggestions on how to fix the problem with its QuickFix utility. For example, say you removed the import for **javax.servlet.http.HttpServletRequest**:

```
import java.io.*;
//import javax.servlet.http.HttpServletRequest;
import javax.servlet.http.HttpServletResponse;
import javax.servlet.ServletException;
import org.apache.struts.action.*;
```

1. You can use the File | New | Class menu item.

2. You select the Project | Properties menu item and click the Libraries tab. Then you click the Add External Jars button and navigate to the directory holding the .jar file you want to add, select it, and click Open.

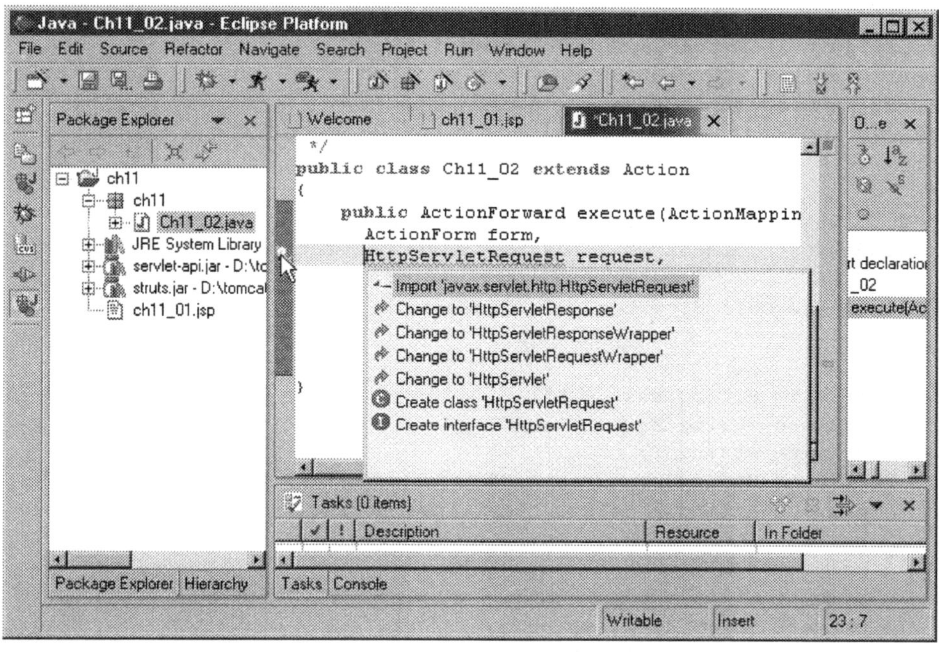

Figure 11-12 Using QuickFix

Now you'll see the line that needs this import marked in red with a wavy underline, as shown in Figure 11-12. Eclipse also displays a QuickFix light bulb icon at left of the line. Clicking the icon displays possible solutions, as shown in Figure 11-12. Selecting one of the offered solutions—the top one here will add an import statement for the **javax.servlet.http.HttpServletRequest** class—will make Eclipse fix the problem for you.

We'll also need the Java code for the form bean in this project, Ch11_03. Create this new class as we've just created Ch11_02, placing it in the package ch11, which will create the file Ch11_03.java. Edit that file to include this code:

```
/*
 * Created on May 20, 2004
 *
 * To change the template for this generated file go to
 * Window&gt;Preferences&gt;Java&gt;Code Generation&gt;Code and Comments
 */
package ch11;

import org.apache.struts.action.*;
import org.apache.struts.upload.FormFile;
```

```
import javax.servlet.http.HttpServletRequest;
import java.io.ByteArrayOutputStream;
import java.io.IOException;
import java.io.InputStream;

/**
 *
 * To change the template for this generated type comment go to
 * Window&gt;Preferences&gt;Java&gt;Code Generation&gt;Code and Comments
 */
public class Ch11_03 extends ActionForm
{

    private String text = "";
    private String X;
    private String Y;
    private String textarea = "";
    private String[] selectItems = new String[3];
    private String[] multiBox = new String[5];
    private boolean checkbox = false;
    private String radio = "";
    private FormFile file;
    private String fileText;

    public String getText()
    {
        return text;
    }

    public void setText(String text)
    {
        this.text = text;
    }

    public String getTextarea()
    {
        return textarea;
    }

    public void setTextarea(String textarea)
    {
        this.textarea = textarea;
    }

    public boolean getCheckbox()
    {
        return checkbox;
```

```
}

public void setCheckbox(boolean checkbox)
{
        this.checkbox = checkbox;
}

public String getRadio()
{
        return radio;
}

public void setRadio(String radio)
{
        this.radio = radio;
}

public String getX()
{
        return X;
}

public void setX(String X)
{
        this.X = X;
}

public String getY()
{
        return Y;
}

public void setY(String Y)
{
        this.Y = Y;
}

public String[] getSelectItems()
  {
        return selectItems;
}

public void setSelectItems(String[] selectItems)
{
        this.selectItems = selectItems;
}
```

```
        public String[] getMultiBox()
          {
               return multiBox;
        }

        public void setMultiBox(String[] multiBox)
        {
               this.multiBox = multiBox;
        }

        private String[] multipleSelect = {"Multi 3", "Multi 5", "Multi 7"};

        public String[] getMultipleSelect() {
               return (this.multipleSelect);
        }

        public void setMultipleSelect(String multipleSelect[]) {
               this.multipleSelect = multipleSelect;
        }

        public FormFile getFile() {
               return file;
}

        public void setFile(FormFile file) {
               this.file = file;
        }

        public String getFileText() {

               try {
                      ByteArrayOutputStream byteStream = new
                          ByteArrayOutputStream();
                      InputStream input = file.getInputStream();

                      byte[] dataBuffer = new byte[4096];
                      int numberBytes = 0;
                      while ((numberBytes = input.read(dataBuffer, 0, 4096))
                          != -1) {
                            byteStream.write(dataBuffer, 0, numberBytes);
                      }
                      fileText = new String(byteStream.toByteArray());
                      input.close();
               }
               catch (IOException e) {
                      return null;
```

```
            }
            return fileText;
        }

        public void reset(ActionMapping mapping, HttpServletRequest request)
        {
        }
}
```

Now that these .java files are under the control of our Eclipse project, we can build the code with the Eclipse Project | Rebuild All menu item. That item will not only compile the project's Java code, but place the compiled code in the webapps/ch11/WEB-INF/classes directory—actually in webapps/ch11/WEB-INF/classes/ch11, since we've placed our code in the **ch11** package.

CRITICAL SKILL 11.7

Edit struts-config.xml

We'll need to update the struts-config.xml file we copied over from webapps/ch06/WEB-INF for this new project. To add that file to the Package Explorer, select Eclipse's New | File menu item, click the ch11 project folder to select it, and enter "struts-config.xml" in the File Name text box. Click the Advanced button, select the Link to File in the file system check box, and navigate to webapps/ch11/WEB-INF/struts-config.xml. Then click the Finish button to add struts-config.xml to the project, making it appear in the Package Explorer.

On the other hand, you can't just double-click struts-config.xml to open it in an Eclipse editor. Eclipse doesn't come with any special editor to handle XML files (although there are specific exceptions, as when you name your XML file build.xml, which Eclipse will treat as an Ant build file), which means that by default, it'll use any editor that's registered itself for XML files, such as the Internet Explorer. So to open struts-config.xml, right-click it in the Package Explorer and select the Open With | Text Editor menu item. That opens struts-config.xml in a simple Eclipse editor (without any syntax highlighting), as shown in Figure 11-13.

There are Eclipse plug-ins, such as XML Buddy, that you can download that will add XML-specific editors to Eclipse. You can find hundreds of free Eclipse plug-ins at http://www.eclipse-plugins.2y.net/eclipse/.

Edit struts-config.xml to change all references to ch06 to ch11. That looks like this in the **<form-bean>** element:

```
<form-bean name="ch11_03" type="ch11.Ch11_03"/>
```

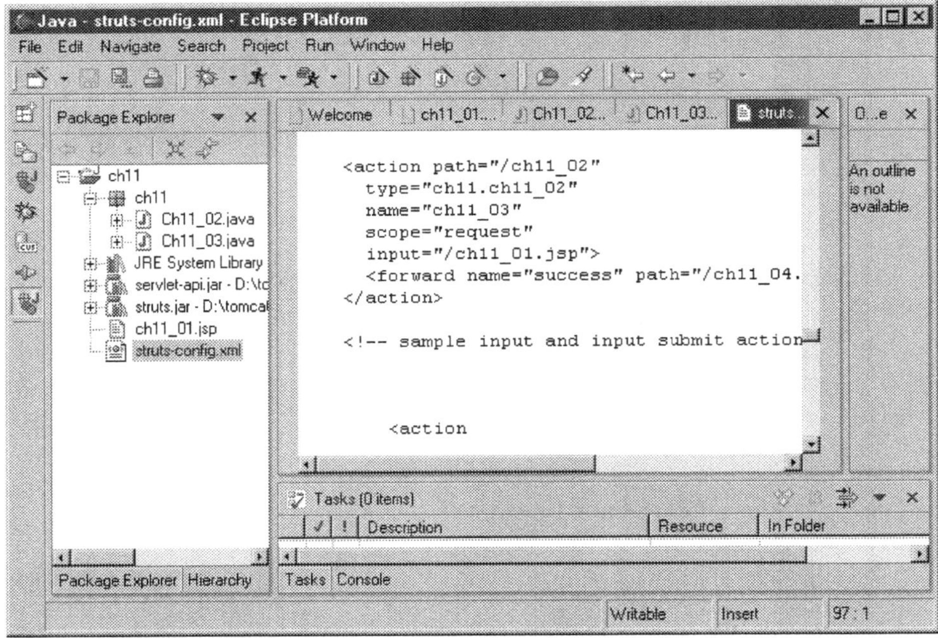

Figure 11-13 Editing struts-config.xml

It looks like this in the **<action>** element:

```
<action path="/ch11_02"
  type="ch11.Ch11_02"
  name="ch11_03"
  scope="request"
  input="/ch11_01.jsp">
  <forward name="success" path="/ch11_04.jsp"/>
</action>
```

Progress Check

1. How do you open a generic XML document in Eclipse?

1. You right-click the XML document in the Package Explorer and select the Open With | Text Editor menu item.

CRITICAL SKILL 11.8

Add the Results Page to the Project

We'll also need to add the Results page, ch11_04.jsp, to the project. Create that file now and store it in webapps/ch11, with these contents:

```
<%@ taglib uri="/tags/struts-bean" prefix="bean" %>
<%@ taglib uri="/tags/struts-logic" prefix="logic" %>

<HTML>
    <HEAD>
        <TITLE>Here's Your Data...</TITLE>
    </HEAD>

    <BODY>
        <H1>Here's Your Data...</H1>
        <h2>The text field text:</h2>
        <bean:write name="ch11_03" property="text"/>
        <BR>
        <h2>The text area text:</h2>
        <bean:write name="ch11_03" property="textarea"/>
        <BR>
        <h2>The checkbox:</h2>
        <bean:write name="ch11_03" property="checkbox"/>
        <BR>
        <h2>The selected radio button:</h2>
        <bean:write name="ch11_03" property="radio"/>
        <BR>
        <h2>The location of the mouse:</h2>
        (<bean:write name="ch11_03" property="x"/>,
        <bean:write name="ch11_03" property="y"/>)
        <BR>
        <h2>The select control selections:</h2>
        <logic:iterate id="select1" name="ch11_03"
            property="multipleSelect">
            <%= select1 %>
            <BR>
        </logic:iterate>
        <BR>
        <h2>The multibox control selections:</h2>
        <logic:iterate id="multibox1" name="ch11_03" property="multiBox">
            <%= multibox1 %>
            <BR>
        </logic:iterate>
        <BR>
        <h2>The file's text:</h2>
        <bean:write name="ch11_03" property="fileText"/>
    </BODY>
</HTML>
```

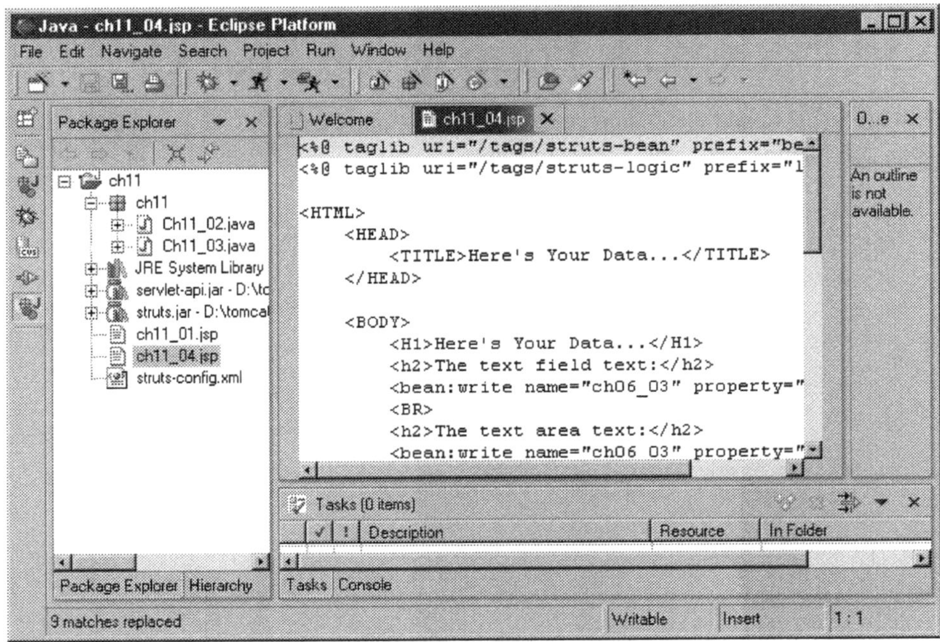

Figure 11-14 ch11_04.jsp in the Package Explorer

Now add this file to the project as we added ch11_01.jsp: select New | File, enter the name ch11_01.jsp in the File Name text box, click the Advanced button, and select the Link to File in the file system check box. Then click the Browse button, navigate to and select webapps/ch11/ch11_04.jsp, click the Open button, and click the Finish button. This adds ch11_04.jsp to the Package Explorer, as shown in Figure 11-14.

Now all the project files are centralized in Eclipse, and you can edit and compile them as needed. It took some work to get to this point, but if you're building a large project that has to be maintained over time, this is a good option.

Build the two .java files now by selecting the Project | Rebuild All menu item. This should create Ch11_02.class and Ch11_03.class and store them in webapps/ch11/WEB-INF/classes/ch11. Then start Tomcat and navigate to http://localhost:8080/ch11/ch11_01.jsp; you should see the Welcome page that appears in Figure 11-15.

You can enter data into this page as you see in the figure and click the Submit button. Doing so will bring up the Results page you see in Figure 11-16, where the data you entered is summarized.

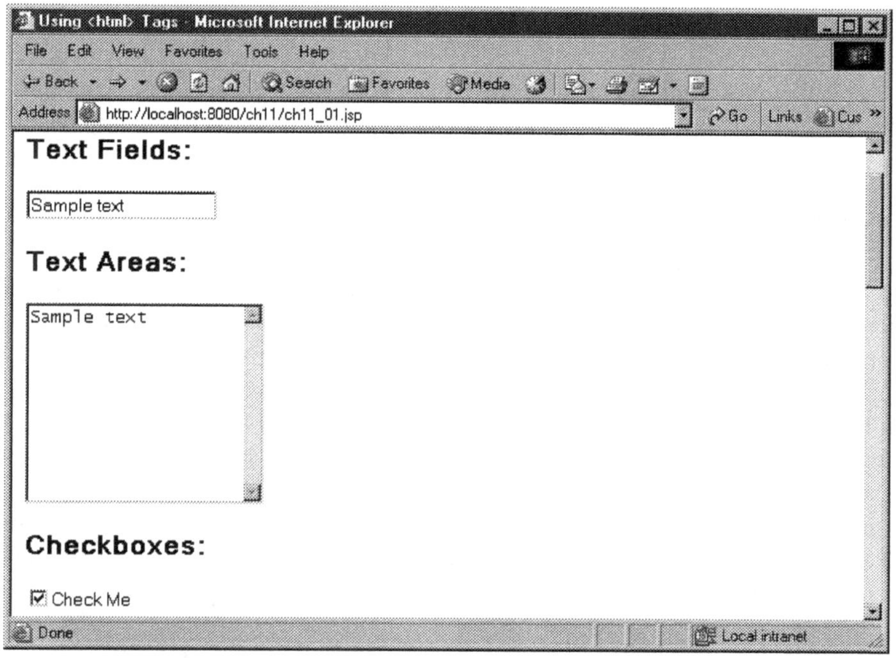

Figure 11-15 The Welcome page

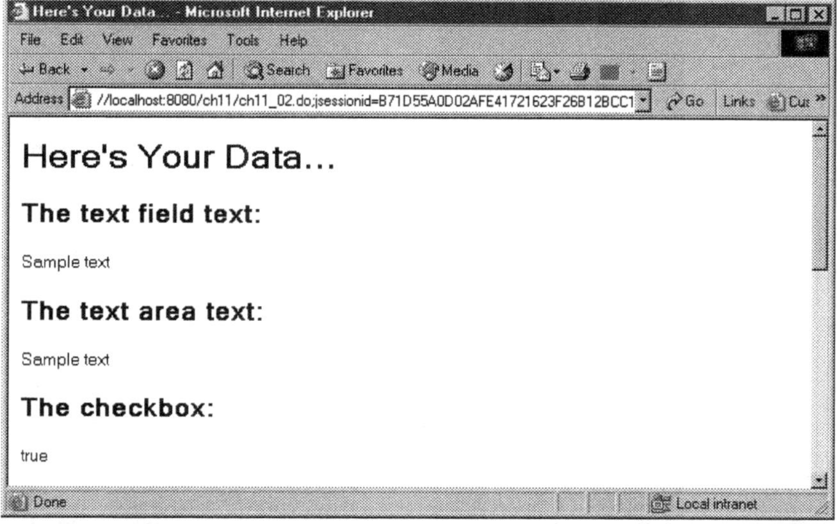

Figure 11-16 The Results page

And that's it—we've installed a Struts project in Eclipse, edited project files, built the project, and now run it. As you can see, there's plenty of value here. Not only does Eclipse centralize all project files and make opening them in an editor easy, but it also catches syntax errors, suggests solutions, and stores the compiled code in the correct Tomcat directories.

CRITICAL SKILL 11.9

Connect Eclipse to Ant

Your Struts deployment needs may exceed what Eclipse can give you, however. There are other options, as well; for example, a great tool for compiling and deploying Struts projects is Ant, the Java build tool. Ant lets you perform remote, FTP-based deployments, create .jar files, and more.

Ant is available as a stand-alone tool, but because Ant is so popular, Eclipse comes with it built in. All we have to do to use Ant is to add an Ant build file, build.xml, to our Eclipse project and set the classpaths that Ant will use in Eclipse. To set the classpaths Ant will use for the build to include servlet-api.jar and struts.jar, select Window | Preferences | Ant | Runtime and click the Classpath tab. Then click the Add JARs button, navigate to and select servlet-api.jar and struts.jar in webapps/ch11/WEB-INF/lib, and click Open, adding those files to the classpath as you see in Figure 11-17.

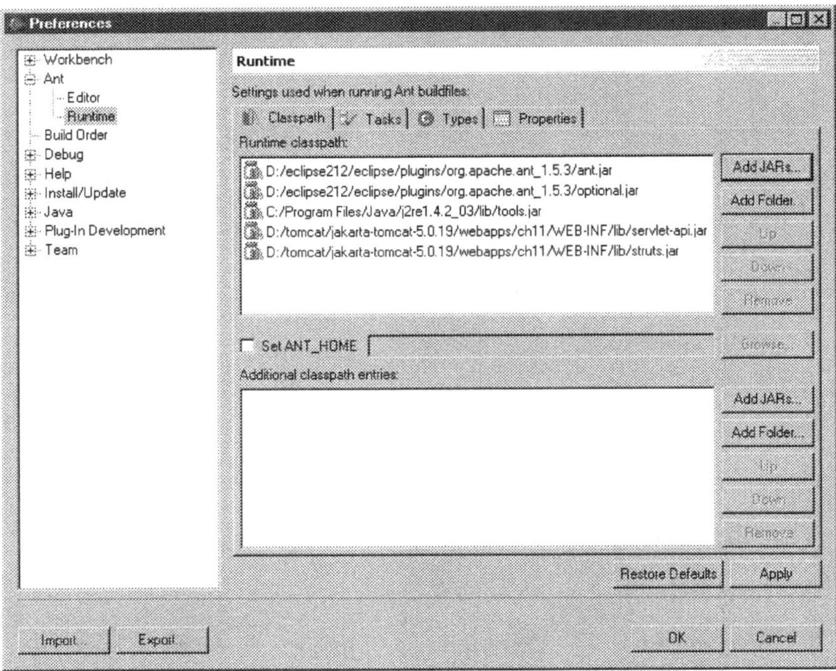

Figure 11-17 Adding .jar files for Ant

Now the version of Ant in Eclipse will be able to find the .jar files it needs for our import statements. The next step is to create the Ant build file.

To create the build file, use the Eclipse File | New | File menu item and create a new file named build.xml (Eclipse has a built-in Ant editor, so although it doesn't open general XML files by default, it'll open build.xml with syntax checking). Eclipse will add that file to the project and give it an icon in the Package Explorer with a small ant, as shown in the Package Explorer at left on Figure 11-18.

The build.xml file starts with an XML declaration and a **<project>** document element. Ant build files are based on targets, and our target will be called "Main Build":

```
<?xml version="1.0" encoding = "UTF-8"?>
<project name="ch11" default="Main Build" basedir=".">
        .
        .
        .
```

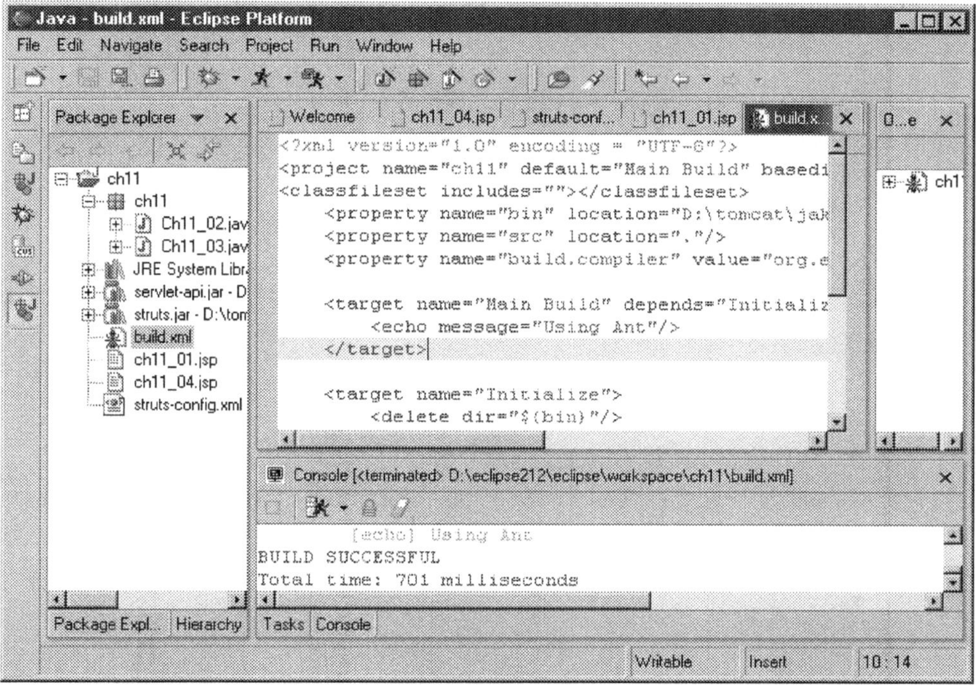

Figure 11-18 Ant's build.xml file

We'll set up a few properties, bin and src, to stand for the output and source folders, respectively. We'll also use the **build.compiler** property to specify that Ant should use the java compiler that comes with Eclipse, **org.eclipse.jdt.core.JDTCompilerAdapter**:

```
<?xml version="1.0" encoding = "UTF-8"?>
<project name="ch11" default="Main Build" basedir=".">
      <property name="bin" location=
          "D:\tomcat\jakarta-tomcat-5.0.19\webapps\ch11\WEB-INF\classes"/>
      <property name="src" location="."/>
      <property name="build.compiler"
         value="org.eclipse.jdt.core.JDTCompilerAdapter"/>
        .
        .
        .
```

The **Main Build** target will depend on two other tasks, **Initialize**, which will clean the output directory, and **Compile**, which will do the actual compilation of our .java files. We indicate this dependency with the **depends** attribute, which means Ant will execute the **Initialize** and **Compile** tasks in order when you execute the **Main Build** target:

```
<?xml version="1.0" encoding = "UTF-8"?>
<project name="ch11" default="Main Build" basedir=".">
      <property name="bin" location=
"D:\tomcat\jakarta-tomcat-5.0.19\webapps\ch11\WEB-INF\classes"/>
      <property name="src" location="."/>
      <property name="build.compiler"
         value="org.eclipse.jdt.core.JDTCompilerAdapter"/>

      <target name="Main Build" depends="Initialize, Compile">
            <echo message="Using Ant"/>
      </target>
        .
        .
        .
```

In the **Initialize** target, we'll delete the output directory and then re-create it in order to make sure no old resources are retained. The **Compile** target will use the Ant <javac> element to compile our .java files and deploy them to the webapps/ch11/WEB-INF/classes directory:

```
<?xml version="1.0" encoding = "UTF-8"?>
<project name="ch11" default="Main Build" basedir=".">
      <property name="bin" location=
          "D:\tomcat\jakarta-tomcat-5.0.19\webapps\ch11\WEB-INF\classes"/>
      <property name="src" location="."/>
      <property name="build.compiler"
         value="org.eclipse.jdt.core.JDTCompilerAdapter"/>
```

```
    <target name="Main Build" depends="Initialize, Compile">
          <echo message="Using Ant"/>
    </target>

    <target name="Initialize">
          <delete dir="${bin}"/>
          <mkdir dir="${bin}"/>
    </target>

    <target name="Compile" depends="Initialize">
          <javac srcdir="${src}"
                destdir="${bin}">
          </javac>
    </target>

</project>
```

To run this Ant build file and deploy the .class files for this project, right-click build.xml in the Package Explorer and select the Run Ant item, opening the ch11 build.xml dialog shown in Figure 11-19.

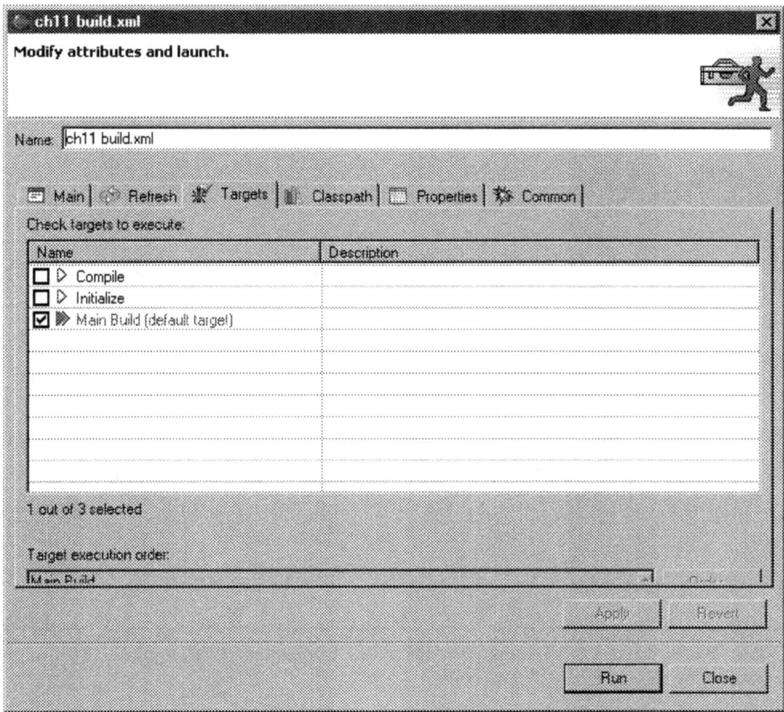

Figure 11-19 Running an Ant build

The default target, **Main Build**, is selected, as you can see in Figure 11-19. To run this target, click the Run button. The dialog disappears and something like this text should appear in the Eclipse Console view:

```
Buildfile: D:\eclipse212\eclipse\workspace\ch11\build.xml

Initialize:
      [delete] Deleting directory D:\tomcat\jakarta-tomcat-
5.0.19\webapps\ch11\WEB-INF\classes
       [mkdir] Created dir: D:\tomcat\jakarta-tomcat-
5.0.19\webapps\ch11\WEB-INF\classes

Compile:
       [javac] Compiling 2 source files to D:\tomcat\jakarta-tomcat-
5.0.19\webapps\ch11\WEB-INF\classes
       [javac] Compiled 188 lines in 2724 ms (69.0 lines/s)
       [javac] 2 .class files generated

Main Build:
        [echo] Using Ant
BUILD SUCCESSFUL
Total time: 3 seconds
```

Progress Check

1. How do you set which classpath Eclipse's version of Ant will use?
2. What's the default name of the file that holds the Ant build instructions?

The project is built successfully, and the .java files were compiled and deployed. This project is relatively simple and the deployment not terribly involved, but Ant is capable of all kinds of advanced deployments, which can be a great help to the Struts developer.

---

1. You select Window | Preferences | Ant | Runtime, then click the Classpath tab. Click the Add JARs button, navigate to and select the .jar files you want, and click Open.
2. build.xml

Ask the Expert

Q: Are there any additional tools for Struts that can be used with Eclipse?

A: You can find Eclipse plug-ins for Struts development at http://www.eclipse-plugins.2y.net/eclipse/, such as Struts Console, Struts Explorer, Easy Struts, Flux4Eclipse, and so on. Some of these tools will even write code for you. Be careful, though: some plug-ins are still not fully developed and will often give you very mixed results.

✓ Module 11 Mastery Check

1. What languages is Eclipse limited to?

   A. Java

   B. Java, C, C++

   C. Java, C, C++, and Cobol

   D. It's not limited to any particular set of languages.

2. Who originally created Eclipse?

   A. IBM

   B. Oracle

   C. Hewlett Packard

   D. Intel

3. What are the three subparts of Eclipse?

   A. The Eclipse workbench, the Plug-in Development Environment, and the debugger

   B. The Eclipse workbench, the editor, and the Plug-in Development Environment

   C. The Eclipse editor, the JDT, and the debugger

   D. The Eclipse platform, the JDT, and the Plug-in Development Environment

4. Which versions of Eclipse correspond to beta versions of software?

   A. Release builds

   B. Stable builds

   C. Integration builds

   D. Nightly builds

5. What's the job of the Eclipse platform kernel?
   A. The kernel displays the visual interface.
   B. The kernel lets you create plug-ins.
   C. The kernel manages the **EclipseWorker** thread.
   D. The kernel loads first and then loads the plug-ins.
6. What component of Eclipse handles Java development?
   A. The Java Development Tools
   B. The Java Development Toolkit
   C. The Development Toolkit
   D. The Java Tools
7. What source control protocol does Eclipse use to interface to code repository servers with?
   A. TCP/IP
   B. CVS
   C. RPS
   D. FTP
8. What's the name used for a collection of Eclipse views and editors?
   A. An Eclipse collection
   B. An Eclipse perspective
   C. An Eclipse set
   D. An Eclipse perspective collection
9. How can you include an existing file in an Eclipse project so that it can stay where it is but you can edit it from inside Eclipse?
   A. Link to it.
   B. Import it.
   C. Copy it.
   D. Refactor it.
10. What Eclipse utility suggests solutions to syntax problems that Eclipse finds?
   A. JDT
   B. Workbench
   C. EasySet
   D. QuickFix

Appendix

Answers to Mastery Checks

Module 1: Creating Web Applications

1. What are the different types of JSP elements?

   A. Scripting elements, methods, directives, and actions

   B. Scripting elements, comments, directives, and schema

   C. Scripting elements, comments, directives, and actions

   D. Scripting elements, comments, commands, and actions

2. What are the different types of JSP scripting elements?

   A. Scriptlets, comments, and expressions

   B. Scriptlets, directives, and expressions

   C. Scriptlets, declarations, and actions

   D. Scriptlets, declarations, and expressions

3. In order, what markup do you use to create JSP scriptlets, declarations, and expressions?

   A. <% and %>, <%! and %>, and <%= and %>

   B. <% and %>, <%? and %>, and <%= and %>

   C. <% and %>, <%$ and %>, and <%= and %>

   D. <% and %>, <%= and %>, and <%! and %>

4. What are the three JSP directives?

   A. page, include, and taglibrary

   B. page, subst, and taglibrary

   C. page, include, and taglib

   D. page, subst, and taglib

5. What JSP action can you use to create a Java object from a JavaBean?

   A. **<jsp:makeBean>**

   B. **<jsp:useBean>**

   C. **<jsp:instantiateBean>**

   D. **<jsp:createBean>**

6. What servlet methods can you use to handle data sent from a HTML form with the GET method?

   A. **doGet**

   B. **doRead**, **doGet**

   C. **doRead**, **service**

   D. **doGet**, **service**

7. Which of these methods can you use to send text back to a browser from a servlet?

   A. A PrintWriter object's **out** method

   B. A ServletWriter object's **out** method

   C. A ServletWriter object's **println** method

   D. A PrintWriter object's **println** method

8. What servlet method can you use to initialize your servlet?

   A. **initialize**

   B. **init**

   C. **start**

   D. **servlet**

9. What is the name of the directory in which you place .class files so they're accessible from JSP?

   A. lib

   B. library

   C. classes and subdirectories as needed to reflect package structure

   D. lib and subdirectories as needed to reflect package structure

10. In JSP, what request object method can you use to read text from a text field?

    A. **getValue**

    B. **getData**

    C. **getParameter**

    D. **getText**

Answers: 1. c. 2. d. 3. a. 4. c. 5. b. 6. d. 7. d. 8. b. 9. c. 10. c.

Module 2: Struts Essentials

1. What does the acronym MVC stand for?

   A. Method, View, Controller

   B. Method, View, Control

   C. Model, View, Controller

   D. Model, View, Control

2. In MVC architecture, the view is often implemented using:

   A. JSPs

   B. Servlets

   C. JavaBeans

   D. HTML

3. How does an action servlet find an action's code?

   A. Using an ActionForm

   B. Using an ActionServlet

   C. Using an ActionConnect

   D. Using an ActionMapping

4. How many custom JSP tag libraries come with Struts?

   A. 4

   B. 6

   C. 8

   D. 10

5. What JSP directive do you use to add support for a Struts tag library in a JSP file?

   A. A JSP **<%@taglibrary%>** directive

   B. A JSP **<%@taglib%>** directive

   C. A JSP **<%@tlib%>** directive

   D. A JSP **<%@library%>** directive

6. What custom JSP tag can you use to create an HTML form that connects to a Struts action named Data?

A. **<html:form method="DataAction">**

B. **<form method="DataAction">**

C. **<html:form action="Data">**

D. **<form action="Data">**

7. What two elements in web.xml set up the action servlet?

   A. **<servlets>** and **<struts>**

   B. **<servlet>** and **<struts>**

   C. **<servlet>** and **<servlet-mappings>**

   D. **<servlet>** and **<servlet-mapping>**

8. In **<action>** elements in struts-config.xml, what attribute do you use to indicate what form bean an action should use?

   A. **<bean>**

   B. **<name>**

   C. **<formBean>**

   D. **<form>**

9. In the **<form-beans>** element in struts-config.xml, what attribute do you use to specify the name of the Java class for the form bean?

   A. class

   B. form

   C. bean

   D. type

10. What objects are passed to the **execute** method of an action?

    A. **ActionForm**, **HttpServletRequest**, and **HttpServletResponse** objects

    B. **ActionMapping**, **HttpServletRequest**, and **HttpServletResponse** objects

    C. **ActionMapping**, **ActionForm**, **HttpServletRequest**, and **HttpServletResponse** objects

    D. **ActionMapping**, **ActionForm**, **ActionForward**, **HttpServletRequest**, and **HttpServletResponse** objects

Answers: 1. c. 2. a. 3. d. 4. b. 5. b. 6. c. 7. d. 8. b. 9. d. 10. c.

Module 3: Handling User Input

1. What custom Struts JSP tag can you use to create an HTML text field?

   A. **<text>**

   B. **<textfield>**

   C. **<html:text>**

   D. **<html:textfield>**

2. To implement a String property named **Data**, what methods should you implement in the action form?

   A. **data**

   B. **dataIn**, **dataOut**

   C. **getData**, **setData**

   D. **getData**, **setData**, **reset**

3. Which JSP directive should you use to connect to a form bean in a Results page?

   A. **<%@ taglibrary uri="/tags/struts" prefix="bean" %>**

   B. **<%@ taglibrary uri="/tags/bean" prefix="bean" %>**

   C. **<%@ taglib uri="/tags/struts-bean" prefix="bean" %>**

   D. **<%@ taglib uri="/tags/bean" prefix="bean" %>**

4. What custom Struts JSP tag do you use to insert bean data to a JSP page?

   A. **<bean:insert>**

   B. **<bean:message>**

   C. **<bean:bean>**

   D. **<bean:write>**

5. When you're writing your own custom JSP tag, what Java class do you typically extend?

   A. **Tag**

   B. **TagSupport**

   C. **TagLib**

   D. **TagLibrary**

6. How do you access data under the name text and insert it in a JSP page using Struts?

   A. **<bean:write name="dataForm" property="text"/>**

   B. **<bean:write name="dataForm" data="text"/>**

   C. **<bean:write name="dataForm" value="text"/>**

   D. **<bean:write name="dataForm" name="text"/>**

7. What method do you override in code for a custom JSP tag to handle the beginning of a tag?

   A. **BeginTag**

   B. **doBeginTag**

   C. **doStartTag**

   D. **BeginOpenTag**

8. What Struts custom JSP tag do you use to insert in a JSP page to display errors, if there are any?

   A. **<html:error>**

   B. **<html:errors>**

   C. **<html:displayError>**

   D. **<html:errorDiv>**

9. What Struts custom JSP tag do you use to loop over arrays of strings?

   A. **<logic:iterate>**

   B. **<logic:loop>**

   C. **<logic:again>**

   D. **<logic:iteration>**

10. What Struts custom JSP tag do you use to display a number of check boxes?

    A. **<html:checkboxes>**

    B. **<html:multibox>**

    C. **<html:checkbox>**

    D. **<html:multiboxes>**

Answers: 1. c. 2. d. 3. c. 4. d. 5. b. 6. a. 7. c. 8. b. 9. a. 10. b.

Module 4: Working with Models and ActionForms

1. On what class do you base the model in a Struts application?

   A. **ActionModel**

   B. **Model**

   C. **ModelFactory**

   D. Your own class

2. What **ActionForm** method do you use to set properties to default values?

   A. **reset**

   B. **default**

   C. **init**

   D. **start**

3. Can an action servlet store data from an HTML form in an action form using the Java **int** datatype?

   A. Yes, **int** datatypes are no problem.

   B. No, an action servlet can only store String and Boolean values in an action form.

4. What **ActionForm** method do you use to check data the user entered?

   A. **check**

   B. **validate**

   C. **dataValidate**

   D. **validation**

5. What two objects are passed to the method used in an action form to validate data?

   A. **ActionForm** and **HttpServletResponse**

   B. **ActionForm** and **HttpServletRequest**

   C. **HttpServletRequest** and **HttpServletResponse**

   D. **ActionMapping** and **HttpServletRequest**

6. What class do you assign to the **<form-bean>** element's **type** attribute when you want to use a **DynaActionForm**?

A. **org.apache.struts.DynaActionForm**

B. **javax.servlet.DynaActionForm**

C. **org.apache.struts.action.DynaActionForm**

D. **javax.servlet.struts.DynaActionForm**

7. What element do you use to set up a custom property in the **<form-bean>** element when you're setting up a **DynaActionForm**?

   A. **<property>**

   B. **<form-property>**

   C. **<custom-property>**

   D. **<property-data>**

8. What two attributes do you use to set up a custom property when using a **DynaActionForm**?

   A. **name** and **size**

   B. **property** and **type**

   C. **type** and **size**

   D. **name** and **type**

9. What **DynaActionForm** method do you use to assign a new value to a property?

   A. **assign**

   B. **change**

   C. **setProperty**

   D. **set**

10. One of the reasons that action forms have their own Struts class and are not just simple beans is that:

   A. Beans don't support text properties.

   B. Unselected check boxes aren't reported by HTML browsers.

   C. Beans can't be serialized.

   D. HTML browsers don't interface to simple beans.

Answers: 1. d. 2. a. 3. b. 4. b. 5. d. 6. c. 7. b. 8. d. 9. d. 10. b.

Module 5: Using Actions

1. What's the full name of the Struts **Action** class?

   A. **javax.servlet.action.Action**

   B. **javax.servlet.struts.action.Action**

   C. **org.struts.action.Action**

   D. **org.apache.struts.action.Action**

2. What **<action>** element attribute specifies the page control should switch to if there's a validation error?

   A. **input**

   B. **error**

   C. **errorHandler**

   D. **exceptionHandler**

3. What values can you set the **<action>** element's **scope** attribute to?

   A. "page" or "session"

   B. "request" or "page"

   C. "request" or "session"

   D. "application" or "session"

4. What **<action>** child element do you use to set up an exception handler?

   A. **<exception>**

   B. **<exceptionHandler>**

   C. **<error>**

   D. **<errorHandler>**

5. What **ActionMapping** method do you use to get all forwards in an action mapping?

   A. **getForward**

   B. **getForwards**

   C. **findForward**

   D. **findForwards**

6. What attribute do you use in an **<exception>** element to specify a custom exception-handling class?

A. **class**

B. **className**

C. **exceptionClass**

D. **exceptionClassName**

7. When using the **ForwardAction** class, what **<action>** element attribute do you use to specify the URL to forward to?

 A. **url**

 B. **forward**

 C. **attribute**

 D. **parameter**

8. What Struts action class is good to add support for legacy code in a Struts application?

 A. **org.apache.struts.actions.LegacyAction**

 B. **org.apache.struts.actions.IncludeAction**

 C. **org.apache.struts.actions.DispatchAction**

 D. **org.apache.struts.actions.ForwardAction**

9. When you're using the **DispatchAction** class, how do you specify the name of the property you'll use to store the name of the action method you want control dispatched to?

 A. You use the **parameter** attribute of the **<action>** element.

 B. You use the **method** attribute of the **<action>** element.

 C. You use the **dispatch** attribute of the **<action>** element.

 D. You use the **attribute** attribute of the **<action>** element.

10. What method do you use in a **LookupDispatchAction**-based class to return a **Map** object telling Struts which methods it should call to dispatch control?

 A. **getMethodMap**

 B. **getMap**

 C. **getKeyMap**

 D. **getKeyMethodMap**

Answers: 1. d. 2. a. 3. c. 4. a. 5. d. 6. b. 7. d. 8. b. 9. a. 10. d.

Module 6: The Struts <html> Tags

1. Which of the following JSP directives would add support for the HTML custom Struts JSP tags?

   A. **<%@ taglib uri="/tags/html" attribute="html" %>**

   B. **<%@ taglib uri="/tags/html" prefix="html" %>**

   C. **<%@ taglib uri="/tags/struts-html" prefix="html" %>**

   D. **<%@ taglib uri="/tags/struts-html-taglib" prefix="html" %>**

2. What Struts HTML tag attribute handles the case where the control loses the input focus?

   A. **focus**

   B. **onfocus**

   C. **ondefocus**

   D. **onblur**

3. What attribute do you use to set the caption of a Submit button using the **<html:submit>** tag?

   A. **caption**

   B. **value**

   C. **name**

   D. **title**

4. What attribute do you use to name a control as far as Struts is concerned so it can retrieve the control's data?

   A. **property**

   B. **name**

   C. **value**

   D. **data**

5. What attributes of the <html:link> tag must you specify exactly one of to set up a link?

   A. **forward** or **action**

   B. **forward**, **href**, or **page**

   C. **action**, **href**, or **page**

   D. **forward**, **action**, **href**, or **page**

6. How do you set the text the hyperlink should display using **<html:link>**?

   A. You use the **value** attribute.

   B. You enclose the text in the body of the **<html:link>** element.

   C. You use a resource bundle key with the prefix **link:**.

   D. It can't be done.

7. What attributes can you use to specify alternate test for an image using **<html:image>**?

   A. **text**

   B. **alt**

   C. **alt** or **bundle** and **altKey**

   D. **alt** or **resource** and **key**

8. What is the datatype of the x and y locations passed to you when handling the mouse location?

   A. **String**

   B. **int**

   C. **long**

   D. **boolean**

9. Which HTML attribute is set to the same value for all multibox check boxes in a group?

   A. **value**

   B. **name**

   C. **property**

   D. **checked**

10. What class holds the data of an uploaded file?

    A. **FormFile**

    B. **File**

    C. **UloadFile**

    D. **StrutsStream**

Answers: 1. c. 2. d. 3. b. 4. a. 5. d. 6. b. 7. c. 8. a. 9. b. 10. a.

Module 7: The Struts <logic> and <bean> Tags

1. Which **<logic>** tag would you use to redirect the browser?

   A. **<forward>**

   B. **<logic:forward>**

   C. **<logic:redirect>**

   D. **<redirect>**

2. Which **<logic>** tag searches for substrings in the text value of a variable?

   A. **<logic:search>**

   B. **<logic:find>**

   C. **<logic:substring>**

   D. **<logic:match>**

3. Which **<logic:empty>** element attribute do you use to specify the bean whose property you're checking?

   A. **bean**

   B. **form**

   C. **name**

   D. **actionForm**

4. When using the **<logic:equal>** tag, which attributes would you use if you wanted to test a bean property against a constant?

   A. **name, property, value**

   B. **name, value**

   C. **name, parameter**

   D. **name, property, value, parameter**

5. Which tag would you use to check if a cookie named **message** exists?

   A. **<logic:present cookie="message">**

   B. **<logic:match cookie="message">**

   C. **<logic:header cookie="message">**

   D. **<logic:search cookie="message">**

6. Which three attributes must you specify exactly one of to use **<logic:redirect>**?

   A. **forward**, **href**, **page**

   B. **forward**, **name**, **page**

   C. **forward**, **name**, **property**

   D. **forward**, **href**, **property**

7. Which **<bean>** tag would you use to create a scripting variable?

   A. **<bean:include>**

   B. **<bean:define>**

   C. **<bean:write>**

   D. **<bean:struts>**

8. Which Struts **<bean>** tag do you use to set the value of a cookie?

   A. **<bean:define>**

   B. **<bean:include>**

   C. **<bean:cookie>**

   D. You can't use a **<bean>** tag to do that.

9. Which Struts tag can you use to determine which browser the user has?

   A. **<logic:browser>**

   B. **<logic:define>**

   C. **<bean:header>**

   D. **<bean:scope>**

10. Which **<bean>** tag can you use to read the data from a text field?

    A. **<bean:header>**

    B. **<bean:parameter>**

    C. **<bean:define>**

    D. **<bean:message>**

Answers: 1. c. 2. d. 3. c. 4. a. 5. a. 6. a. 7. b. 8. d. 9. c. 10. b.

Module 8: Creating Custom Tags

1. What JSP directive do you use to connect a tag library prefix with the tag library's .tld file?

   A. **<% taglibrary %>**

   B. **<%@ taglibrary %>**

   C. **<%@ taglib %>**

   D. **<% taglib %>**

2. Which element do you use to set up a tag library in a .tld file?

   A. **<name>**

   B. **<taglib>**

   C. **<%taglib%>**

   D. **<%@taglib>**

3. What elements are required inside a **<tag>** element in a .tld file?

   A. The **<taglib>** and **<class>** child elements are required.

   B. The **<tagname>** and **<class>** child elements are required.

   C. The **<name>** and **<class-name>** child elements are required.

   D. The **<name>** and **<tag-class>** child elements are required.

4. What class do you base the Java code for a custom tag on?

   A. **TagSupport**

   B. **Tag**

   C. **TagLib**

   D. **TagLibrary**

5. What method do you use to handle the case where the end of an element is encountered?

   A. **endElement**

   B. **doEndElement**

   C. **doEndTag**

   D. **doEnd**

6. How can you access a **JSPWriter** object in your tag's code that will enable you to write to the result web page?

   A. You can call **pageContext.getOut()**.

   B. You can call **page.getWriter()**.

   C. You can call **servletContext.getWriter()**.

   D. You can call **pageContext.getWriter()**.

7. What child element is required inside the .tld file **<attribute>** element?

   A. **<class>**

   B. **<type>**

   C. **<length>**

   D. **<name>**

8. What method do you use in the Java code for a tag to pass data to a web page?

   A. **pageContext.setValue**

   B. **pageContext.setParameter**

   C. **pageContext.setAttribute**

   D. You can't use a method to do that.

9. Which interface must you implement to create an iterating tag?

   A. **Iterate**

   B. **IIterate**

   C. **Iteration**

   D. **IterationTag**

10. When you don't want to iterate any more in an iterating tag, what constant should you return from the **doAfterBody** method?

    A. **STOP_ITERATION**

    B. **CANCEL**

    C. **SKIP_BODY**

    D. **EVAL_PAGE**

Answers: 1. c. 2. b. 3. d. 4. a. 5. c. 6. a. 7. d. 8. c. 9. d. 10. c.

Module 9: The Struts Validator Framework

1. What class do you use in your form bean to support validation?

   A. **ActionForm**

   B. **ValidationForm**

   C. **ValidatorForm**

   D. **ValidatorActionForm**

2. What class do you use in the **<plug-in>** element to work with the Validator framework?

   A. **org.apache.struts.ValidatorPlugIn**

   B. **org.apache.struts.validation.ValidatorPlugIn**

   C. **org.apache.validator.ValidatorPlugIn**

   D. **org.apache.struts.validator.ValidatorPlugIn**

3. What file do you use to set up your own validation rules?

   A. validator.xml

   B. validation.xml

   C. validation-rules.xml

   D. validator-rules.xml

4. What element do you use inside a <plug-in> element to specify where to find the two XML files used to set validation rules?

   A. **<set-property>**

   B. **<property>**

   C. **<filename>**

   D. **<location>**

5. What standard rule lets you specify maximum length?

   A. **length**

   B. **maximumLen**

   C. **maxLen**

   D. **maxLength**

6. What standard rule(s) do you use to specify maximum and minimum integer values?

   A. **max** and **min**

   B. **maxInt** and **minInt**

   C. **integerRange**

   D. **intRange**

7. What standard rule do you use to make sure the user enters data in the corresponding field?

   A. **necessary**

   B. **standard**

   C. **requirement**

   D. **required**

8. What variable do you use to set the minimum value of an integer range?

   A. **minimum**

   B. **min**

   C. **minInt**

   D. **minInteger**

9. What element do you use to set the first argument passed to an error string?

   A. **<arg0>**

   B. **<arg>**

   C. **<argument>**

   D. **<arg1>**

10. What two elements do you use to set up a constant's name and contents?

    A. **<name>** and **<contents>**

    B. <**constant**> and <**contents**>

    C. **<constant-name>** and **<constant-value>**

    D. **<constant-name>** and **<constant-contents>**

Answers: 1. c. 2. d. 3. b. 4. a. 5. d. 6. d. 7. d. 8. b. 9. a. 10. c.

Module 10: The Tiles Framework

1. What element do you use with struts-config.xml to install Tiles?

   A. **<struts-configuration>**

   B. **<tiles>**

   C. **<tiles-config>**

   D. **<plug-in>**

2. What element do you use to associate a definition file with Tiles in struts-config.xml?

   A. **<config-file>**

   B. **<set-property>**

   C. **<tiles-definition>**

   D. **<definition>**

3. What attributes do you use to associate a definition file with Tiles in struts-config.xml?

   A. **property** and **value**

   B. **config** and **item**

   C. **config-file** and **item**

   D. **configuration** and **item**

4. What .tld file comes with Struts 1.1 to support the Tiles custom tags?

   A. **tiles.tld**

   B. **struts-tiles.tld**

   C. **tiles-taglib.tld**

   D. **tiles-library.tld**

5. What is the effect of setting the **<tiles:insert>** element's flush attribute to **true**?

   A. The Struts input stream will be flushed.

   B. The Struts output stream will be flushed.

   C. The current page's input stream will be flushed.

   D. The current page's output stream will be flushed.

6. You use **<tiles:put>** elements inside which other element?

   A. **<tiles:insert>**

   B. **<tiles:list>**

   C. **<tiles:putList>**

   D. **<tiles:attribute>**

7. What Tiles element can you use to recover the value of a Tiles attribute as text?

   A. **<tiles:text>**

   B. **<tiles:getAsText>**

   C. **<tiles:getAsString>**

   D. **<tiles:astext>**

8. What elements do you use to create a list of tiles?

   A. **<tiles:list>** and **<tiles:put>**

   B. **<tiles:putList>** and **<tiles:add>**

   C. **<tiles:putList>** and **<tiles:put>**

   D. **<tiles:list>** and **<tiles:add>**

9. What attribute in the **<tiles:useAttribute>** element sets the name of the variable to be created?

   A. **id**

   B. **name**

   C. **variable-name**

   D. **ref**

10. What element do you use to invoke a Tiles definition?

    A. **<tiles:definition>**

    B. **<tiles:put>**

    C. **<tiles:def>**

    D. **<tiles:insert>**

Answers: 1. c. 2. b. 3. a. 4. b. 5. d. 6. a. 7. c. 8. b. 9. a. 10. d.

Module 11: Using Eclipse with Struts

1. What languages is Eclipse limited to?

   A. Java

   B. Java, C, C++

   C. Java, C, C++, and Cobol

   D. It's not limited to any particular set of languages.

2. Who originally created Eclipse?

   A. IBM

   B. Oracle

   C. Hewlett Packard

   D. Intel

3. What are the three subparts of Eclipse?

   A. The Eclipse workbench, the Plug-in Development Environment, and the debugger

   B. The Eclipse workbench, the editor, and the Plug-in Development Environment

   C. The Eclipse editor, the JDT, and the debugger

   D. The Eclipse platform, the JDT, and the Plug-in Development Environment

4. Which versions of Eclipse correspond to beta versions of software?

   A. Release builds

   B. Stable builds

   C. Integration builds

   D. Nightly builds

5. What's the job of the Eclipse platform kernel?

   A. The kernel displays the visual interface.

   B. The kernel lets you create plug-ins.

   C. The kernel manages the **EclipseWorker** thread.

   D. The kernel loads first and then loads the plug-ins.

6. What component of Eclipse handles Java development?

A. The Java Development Tools

B. The Java Development Toolkit

C. The Development Toolkit

D. The Java Tools

7. What source control protocol does Eclipse use to interface to code repository servers with?

A. TCP/IP

B. CVS

C. RPS

D. FTP

8. What's the name used for a collection of Eclipse views and editors?

A. An Eclipse collection

B. An Eclipse perspective

C. An Eclipse set

D. An Eclipse perspective collection

9. How can you include an existing file in an Eclipse project so that it can stay where it is but you can edit it from inside Eclipse?

A. Link to it.

B. Import it.

C. Copy it.

D. Refactor it.

10. What Eclipse utility suggests solutions to syntax problems that Eclipse finds?

A. JDT

B. Workbench

C. EasySet

D. QuickFix

Answers: 1. d. 2. a. 3. d. 4. b. 5. d. 6. a. 7. b. 8. b. 9. a. 10. d.

Index

A

B

C

D

E

F

G

H

I

J

K

L

M

N

O

P

Q

R

S

T

U

V

INTERNATIONAL CONTACT INFORMATION

AUSTRALIA
McGraw-Hill Book Company
Australia Pty. Ltd.
TEL +61-2-9900-1800
FAX +61-2-9878-8881
http://www.mcgraw-hill.com.au
books-it_sydney@mcgraw-hill.com

CANADA
McGraw-Hill Ryerson Ltd.
TEL +905-430-5000
FAX +905-430-5020
http://www.mcgraw-hill.ca

GREECE, MIDDLE EAST, & AFRICA (Excluding South Africa)
McGraw-Hill Hellas
TEL +30-210-6560-990
TEL +30-210-6560-993
TEL +30-210-6560-994
FAX +30-210-6545-525

MEXICO (Also serving Latin America)
McGraw-Hill Interamericana Editores
S.A. de C.V.
TEL +525-1500-5108
FAX +525-117-1589
http://www.mcgraw-hill.com.mx
carlos_ruiz@mcgraw-hill.com

SINGAPORE (Serving Asia)
McGraw-Hill Book Company
TEL +65-6863-1580
FAX +65-6862-3354
http://www.mcgraw-hill.com.sg
mghasia@mcgraw-hill.com

SOUTH AFRICA
McGraw-Hill South Africa
TEL +27-11-622-7512
FAX +27-11-622-9045
robyn_swanepoel@mcgraw-hill.com

SPAIN
McGraw-Hill/
Interamericana de España, S.A.U.
TEL +34-91-180-3000
FAX +34-91-372-8513
http://www.mcgraw-hill.es
professional@mcgraw-hill.es

UNITED KINGDOM, NORTHERN, EASTERN, & CENTRAL EUROPE
McGraw-Hill Education Europe
TEL +44-1-628-502500
FAX +44-1-628-770224
http://www.mcgraw-hill.co.uk
emea_queries@mcgraw-hill.com

ALL OTHER INQUIRIES Contact:
McGraw-Hill/Osborne
TEL +1-510-420-7700
FAX +1-510-420-7703
http://www.osborne.com
omg_international@mcgraw-hill.com

Mc
Graw
Hill
OSBORNE
www.osborne.com

www.ingramcontent.com/pod-product-compliance
Lightning Source LLC
Chambersburg PA
CBHW080145060326
40689CB00018B/3863

* 9 7 8 0 0 7 2 2 5 6 5 9 8 *